# Reflexive Democracy

## Studies in Contemporary German Social Thought (partial listing)
Thomas McCarthy, general editor

# Reflexive Democracy

Political Equality and the Welfare State

*Kevin Olson*

The MIT Press    Cambridge, Massachusetts    London, England

MIT Press books may be purchased at special quantity discounts for business or sales promotional use. For information, please email special_sales@mitpress.mit.edu or write to Special Sales Department, The MIT Press, 55 Hayward Street, Cambridge, MA 02142.

This book was set in Baskerville by Graphic Composition, Inc. and was printed and bound in the United States of America.

Library of Congress Cataloging-in-Publication Data

Olson, Kevin.
Reflexive democracy : political equality and the welfare state / Kevin Olson.
    p.   cm.—(Studies in contemporary German social thought)
Includes bibliographical references and index.
ISBN 0-262-15116-2 (hc : alk. paper)
1. Welfare state. 2. Democracy. I. Title. II. Series.
JC479.O39   2006
320.51'3—dc22

10  9  8  7  6  5  4  3  2  1

For my family

# Contents

# Contents

# Acknowledgments

I'm grateful to a number of colleagues, mentors, and friends for their encouragement and careful criticism. Nancy Fraser originally sparked my interest in many of the themes discussed here, and her subsequent inspiration will be easily recognizable to anyone familiar with her work. Thomas McCarthy has shown me many times that the force of the better argument does indeed win out. His own better arguments have greatly influenced my thinking in this book. John McCumber has been a source of advice and encouragement throughout this project, and he continues to make Southern California an intellectually exciting place to live. Warm thanks to Joel Anderson, Kenneth Baynes, Robert Goodin, Joseph Heath, Terrence Kelly, Ann Shola Orloff, Shawn Rosenberg, Philip Selznick, Christopher Zurn, and the anonymous reviewers for their thoughtful comments on many of the ideas put forward here. I'm also very grateful to John Covell at the MIT Press for his interest in this project. I've benefited greatly from conversations with many others as well, particularly Amy Allen, Elizabeth Allen, Lisa García Bedolla, David Easton, David Theo Goldberg, Pauline Kleingeld, Kristen Monroe, Erin McKenna, Darrell Moore, Harvey Rabbin, Kamal Sadiq, Jennifer Schaffner, Michael Szalay, and Katherine Tate.

I would like to thank the University of Heidelberg, the Swedish National Institute for Working Life, and the archives of the *Institut Mémoires de l'Édition Contemporaine* for access to their collections. A Faculty Career Development Award from the University of California provided welcome support for this project. Some of the material in this book has previously appeared in another form. Chapter 3 is a revised and expanded version of "Recognizing Gender, Redistributing Labor," *Social Politics* 9:3 (2002): 380–410. Chapter 7 expands upon "Do Rights Have a Formal Basis? Habermas' Legal Theory and the Normative Foundations of the Law," *Journal of Political Philosophy* 11:2 (2003): 273–294. The book also draws in several places on substantially revised portions of "Democratic Inequalities: The Problem of Equal Citizenship in Habermas's Democratic Theory," *Constellations* 5:2 (1998): 215–233; and "Welfare, Democracy, and the Reflexive Legitimacy of the Law," *Studies in Law, Politics, and Society* 29 (2003): 89–113.

Above all, warmest thanks to my parents, Richard and Florence, for encouraging my "projects" for many years, and to my sisters, Shannon and Mikaela, for aiding and abetting. Special thanks to Alaïa, Annika, Driscoll, Melena, and Tahina for being such wonderful muses, and to the rest of my extended family in Irvine and beyond for many welcome diversions. And of course Ulrike has my gratitude for making sure that work does not expand to fill the time allotted to it.

# 1

## The Conceptual Crisis of the Welfare State

The welfare state has been a subject of major controversy over the past several decades. The neoliberal political revolutions of the 1980s—Reaganism in the United States, Thatcherism in the U.K.—got their focus and raison d'être largely by promising to dismantle the governmental formations built up during the previous half century. These reform movements promised smaller government, lower taxes, an end to entitlements, and a host of social benefits that would accrue from self-reliance rather than governmental largesse. Thus the electoral success of people like Reagan, Thatcher, and their epigones Bush and Major was gained largely through promises to renegotiate the social contract, to restructure basic forms of government and relations between state and society. The success of this logic can be seen in its uptake well outside the boundaries of conservatism. Bill Clinton and Tony Blair took office as members of progressive, populist parties, but their ideological orientation showed the influence of Reagan and Thatcher as much as Roosevelt or Beveridge.

At the same time, the collapse of the communist East in 1989 was heralded as the end of socialism, even the "end of history." When Hegel first foretold the end of history, however, he assumed that self-interest would be sublated in a universalist, communally oriented ethical life. The history that ended in 1989 seems to have had the opposite effect: it universalized self-interest through capitalism. While the residents of the former Eastern Bloc greeted their newfound civil and political freedoms with justified enthusiasm, many were quickly nostalgic for the social services provided by the old communist regimes. The price of freedom, in this case, was the vertigo of personal insecurity in a poorly regulated market economy.

The welfare-providing functions of the state have emerged as a primary bone of contention, then, in both the democratic West and the post-communist East. In the West, the growth of postwar welfare states has caused concern about the proper domains of state action, the allegedly negative effects of welfare upon its recipients, and the economic costs of social policy. In the East, a different set of debates has arisen over similar issues. In the rush to capitalism and democracy, it is not clear what should become of social programs that were intertwined with the communist legacy. The momentum of sweeping reform has raised many questions, but given policy makers, academics, and newly empowered citizens little time to find the answers. The result of these controversies in both West and East has been a retreat from socialist and social-democratic approaches to politics, accompanied by broad repeals of much social policy. Ironically, then, the revolutions of the 1980s—both neo-liberal and anti-communist—have landed West and East at the same impasse. That is the stand-off between those who believe that social and economic problems can be resolved by appealing to something like a welfare state and those who think the welfare state is part of the problem.

Important questions have emerged from these debates. It is no longer clear how we should define the proper ends and means of contemporary welfare states. There is little consensus on what welfare ought to do or how it ought to function. These are fundamental issues of what government is for, what citizens are entitled to, and what kinds of social and political relations we want to have. It is also unclear what kind of state we need to cope with contemporary social, political, and economic problems. Global changes in the social and institutional world are rapidly outdistancing our understanding of the state's capacities.

It is no accident that these parallel lines of controversy originated when they did, nor is it an accident that they have converged during the past decades. The crises of the welfare state have occurred during substantial changes in social, cultural, political, and economic conditions. Both West and East have felt the effects of globalization, immigration, ethnic and racial tensions, and changing family structures. The result is substantial difficulty of coming to political agreement over the kind of social relations and government we ought to have.

The welfare-state project has often been referred to as a middle path or third way. This path is usually seen as threading between two equally unsavory alternatives: state-planned socialism and laissez-faire capitalism. The unsavoriness of the alternatives is rooted in the socioeconomic problems characteristic of each. Socialism based on a command economy is held to be bureaucratic, paternalistic, and unproductive. Capitalism built around unregulated markets, in contrast, is inegalitarian, crisis prone, and cruel. The middle path, then, is theorized as a governmentally tamed capitalism that uses state institutions to harness the productive energies of a market economy while simultaneously shielding people from its undesirable side effects.

Because the middle path traverses a distinctly economic landscape, the welfare state has largely been understood in economic terms. This vision centers above all on labor and production. It is a model populated by workers and capitalists. In general this model directs its attention to the conditions under which labor is bought and sold, and more particularly, to the conditions under which some people are rendered vulnerable within the market. Here equality is construed in economic terms, while social problems are theorized in a vocabulary of production processes and distribution patterns. As a result, the welfare state is largely seen as a redistributive and regulatory mechanism, one that acts as a counterweight to the capitalist economy. Because this model devotes its attention so strongly to issues of labor, I will call it the *labor market paradigm*. That name refers to the normative core of most contemporary thinking about the welfare state: the idea that it exists to pursue a set of social ideals defined in opposition to the economy.

The labor market paradigm is built above all on notions of preventing poverty, class inequality, and the vulnerability of workers to employers. Criticism of these problems has won varying degrees of acceptance among the developed nations. In Scandinavia it has promoted a famously comprehensive and solidaristic welfare state. It has also given rise to well-developed welfare regimes in many other nations since the beginning of the twentieth century. In recent decades, however, the values on which this model is based have come under increasing fire. In liberal states, poverty is often seen as a motivational failure on the part of individuals. Market intervention, similarly, is seen as an unwarranted intrusion of the state into civil society. The logic of markets and individual initiative has gained increasing dominance as a rationale for rolling back many welfare programs and reformulating others. One of the primary problems of the welfare-state project today, then, is the erosion of the very ideals that once supported it. The public provision of goods and services is more and more delegitimated, and individuals must find their own way in the market.

I believe that many of the welfare state's current problems can be attributed to its focus on economic issues. An institution that sells itself as a solution to problems of class, distribution, and market regulation stakes its political fortunes on public uptake of those issues. As new struggles have broken out since the 1960s, however, class has received strong competition from race, gender, and ethnicity as a flashpoint of social conflict. To the extent that class issues still occupy center stage, they are usually admixed with such other concerns. Poverty, for instance, is often seen in the public mind as race-poverty ("the underclass") or gender-poverty ("welfare mothers"). Immigration is a highly ethnicized economic issue, typically seen as a matter of "them" taking "our" jobs. Globalization simply relocates the same problem: "they" take "our" jobs over the border. In short, contemporary economic issues are overlaid with complex social and identitarian concerns. Models of the welfare state that ignore this complexity risk irrelevance.

A narrow focus on economic issues also places welfare on shaky normative grounds. Redistribution can be rejected for the same kinds of reasons that it is embraced. If the pattern of goods distribution is the primary bone of contention, reasons for one pattern are difficult to privilege over reasons for another. When the welfare state is conceived as a means of poor relief or a functional counterweight to the market, it is forced to compete on ideological grounds with neoliberal conceptions of market freedom, moral hazard, and property rights. It invites debate, in other words, about which set of normative concepts should rule our economic life. Outside of the Scandinavian states, there has been little public consensus over that issue. Instead, it has fueled a great deal of the controversy in recent welfare debates.

It is politically fashionable to refer to the welfare state's problems as "crises." These crises are usually portrayed as fiscal, often with moral overtones of the alleged social pathologies perpetuated by welfare. I believe that there is a crisis of sorts, but not the one identified by political rhetoric. Our public understanding of the goals and means of welfare has fallen behind the times. The political conflicts dogging the welfare state reveal an ambivalence about many nineteenth- and twentieth-century philosophical projects. These controversies mark, in other words, a *conceptual* crisis. Many of the past century's guiding ideals have fallen behind the times, leaving the welfare state without a clear normative understanding of the goals it should be pursuing in modern society.

The conceptual crisis has occurred despite much innovative work in philosophy and the social sciences. Theorists of distributive justice have made great strides in clarifying norms of property and possession. Empirical researchers have developed subtle comparative understandings of different welfare regimes. Yet this solid and commendable work has not gained the political influence it deserves. Its uptake in the public sphere has been nowhere near the uptake of much less well-developed neoliberal arguments against the welfare state. This fertile area of study has not performed the public function one would expect—providing ways of thinking about how things could be otherwise.

To resolve the conceptual crisis, we must incorporate the best of this work into a more solid normative perspective on the welfare state. Although the economic import of welfare policies is frequently noted, their political and cultural functions are much less frequently remarked on. This is a singular lapse, because welfare sits right on the seam where politics, culture, and the economy meet. It would be a mistake, then, to focus on the distributive and class-structuring properties of welfare to the exclusion of its political and cultural aspects. In spite of the inherently political and cultural character of the current crises, however, fairly little attention has been devoted to these aspects of the welfare state.

To be sure, there are many exemplary studies of the politics of welfare. They have traced the mobilization of farmer-labor coalitions, the struggle of unions for better work conditions, market regulation, and wage concessions, and the expansion of citizenship and social rights. This enterprise emphasizes description over prescription, however. It has scarcely begun to draw on the rich normative resources of political theory. This has been a missed opportunity for both political theorists and for our understanding of the welfare state.

Issues of culture and identity have also been treated in the welfare state literature, but again, in a primarily descriptive sense. Race, for instance, has been revealed as the unacknowledged elephant-sitting-in-the-corner of the American debate. Attacks on the U.S. welfare regime have been shown to play on racial politics in an adept way. Further, race has been shown to be the principal lens through which the American electorate perceives welfare. While these studies would connect well with the rich normative understandings of race developed in the humanities and cultural studies, those connections have not been made in a systematic way. As a result, many actual welfare states—including Scandinavian ones—currently founder on racial controversy while the well-developed literature on race has contributed little to our normative understanding of welfare.

Things stand a bit better when it comes to gender issues. Feminists were the first to challenge the welfare state's focus on wage labor and the official economic sphere. They have shown that the state has an important role to play in gender equity. The way a state awards benefits, the way it conceptualizes recipients, and the kinds of goals it pursues all have a strong influence on gender relations in a given society. Welfare states can enable or hinder women's access to the labor market. They can institutionalize and naturalize particular conceptions of marriage, domesticity, the family, and gender roles. At the same time, gender norms structure the welfare state itself. They naturalize particular issues as proper subjects of state concern while marginalizing others. To promote gender equity, feminists argue, careful consideration must be given to the complex character of welfare as a set of institutions that are simultaneously economic, cultural, and political. Feminists provide a good model of the way that normative ideals of gender equity can be combined with a subtle analysis of the social construction of gender norms *and* the ways that social policy structures and is structured by such norms. They effectively thematize the role of welfare in the politics of everyday life, simultaneously holding a focus on formal state politics and the daily politics of gender norms.

In this book I will argue that our understanding of welfare needs more of the kind of changes innovated by feminists. To develop a normatively persuasive conception of the welfare state, we must take greater notice of politics and culture as they are connected with the welfare state's traditional concerns. In the coming pages I will refer to this new direction as a *political turn*. Such a turn holds great promise for putting the welfare state on new grounds. It taps into culturally deep-seated values of political equality to provide a powerful set of arguments for welfare. These ideals stand out in sharp contrast against the background of economic, cultural, and political inequalities that undermine the equality of political participation. Political equality thus furnishes the welfare state with a new and important purpose. At the same time, this goal specifies conditions under which the state must ensure its own normative basis in actual democratic deliberation. A welfare state promoting political equality must foster a public sphere capable of formulating and legitimating welfare legislation itself. Politics, then, provides a normative key to rethinking welfare in a double sense: the welfare state both promotes political equality and depends upon it. In a very important sense, such a state reflects back upon itself, providing its own grounds of political legitimacy. I will call this kind of politics *reflexive democracy*.

It is not surprising, of course, to point out that welfare is political. Social policy is legislatively authored, legally encoded, and administratively enacted. It is political literally from start to finish. More broadly, the classic chapters in the history of welfare tell a story of dynamic political struggles at the interface of state and society. The Bismarckean welfare state, for instance, was a political attempt to neutralize competing socialist parties while containing the power of an emergent capitalist class. The first two centuries of British poor laws trace the politics of the enclosure movement and the broader economic changes that surrounded it. The postwar Swedish welfare state was made possible by a political alliance between labor and farmers, the famous "red-green coalition." And many elements of the American War on Poverty pitted a progressive federal government against conservative and racist municipalities.

Against this background, a political turn in the welfare state begins to sound like a quaint attempt to declare the obvious. It is intended somewhat differently, however. While actually existing welfare states are deeply political, political grounds have never been used as the basis for *justifying* welfare. The theoretical justification of welfare programs, when it is attempted at all, is typically based on distributive criteria. Reflexive democracy takes a different tack, providing distinctively political rather than economic reasons for welfare. It provides a normative conception of the *politics* of welfare, equal in normative sophistication and complexity to their actual practice.

To develop such a view, I will outline a conception of welfare centered on carefully reconfigured ideals of political equality, democratic legitimacy, and citizenship. This view attempts to show how deeply intertwined welfare is with political processes, the formation of legitimate laws, and cultural struggle. It reveals deep-seated egalitarian norms at the heart of the welfare state—norms derived not from economic, but political equality. This view is not designed to replace our more traditional, economic concerns. Rather, it strengthens arguments about economic justice by providing them with a more solid normative basis. The result is a new genre of justification for welfare, developed out of insights about the material bases of democratic equality. This view is intended both as a contribution to our understanding of democracy and as an attempt to resolve some of the impasses currently faced by the welfare state.

## 1.1   The Contemporary Impasse

To outline some of the motivations for my approach, it is useful to consider a particular case. The United States provides a good illustration of the contemporary problems of the welfare state: conceptual exhaustion, delegitimation, and calls to dismantle social programs. In recent years the United States' welfare system has increasingly emphasized personal responsibility, a strong distinction between deserving and undeserving poor, and enforcement of the work ethic. This system places great weight on market freedom and economic initiative while discrediting collective responsibility. This can be seen particularly in its recent history.

In the late summer of 1996, Bill Clinton delivered on his campaign promise to "end welfare as we know it," signing into law the Personal Responsibility and Work Opportunity Reconciliation Act of 1996. The most prominent feature of this law is the termination of federal welfare entitlements. The act—often called the PRA—overrides key elements of the Social Security Act of 1935. In particular, it replaces the most visible and controversial component of the American welfare system, Aid to Families with Dependent Children (AFDC) with a block grant program to states, Temporary Assistance for Needy Families (TANF). The new welfare system thus holds true to a Republican commitment to return welfare to local control. This commitment does not allow states free rein in spending federal welfare dollars, however. The U.S. Congress announces a strong social agenda in its preface to the bill, one that imposes federal restrictions on the shape and dimensions of state welfare programs.

The dramatic institutional changes brought about by this law have been widely remarked upon, but its social and cultural significance has only begun to be assessed. Most obviously, the symbolic import of the shift from *social security* to *personal responsibility* says volumes. It signals the end of federal commitments to a society-wide system of security, announcing the need for individuals to take responsibility for their own fates. This law marks an important milestone in American culture, then. It caps two decades of rollback in New Deal social programs, exemplifying a shift from the progressive politics of the Depression to a neoliberal paradigm of self-sufficiency and minimal government.

"Responsibility" is employed in a double sense in the PRA. Most prominently, the act's introductory remarks focus on reproductive and parental responsibility. They state that, "Promotion of responsible fatherhood and motherhood is integral to successful child rearing and the well-being of children."[1] The principal concern of these remarks is out-of-marriage birth, which is held to raise newborns' risks of having a low birth weight, low verbal skills, and lower educational aspirations. It is also held to reduce their chances of having an intact marriage in adulthood and to increase their likelihood of suffering child abuse and child neglect, and of becoming teenage parents themselves. The absence of a father, the Congress notes, has negative effects on school performance and peer adjustment.

Intercut with these psychological, social, and medical harms, however, is the problem of cost. The authors of the bill pointedly note the welfare costs of births to single mothers. They note that young women giving birth are more likely to go on public assistance and likely to stay there longer than older mothers. Moreover, past increases in AFDC rolls were closely related to increased births among unmarried women. Congress thus implements stiff measures to cut costs and prevent moral hazard. The PRA places a two-year limit on continuous receipt of benefits and a lifetime cap of five years. It requires thirty hours of work per week from single parents and thirty-five hours in total from two-parent families. It also gives states incentives for moving people off the rolls and mandates targets for work participation of those receiving benefits. As a result of its cost-saving efforts, Congress managed to cut $55 billion out of the welfare budget over the first six years of implementation.

The PRA's double conception of responsibility is a complex blend of social and fiscal considerations, which are twisted together in complicated ways. On one hand are considerations about the social, psychological, and medical well-being of children, and on the other are concerns about the runaway costs of caring for them. Parents are enjoined to be responsible not simply for the well-being of their children, but also in order to decrease state spending. This conception has a strong neo-liberal flavor.[2] It is a notion of responsibility in which self-sufficient economic actors pursue their own well-being in the marketplace. Correspondingly, this act encodes a vision of government in which the state's role is largely minimal and negative. It is a minimal role in the sense of encouraging individual self-sufficiency. It is negative because it establishes a system of constraints and incentives to promote individual economic activity, rather than actively supporting the lives and goals of its citizens. As a result, the PRA's notion of responsibility implicitly assumes a zero-sum balance between the responsibilities of the state and those of individuals. Responsibilities, in this view, are allocated by choosing a point on a continuum. This point distinguishes that which is properly the state's domain from that which ought to be undertaken by individuals. If fathers took financial responsibility for their children, the state would not have to. If welfare recipients took responsibility for their own sustenance, the state would not have to. In this sense the PRA's conception of responsibility incorporates not only notions of minimal and negative government, but also the neo-liberal idea that the art of governing consists of drawing a line between individual and state. Anything the state abjures, in this picture, becomes the province of individual initiative.

When responsibility is seen as a line drawn between the state and its citizens, the primary problem lies in deciding where the line ought actually to be drawn. For neoliberals the line would presumably fall close to the state's end, allocating most responsibilities to individuals. For progressives, in contrast, the line would presumably fall close to the individuals' end of the spectrum, leaving a large number of tasks in the domain of state action. Justifications for drawing the line in one place or another are typically moral in character. They typically rely on morally grounded ideas of dependency, laziness, and economic individualism on one side, and equality, collective responsibility, and economic justice on the other.

Lawrence Mead's "new paternalism" is the most carefully worked-out version of the neo-liberal position. It allocates responsibilities through an account of the moral obligations of citizenship.[3] Mead observes that the conception of citizenship operative in American social policy emphasizes benefits and entitlements without corresponding obligations. Opposing this conception, he draws on a countertradition in American politics that he calls civic conservatism. In this conception, benefits and obligations go hand in hand. Citizens can expect to benefit from social membership only if they contribute to the polity. These obligations are conceived specifically in terms of labor. To receive welfare benefits, citizens should be expected to work. The discipline of work is not an unfair burden, then, but a social obligation. This, Mead claims, is an attitude toward social obligation that is common in contemporary American culture, and it is crucial to defining what it means to be a full participant in American society.

Mead's critique of the American welfare system was influential in establishing the paternalist measures adopted in the PRA. People normally expect to be independent and self-supporting, he claims, so it is unreasonable for welfare recipients to receive benefits without corresponding obligations to work. Moreover, work requirements would have the beneficial effect, he argues, of attenuating social and behavioral problems resulting from welfare. From this perspective, work is a vital component of citizenship, a social obligation, and a moral corrective.

The progressive position, in contrast, typically focuses on the social consequences of poorly regulated markets. Progressives typically rely, in other words, on what I have called the labor market paradigm to justify welfare benefits. Insofar as the PRA succeeds in moving people into jobs, critics fear that such jobs will be found only in the lowest tier of the market. Further, they fear that such jobs are dead-end positions that fail to teach people employable skills or allow them to move up the employment ladder. Additionally, many have voiced the concern that cyclical economic downturns will perpetually reverse any gains in putting the poor to work, unemploying those who succeeded in leaving the welfare rolls and stranding those trying to leave. Backgrounding these concerns is the fear that the PRA puts welfare recipients between a rock and a hard place. Their choice is either a temporary welfare benefit with work requirements or employment in the lowest-paid and most unstable tiers of the American economy.

From this perspective, the PRA can be seen as a functional adjunct to the economy. It contains the poor and unemployed for short periods of time, but forces them back into the labor market as quickly as possible. In this sense, the PRA is a residualist social policy of the kind described by Richard Titmuss.[4] Residualist policies are designed to function in tandem with market imperatives, so that they only serve as a temporary and undesirable last resort when market and family have failed. Because of its orientation towards the market, the PRA also exemplifies Piven and Cloward's celebrated argument that American welfare functions to maintain a reserve army of capitalist labor.[5] Such an orientation is typical of the American welfare system and ones similarly descended from the British Empire.[6] It shows the legacy of Anglo-American liberalism, particularly the possessive individualist strand that emphasizes self-sufficiency, personal property rights, and minimal government.[7] Here the PRA follows a long lineage of British social policy that can be traced at least from the Elizabethan Poor Laws' concern with "setting the Poor to Work";[8] to John Locke's dictum that "true and proper relief of the poor . . . consists in finding work for them, and taking care they do not live like drones upon the labour of others";[9] through disciplinary work house schemes designed to "extirpate mendicity and habitual depredation";[10] to the Poor Law Amendment Act of 1834.[11] It also continues trends in the evolution of the American AFDC program. This begins with the first work requirement in 1967, administered through the Work Incentive Program (WIN); continuing to work regulations in the Nixon Administration's never-implemented Family Assistance Plan; and blossoming into full-blown workfare in the Reagan Administration's Community Work Experience Program (CWEP) and Job Opportunity and Basic Skills program (JOBS).[12]

Residualist welfare provision is problematic for several reasons. Most prominently, it leaves people vulnerable in the labor market. When workers have no choice but to take the first job they can find, they are trapped in a position of competing against one another for wages and positions. As a result, their bargaining leverage goes down. The economic and legal system creates structural asymmetries between workers and employers in which those with capital can buy labor at a discount and those without capital must sell it. In this sense, the structure of the capitalist economy—reinforced by measures like the PRA—is coercive in an asymmetrical sense.[13] It places workers in a situation of unfair vulnerability relative to employers.

From this perspective, the PRA's primary failure lies in making people more beholden to the market rather than less. It fails to decommodify labor in ways that would improve the bargaining position of workers, and it fails to shield them from economic forces. By instituting work requirements and capping benefits, the PRA does the opposite of protecting workers: it gives welfare recipients a strong push to commodify their labor rather than rely on out-of-market benefits for sustenance. The law, in this case, fails to protect poor people and acts simply as part of the market mechanism.

The tensions between conservative and progressive critiques of the PRA ably demonstrate a point I will make in chapter 7. Each of these positions is based, in different ways, on an interpretation of American political and legal culture. The progressive position rests on commitments to equality and protecting workers from exploitation. Mead's civic conservatism, similarly, is rooted in obligations of self-sufficiency and work held to be deep commitments in American culture. These theories are problematic in the same way, even though their points of view are diametrically opposed. Each tries to read normative claims directly out of our political culture, becoming mired in all of the contradictory principles and commitments that mark any actual culture. When we use such observations as a normative starting point, it is no wonder that we can reach two such opposite conclusions.

These conflicting claims illustrate a general point about the justification and criticism of welfare regimes. If welfare programs are justified by a moral critique of the economy they are subject to rejection on similar grounds. Some people embrace robust notions of distributive equality and worker protection, while others support economic individualism, minimal government, and strong property rights. To justify welfare as a counterweight to the labor market opens it to rejection for similar reasons. Thus arguments over the size and shape of a redistributive welfare state easily become mired in zero-sum struggles over mine and thine, over the proper role of the state and the border between individual and society. In this case redistribution and regulation are counterposed to individualist economic interests like tax relief and property rights. To resolve this dispute, there would have to be some theoretically decisive way to fix the line between self-sufficiency and mutual obligation. A philosophical justification for one position or the other would decide the issue. To date, however, no decisive position has emerged.

In the absence of a firm philosophical basis, each of these opposing positions is reduced to the status of a moral recommendation. Each seems appealing to its constituents because it has some currency in our culture. Some believe it is bad for people to have to scramble for survival, whether this means unemployment or working in low-status, low-wage jobs. They conclude that law and social policy should be used to correct this problem. Others believe that talent and hard work should be the only determinants of one's fortune, and they are not willing to support policy measures to make up the difference for those who achieve less. This, however, is as far as such arguments can go. From a moral-economic standpoint, there are many conflicting ideas about the proper relations between states, markets, and individuals. Lacking a more formidable justification, there is no decisive way to choose among them, nor even to decide whether "responsibility" is a productive way to think about such issues.

This impasse illustrates some of the conceptual problems that welfare encounters today. Our most fertile lines of research on economic justice still cannot effectively counter charges like Mead's. In the end, their arguments and his each make similar assumptions. Absent some way to decide the issue one way or another, we are left with contradictory assertions about economic structure and social relations. The result of this philosophical deadlock is lack of a clear vision of the welfare state's proper function. This lack leaves it primed for political controversy, delegitimation, and deadlock. To put the welfare state on more solid grounds, we need a firmer normative basis for making claims about what the state should be doing and how it should be doing it.

## 1.2 Philosophical Norms and Actual Societies

Robert Goodin provides a valuable direction out of this impasse. He attacks the facile use of "responsibility" for thinking about welfare reform. Goodin's approach is based on an analysis of the market's internal logic. He argues that the market's tendency to generate exploitable vulnerabilities creates corresponding responsibilities. The people who benefit most directly from such vulnerabilities thereby create obligations to shield the vulnerable from harm. Before vulnerable people can be held individually responsible to provide for their own needs, our collective responsibilities to protect them from harm must first be discharged.[14] The American welfare reforms go wrong, then, because the welfare state ought to be the means to protect the vulnerable rather than a tool for enforcing work discipline upon them. Goodin makes a key methodological innovation here. He draws a justification for the welfare state out of the market itself. The welfare state, he claims, fulfills the moral *presuppositions* of the market.

We could not morally embrace the logic of the market, he argues, without also protecting people made vulnerable by it. The welfare state is the means for living up to our moral principles and legitimating the market.

Such an argument is important because it justifies welfare based on presuppositions of the practices that we already engage in. I will continue this general line of thought, though traversing somewhat different ground. My focus will be on the ways that welfare can fulfill presuppositions of our present *political* practices. This line of investigation traces deep connections between political participation and welfare. It provides a justification that avoids many of the problems I have detailed in economic arguments. Although the state's economic functions are a continuing source of controversy, there is a long tradition supporting political equality in democratic societies. Political equality is, after all, one of the animating ideals of democracy. Whereas economic arguments run aground on their lack of moral consensus, arguments about democracy and political equality secure agreement much more easily.

Following these insights, I will pursue an approach in which welfare is justified on political grounds. The chapters to follow outline a view based on commitments we already hold to values of political equality. This line of reasoning exploits an important but often overlooked insight: welfare is not simply a means of redistribution nor simply a counterweight to the market. It is more generally an institutional mechanism for realizing collective goals of many different kinds. This approach moves away from a focus on redistribution and class, toward a focus on political equality.

To see what is distinctive about this approach, it is worth thinking in more detail about the claim that debates over the welfare state tend to degenerate into struggles over conflicting moral intuitions. Max Weber made a similar criticism of late nineteenth-century welfare law. He wrote that

New demands for a "social law" to be based upon such emotionally colored ethical postulates as "justice" or "human dignity," and directed against the very dominance of a mere business morality, have arisen with the emergence of the modern class problem. . . . Such a concept as economic duress, or the attempt to treat as immoral, and thus as invalid, a contract because of a gross disproportion between promise and consideration, are derived from norms which, from the legal standpoint, are entirely amorphous and which are neither juristic nor conventional nor traditional in character but ethical and which claim as their legitimation substantive justice rather than formal legality.[15]

Much contemporary thinking about welfare, I believe, is based on such "emotionally colored ethical postulates." It formulates agendas for social policy based on substantive conceptions of justice—in this case, ones that enjoy some currency in our culture but no unanimity nor solid philosophical basis. This line of thinking runs into problems because it is *external* to the practices it is designed to criticize. It draws on moral paradigms brought in from outside to evaluate welfare regimes. Such an approach is only contingently associated with the regime it evaluates. It captures one set of opinions on the structure of the economy and the social role of the state. Unfortunately, however, we have not yet succeeded in arguing that any particular perspective gives us a better appraisal of the sociomoral consequences of welfare than any other.

Weber, of course, was a proponent of a highly formal *Rechtsdogmatik,* an academic working up of the body of law into an internally consistent, rigorously neutral doctrine. I will not follow that path here, though I will focus on the legal foundations of the welfare state. Instead I will elaborate a new paradigm for thinking about the political and cultural effects of welfare. Unlike the "social law" Weber criticizes, this one is developed from a perspective *internal* to the law. It criticizes welfare regimes based not on their socioeconomic effects, but on their role as important functional elements in a system of laws. This point of view does not import ethical principles to criticize the law, but takes its philosophical bases from the law itself. It is thus formal in the sense that Weber describes. Perhaps surprisingly, however, this position is also *substantive* in Weber's sense. It makes concrete proposals about the structure and character of society, particularly regarding the state's responsibilities toward its citizens. In this sense, it stipulates the kinds of substantive goals and outcomes that Weber found so abhorrent in late nineteenth-century welfare law. The advantage of this position is precisely that it undoes Weber's distinction and manages to be substantive and formal at the same time. It is a conception of welfare that derives its normative force from the formal character of law, but that also has the specificity and critical distance to say something substantively useful.

Participatory equality is the normative basis of this conception of the welfare state. This idea is based on an analysis of welfare as part of a system of laws. Every day we engage in cooperative practices with other people. Our economy and political system are large-scale examples of this. Small-scale, face-to-face interactions are also a part of it. The most basic presupposition of this kind of cooperation is that people must be able to agree to the terms under which they cooperate. In a modern, complex society, the terms of cooperation are typically legal. They spell out rules and norms for cooperative interaction. For people to be able to agree on these terms, however, they must be able to participate equally in the political processes that form the laws. Thinkers as diverse as Mill, Hegel, and Rawls have pointed out, however, that equal participation cannot be a purely formal concern. The material well-being of citizens has a direct bearing on their ability to function as democratic decision-makers. Citizens must be sufficiently equal and sufficiently free to participate in the core functions of their society. To guarantee the equality of citizens, a system of laws must include some kind of equality-promoting measures. The law is thus self-referential: it needs the equal participation of citizens to ensure its own legitimacy, but it also must promote that equality itself. Welfare sits at the heart of this self-referentiality because it is a crucial part of the legal apparatus producing equal participation.

The self-referential character of the law sows the seeds for a vicious circularity. The welfare state must guarantee the participatory equality of its citizens in order to legitimate itself. At the same time, it depends on equal participation for its own legitimacy. Herein lies the problem: equal participation is a precondition for equal participation. This paradox is best solved, I believe, by inserting a guarantee of enablement into the circle from the start. If citizens are guaranteed the means for participatory equality regardless of circumstance, the vicious downward spiral of inequality and marginalization is avoided. In its place we have a virtuous circle in which policies supporting citizen participation can be drawn up through citizen participation. This conception of politics is doubly democratic: it is based on participation and oriented to supporting it. It is, in short, a *reflexive* conception of democracy, one in which democratic politics circles back to sustain the very conditions of equality that make it possible.

The guarantee of participatory equality at the heart of reflexive democracy is best encoded in a notion I call reflexive citizenship. It is a conception of citizens' rights that guarantees people the forms of agency needed to circle back, reflexively, to set the terms of their own citizenship. This includes, most importantly, their ability to devise policies ensuring their own equality. Reflexive citizenship specifies a set of core tasks for the welfare state right from the start. The state must ensure its own basis of legitimacy by safeguarding the material conditions of political participation. Any other functions the state incurs, I claim, must be based on this initial guarantee of participatory equality.

A focus on participatory equality provides a unique justification for welfare states. It is internally rooted in our own practices instead of being imposed from outside. This argument is not based on moral intuitions, but on commitments of a much more mundane kind. These are the ones we make going about our daily business of interacting with one another. These implicit values are revealed by our practices, not deduced from some more abstract ethical theory.

A particular kind of welfare state is needed to support the democratic commitments that arise from our daily interactions. The conception I will outline is oriented toward promoting equal opportunities in the political and cultural spheres. As such, it is most concerned to underwrite particular kinds of capacities and target inequalities that have a particularly political significance. In this view the state is justified on political and legal grounds, rather than as a vector of redistribution and economic regulation. This is not to say, however, that such a state would not have important redistributive consequences. Because it is justified as a means for equalizing the material conditions needed for its own legitimation, such a state would certainly exercise a redistributive function in the course of its other duties. Equally important, this vision promotes redistribution in an indirect sense. The political sphere is the arena in which citizens formulate policy, structure the economy, and set tax rates. When previously marginalized citizens have equal opportunities to participate, they will be able to raise redistributive claims in the political sphere as they see fit.

The most distinctive feature of this line of justification is its minimalism. Here the welfare state is defined in relation to political and cultural practice. When welfare supports equal political agency, citizens are able to decide how best to support their own ongoing equality and agency as citizens. This view is minimal in the sense that it does not draw on substantive social ideals of equality or justice. There is no utopian vision in this conception. Rather, it relies on a lean analysis of practice, identifying presuppositions and consequences of practices we have already adopted. As a form of justification, this argument is morally parsimonious.

This view has important implications for many other normative problems. When citizens have the ability to ensure their own participatory agency, they are placed on an equal footing in the public sphere. Equal opportunities to participate in turn allow each person the same chances to express her views and translate them into laws, policies, or norms. As a result, the political sphere becomes more than just an arena for horse trading and compromise. In a deep way, it reflects the basic presuppositions of social cooperation itself: the idea that people entering cooperative endeavors should be able to agree on the terms under which they will cooperate. This participatory arena is a space in which the norms regulating cooperative endeavors can be worked out. Equal participation thus becomes the means through which other norms, values, and goals are developed. As such, many other problems of social justice can be dissolved into such a conception of democratic equality. We need not devise philosophical answers for all such questions if we have some way of ensuring that the deliberations of actual citizens are fair and thoroughly democratic.

At the same time, a political turn toward reflexive democracy actually *removes* some previously contentious issues from discussion. This view narrows the scope of what can be democratically decided in certain key senses. Democratic citizens cannot consistently endorse practices that would disenfranchise themselves or other citizens. Strongly punitive, exclusionary, or racially and sexually biased welfare programs are thus off-limits because they would undermine the democratic bases of the welfare state itself. Similarly, an inadequately redistributive welfare state would fail to promote sufficient participatory equality. Excesses of state power, domination, or bureaucracy that interfere with the democratic agency of citizens would also be ruled out of bounds by my view. In each of these cases, democracy itself places normative limits on the political outcomes of democratic deliberation. As I will argue in the following pages, it would be normatively inconsistent for citizens to establish a system of laws that undercuts reflexive democracy. Here we see that a political turn has many implicit consequences for social and cultural equality, distributive justice, and the critique of power. Posing questions about the welfare state in democratic terms, then, simultaneously *answers* many of those same questions. It puts many safeguards in place against the runaway use of democracy to disenfranchise or dominate members of the polity.

In the coming pages, I will argue that reflexive democracy provides us with a powerful solution to many problems of the welfare state. By focusing on participatory equality, we establish a level playing field for adjudicating thorny issues of distribution, property, and policy design. Such a political turn also provides a basis for resolving difficult issues of political and cultural justice. The kind of participation required for reflexive democracy is possible only under very specific economic, cultural, and political conditions.[16] To secure these conditions, reflexive democracy in turn places many limits on economic, cultural, and political life. This conception is based *normatively* in politics, but it has wider implications for many other spheres of human interaction. Reflexive democracy thus goes hand in hand with broader projects of justice, but it gives politics pride of place as the normative cornerstone of an economically, culturally, and politically just society.

## 1.3 Democracy and Law as a Basis for the Welfare State

In spite of its minimal burdens of justification, the view I will develop produces a distinctive vision of the welfare state. The idea of reflexive democracy sets qualitative standards for welfare. Citizens must support their own participatory agency in order to sustain it in a reflexive sense. The welfare state is the institutional mechanism for ensuring that the conditions of reflexivity are met. To ensure a virtuous circularity of citizen participation, the state must maintain equal opportunities for political participation. Such opportunities must be *actually* equal because they have a very important function to fulfill. They cannot simply be a formal legal guarantee that is never realized in practice. To make opportunities actually equal, the welfare state must counteract social conditions that undermine participatory equality.

Participatory inequality has been studied thoroughly in the empirical literature. I use this work as a point of entry for a richer and more concrete description of reflexive democracy. The conditions undermining participatory equality include certain economic inequalities, particularly when they are so onerous that some people cannot participate because their health and well-being are in jeopardy. The recipients of means-tested welfare benefits are particularly prone to such inequalities. The conditions undermining participation also include inequalities less often seen as falling within the welfare state's domain. Unequal participatory skills stand out as particularly troubling. People's abilities to participate in political and cultural life seem to be associated with the degree to which they get to practice such skills in daily life. Having a high-status job, for instance, allows one to cultivate such skills, while a low-status job does not. The welfare state has a unique capacity to rectify this situation because welfare policy itself could be formulated to help equalize people's chances to develop such skills.

Because this conception emphasizes people's agency to do particular kinds of things, and because it requires actually equal opportunities, I draw on Amartya Sen's notion of capability equality. Sen's work provides a compact way to show exactly how the welfare state could go about promoting agency. Most strikingly, it suggests that one of the best ways to promote participatory equality may be to focus on the form rather than the content of welfare. Allowing people to participate in the administration of welfare encourages them to develop participatory skills. In this case, the form in which benefits are delivered could have as much effect as the content of goods and services that the state provides.

The result is a distinctive model of the welfare state. This state draws its goals from the political sphere. It serves as a support mechanism for the agency of citizens and thus focuses on providing them with the skills and resources needed to participate on an equal footing with others. This is a reflexive state, one dedicated above all to creating a virtuous circularity within its own democratic base. This conception is egalitarian and universalist, but in a qualitatively unique sense. It is dedicated to promoting a status that allows citizens to become equal in their cooperative interdependence. More concretely, this notion of the welfare state is centered on promoting agency rather than simply equalizing the possession of goods and resources.

The conception I am outlining is rooted in characteristically democratic values. The three most central of these are popular sovereignty, political inclusion, and equal opportunity. Popular sovereignty is the central value of all democracy. It claims that people should be able to author the laws under which they live. Political inclusion has been central to the democratic tradition for centuries as well, as the franchise has expanded to ever larger circles. This value recognizes that departures from the norm of popular sovereignty are hard to justify, and that sometimes extra measures must be taken to ensure that all people can exercise their sovereignty. Equal opportunity is an allied concept. It is primarily rooted in modern notions of distributive justice, but it can also be employed to theorize political inclusion more precisely. To a large extent, then, many of the ideas that I will draw on here are familiar and widely accepted. They are already part of the political culture of contemporary democratic societies. As I will argue, though, the wide *acceptance* of these values is nothing one should rely on to justify a welfare state. Much more important is the fact that these ideals are *presupposed* in practices in which we already engage.

With this brief outline as background, I can now sketch an even briefer response to the recent American welfare reforms. These reforms were directed at the very bottom of the American safety net. Temporary Assistance for Needy Families is a program designed for unemployed people with children. It provides temporary emergency relief, one that mitigates the effects of poverty on children while enforcing strict work rules for parents. As such, it does not promote the skills or resources needed to raise people to higher levels of material prosperity, nor does it effectively move them into sustainable employment. One of the most damaging effects of this policy is not its reproduction of poverty per se, however, but its systematic failure to promote political equality. TANF does not provide adequate opportunities for people to acquire the skills and resources they would need to participate as equals in politics. As a result, the voice of welfare recipients is significantly muted compared to other citizens. They are thus less able to participate in forming the very programs designed to benefit them. Not only is the poverty of such people reproduced, then, but they are further deprived of the political means to alleviate their condition and demand equal citizenship. In this sense, political marginalization plus poverty is even worse than poverty alone.

In the coming chapters I will articulate more clearly why political marginalization is such an important problem. I will claim that systematic inattention to participatory equality results in vexing paradoxes for democracy, violates commitments basic to American political practice, and ultimately undercuts the legitimacy of our political and legal system. These, however, are tendentious claims that one should not make lightly. It will take seven chapters to redeem them adequately. At the end I will return to the example of American welfare reform in much greater detail, providing a fuller exposition of the position I have only sketched here.

## 1.4 Overview

To develop the view I have just described, I will outline three idealized genres of argument about the welfare state. In order of their appearance, they are the labor market paradigm, the feminist paradigm, and the deliberative-democratic paradigm. Each of them highlights the benefits and drawbacks of a particular approach to welfare. Each is rooted in well-known work in political theory, but work that is heavily modified under my scrutiny. None of the paradigms is the product of any one person's view; rather, each is a composite. The three paradigms are thus ideal-typical in nature. Each represents the characteristic features of a particular way of thinking about welfare. The book's argument will unfold as I show how each resolves problems of its predecessor, creating its own difficulties in the process.

Chapter 2 outlines the first of these, the *labor market paradigm*. This paradigm reconstructs the normative core of the predominant view of the welfare state. As the name implies, this is the idea that the state ought to shield workers from exploitable vulnerabilities in the labor market. To examine its normative potential, I outline three distinct strands: the *comparative* approach exemplified by Gøsta Esping-Andersen's work; the *structural* approach of John Roemer; and the *moral-theoretic* approach of Robert Goodin. The comparative approach produces a rich analysis of the connections between welfare policy, markets, and social relations. It is analytically sophisticated but normatively weak. The structural approach packs a strong normative punch but is built on overly stylized assumptions about rationality and social structure. These assumptions compromise its usefulness. The moral-theoretic approach successfully avoids both of these problems, providing a more robust normative basis for the labor market paradigm.

All three strands of the labor market paradigm share a common problem. To make sense of its normative commitments, this paradigm must ultimately go beyond the economic sphere to address the social, cultural, and political bases of market vulnerability. The most defensible basis for making claims about exploitable vulnerabilities, I believe, is through politics itself. I use Albert Hirschman's concepts of exit and voice to outline a framework for thinking about such problems. Exit and voice fuse politics and economics, allowing the integration of economic issues with other social concerns. This perspective resolves labor market problems by shifting the normative burden to the political sphere. Now we must ask how political processes can be conducted in a fair and equitable way, ensuring that all citizens have an equal chance to voice their concerns and participate in forming the laws, norms, and policies under which they live. Answering that challenge is the central task of this book.

Chapter 3 shows why voice is such an important feature of the welfare state. Although the labor market paradigm provides us with valuable critiques of inequality and vulnerability, it construes them too narrowly as problems of class. When we look at inequality and vulnerability more broadly, we see that they are often articulated along gender lines as well. Feminists have successfully shown how states, markets, and families are structured by gender distinctions, at the same time that states, markets, and families reproduce such distinctions. The *feminist paradigm* is built around this critique of gender inequities and the injustices that result from them. It outlines a degendered and degendering welfare state, one that would use social policy to promote women's economic, cultural, and political equality while shielding them from gender-based injustice and domination. A principal point of attack for feminists has been the material bases of gender norms. The gender division of labor is a chief one of these. Feminists have outlined welfare programs designed to blur the lines between breadwinning and caregiving roles, degendering labor and encouraging men to share caregiving responsibilities. By undermining taken-for-granted ideas of masculine and feminine labor, such policies are designed to destabilize gender norms in a broader sense.

Focusing on Nancy Fraser's "universal caregiver state" as an exemplar of this strategy, I claim that such policies run aground to the extent that they do not account for the joint effects of choice and enculturation in people's use of welfare benefits. In a patriarchal society and a democratic state, people's choices reproduce the gender norms of their own socialization. This has been observed during the past three decades of Swedish welfare policy, which I examine as an extended case study. To foil this paradox, welfare regimes must try to promote gender equity in a broader sense by ensuring that women have cultural agency equal to men's. Cultural agency provides women with increased voice to challenge and renegotiate gender norms. To figure out what equality might mean in a cultural sense, I turn to Amartya Sen's work on capability egalitarianism. This work provides elegant means to theorize the kinds of cultural struggles with which feminists are concerned. It shows that the feminist paradigm can succeed only if the welfare state is conceived as a means for providing women with particular kinds of agency. This modification of the feminist paradigm further develops the notion of voice in both a political and cultural sense.

Chapter 4 continues the line of argument developed in chapters 2 and 3, outlining a distinctively political conception of the welfare state. Earlier I claimed that our normative understanding of welfare should be based on a conception of politics rather than norms of economic justice. We should, in other words, make a *political turn* in our view of welfare. The labor market and feminist paradigms provide the initial moves in such a turn, but neither has the resources to develop an autonomous, free-standing conception of politics appropriate for the welfare state. These paradigms show what is required for a political turn, however. The desiderata derived from them form the basis for a view named the *deliberative-democratic paradigm*.

The deliberative-democratic paradigm centers around a core commitment called the *participatory ideal*. That is the idea that citizens should have equal abilities to participate in forming the norms, laws, and policies under which they live. T. H. Marshall provides a rich vein of insights for this view, contributing especially to our understanding of the functional relations between democracy, law, and welfare. Unfortunately, though, Marshall's work is limited by its lack of a normative dimension. It describes the relations between political, civil, and welfare rights in admirable detail, but cannot explain how or why a welfare state should incorporate these elements.

Jürgen Habermas fills this lacuna well, adopting Marshall's basic framework but adding powerful normative resources to it. He claims that rights are justified to the extent that they support citizens' autonomy. This includes whatever welfare rights are needed to provide autonomy's material basis. When such basic rights are guaranteed, citizens can develop other measures that they see as important to promoting their own freedom and political participation. Habermas, then, articulates a crucial normative dimension in the participatory ideal.

While the participatory ideal fulfills the desiderata for a political turn in the welfare state, it is not without problems. Chapter 5 details an important one of these. The ideal stipulates that the welfare measures necessary to ensure equality must be developed through the participation of their recipients. On one hand welfare exists to ensure political agency, on the other hand it depends upon it. The participatory ideal is thus circular. It depends on exactly the same processes it is designed to safeguard. There is, in short, a vicious circle between the legitimation of welfare rights and their justification. This circularity is not simply an artifact of the participatory ideal, but a fundamental paradox of constitutional democracy. I call it the *paradox of enablement*. The paradox is a significant problem because it short-circuits the relation between democratic equality and democratic legitimacy, ensuring that the participatory ideal can never get off the ground.

Jürgen Habermas's work provides a concrete example of the paradox. The problem crops up in Habermas's conception of rights. I experiment with a promising solution, drawing on Habermas's ideas about the evolutionary development of constitutions. This strategy merely illustrates the intractability of the problem, however. Fortunately it also suggests a different approach: a conception of welfare rights justified as a necessary precondition of democratic deliberation. This solution eliminates the problem of circularity because welfare rights are guaranteed from the start as a means to ensure democratic equality. Welfare rights are a necessary component of citizenship in this view, rather than a contingent patchover for other problems.

Chapter 6 continues the line of thought in chapter 5, developing the idea of reflexive democracy as a solution to the paradox of enablement. To resolve this paradox, citizens must be able to ensure that they will not be excluded from political participation. They must, in other words, be able to participate as equals in defining the very meaning of citizenship, particularly the laws and policies that sustain political agency. A nonparadoxical conception of citizenship is therefore *reflexive* in form: it provides citizens the means to ensure the bases of their own equality. When citizens have this capability, democracy itself becomes reflexive. Reflexive citizenship is thus a core legal and procedural element of the broader concept of reflexive democracy.

Reflexive citizenship foils the paradox of enablement by creating a virtuous circle between participation and the means needed to sustain it. It does not resolve the paradox in one stroke, however. Instead, it establishes a standard for actual, democratic processes of constitutional reform—an improved version of the evolutionary approach outlined above. It allows citizens to judge their progress toward a goal inherent in their own ideals about participation. Reflexive citizenship thus adds teleology to constitutional democracy, providing the grounds for people to resolve the paradox of enablement themselves.

To make the idea of reflexive citizenship more concrete, I outline some of the rights and policies that would be included in such a scheme. Amartya Sen's work on capability equality again provides a useful way to think about a conception of citizenship that promotes the agency of its citizens. In sketching more concrete details of such a view, I also provide a much more specific account of the kinds of equality and sufficiency required for the participatory ideal.

Chapter 7 moves from issues of citizenship and participation to issues of justification. Citizenship is a legal status encoded in constitutions and statutes. Because the view I am outlining is constitutional in its basic structure, I now turn to examine the normative foundations of law as a basis for welfare regimes. I draw again on Habermas's work as an entrée into these issues.

The key problem is to decide how a theorist can say anything compelling about the content of the law, if legitimate laws are solely created by sovereign citizens. More specifically, the question is how one can claim that citizenship ought to be a reflexive status guaranteeing equal capabilities of certain kinds. Such a view seems to have an awkward relation to the democratic deliberation of actual citizens because it preempts many of their own decisions about citizenship and rights. In response to these concerns, I note that the normative claims of this theory ultimately arise from citizens' actual practices and are not imposed on them from elsewhere. This view finds a principled perspective for legal criticism *within* the positing of the law itself. It connects actual legal and political practices with more abstract philosophical principles. It suggests that philosophical conceptions of democracy, citizenship, and constitutional rights can be derived from the actual practices of real citizens. If this can be accomplished, there would be no tension between my theoretical analysis of reflexive democracy and the actual positing of laws and constitutions.

Chapter 8 concludes the volume by drawing its various lines of argument together into a normative view of reflexive democracy and welfare state citizenship. Building on chapter 7, I establish a basis for this view by outlining some of the implicit presuppositions of constitutional democracy. I show that the cooperative structure of our social and political interactions carries important normative consequences. The modern state is an institutional structure designed to organize a highly complex system of social cooperation. People entering into cooperative relations must be able to agree to the terms under which they cooperate. The state is legitimate, therefore, only when citizens are guaranteed actually equal opportunities for participation. Thus arises the paradox of enablement that I detail in chapter 5: the welfare state depends on equal political participation to legitimate itself, but at the same time it exists to ensure equal participation. The democratic-constitutional state is thus internally self-referential: in order to legitimate itself, it must provide the political bases of its own legitimacy. To avoid the potentially vicious circularity of this situation, a finely tuned welfare regime must ensure political equality by providing particular capabilities for its citizens. These are ongoing guarantees to particular forms of political agency—those at the core of reflexive democracy. Reflexive democracy is thus a basic presupposition of our present forms of social cooperation. It is justified by practices we already engage in.

There is much to gain by looking beyond classic economic justifications for the welfare state. Norms of participation and political equality provide a minimal but fecund justification for welfare rights, giving contemporary welfare states a much more solid normative foundation and making their core functions much less prone to controversy. This argument describes a qualitatively different focus for welfare, one promoting equal opportunities for democratic participation. Before we can outline that view, however, it is first necessary to take a much closer look at the classic, social-democratic model of the welfare state. There is still much to learn from this rich body of thought.

# 2

# Vulnerability, Exploitation, and the Market

A "welfare state" is a state in which organized power is deliberately used (through politics and administration) in an effort to modify the play of market forces. . . .

—*Asa Briggs* [1]

Originally conceived as a means of "poor relief," the welfare state has been dialectically intertwined with the economy since its inception. At times it has been employed as a countermeasure to the economy, sheltering workers from the side effects of capitalism. At times it has functioned as an adjunct to the capitalist market system, maintaining a steady supply of healthy labor and stabilizing the economy's cyclical fluctuations. Sometimes it has performed both of these functions at once. The Elizabethan Poor Laws, for instance, provided poverty relief to economically marginalized citizens in sixteenth- and seventeenth-century England, but also mandated corporal punishment for those able but unwilling to work. The parish rates of the Speenhamland system provided comprehensive though paternalistic protection to displaced agricultural workers. The Poor Law Amendment Act of 1834, in contrast, reimposed the imperatives of the market and provided workers with strong incentives to engage in paid employment. The first full-blown welfare state—Bismarck's conservative German regime of the 1880s and '90s—was intended to capture the loyalty of workers by sheltering them from the insecurities of the labor market. Postwar welfare policies in Scandinavia and Britain aimed at even more comprehensive forms of social protection, also designed to bridge the gaps left by paid employment. And recently we have seen a return to more punitive, market-oriented welfare programs in the Clinton–Blair version of the Third Way.

Although history abounds with ideas about the relation between welfare states and markets, the intellectual origins of our present view come out of late nineteenth-century socialism. When revisionists like Eduard Bernstein gave up on revolution in favor of a gradualist strategy of social reform, they established the basis for a critical understanding of the relation between state policy and markets. This position focuses on the state's ability to counteract the side effects of capitalism. To the dismay of their orthodox Marxist colleagues, these early social democrats became participants in the critical project of rethinking the nascent welfare state rather than opponents of its very existence.

The *labor market paradigm* that I will outline captures key features of this classic model. It is the line of thought that connects the views of Eduard Bernstein, William Beveridge, Richard Titmuss, and Franklin Roosevelt with contemporary theories of social democracy and market socialism. There is, of course, no single, orthodox version of the labor market paradigm, and no single person will subscribe to the totality of the view I outline. Rather, there are scores of normative approaches to the market economy and hundreds more agendas aimed at correcting its problems. The question is, which of these many approaches gives us the best insights into the problems faced by the welfare state? To make this scene surveyable, I will construct an ideal-typical model of this paradigm. I will identify a core feature that connects all of the various strands and use it to assess the merits and drawbacks of this venerable justification of the welfare state.

The central thesis of the labor market paradigm is that the welfare state should shelter workers from exploitation in the labor market. Exactly what this problem is or how it can best be analyzed is by no means universally agreed on, however. There are many different and competing answers to the question of what is wrong with capitalist labor markets and what the welfare state should do about it. To delineate the labor market paradigm, I will examine three distinctive approaches. Together they provide a good characterization of the many different things that fit under the paradigm's large tent. For ease of exposition, I will focus on three individual thinkers, Gøsta Esping-Andersen, John Roemer, and Robert Goodin. I chose these three because each frames his particular approach with exemplary rigor and insight. To emphasize that I intend these thinkers to represent broader streams of thought, I will label their positions the comparative approach, the structural approach, and the moral-theoretic approach, respectively. These labels do not do justice to the richness of each position, but I hope my discussion will compensate for that limitation.

I have chosen to begin with problems of work and labor because these issues form the primary source for our current understanding of the welfare state. This starting point provides a good opportunity to indicate future directions and paths not yet taken. By focusing too narrowly on economically generated problems, the labor market paradigm is inattentive to other forms of inequality and exploitation. This weakens its own normative basis. To produce a robust conception of the welfare state, we must consider economic issues in the same breath as political and cultural ones. In criticizing this economic one-sidedness, I will claim that the normative bases of the labor market paradigm should be enriched by insights from political theory. To successfully indict the problems of the labor market, we should develop a better account of the political basis for normative claims about the economy. At the same time, however, we must be aware of the ways in which economic vulnerabilities undercut political participation and voice. The labor market paradigm can benefit greatly from the insights of political theory, then, but it has much to offer our understanding of politics as well.

## 2.1 The Comparative Approach

Gøsta Esping-Andersen has developed the most sophisticated version of what I will call the *comparative approach*. He takes seriously questions like Emile Durkheim's celebrated query, "What is the state? Where does it begin, where does it end?"[2] Esping-Andersen notes that the functional borders between states, markets, and families are often blurred. The state interacts dynamically with markets and families, regulating them, drawing taxes from them, and collectivizing certain tasks, risks, and responsibilities. Markets, similarly, often perform functions that could otherwise be allocated to the welfare state or family members—providing health, education, job training, retirement, and other resources required for daily life. Families, in turn, are forced to shoulder any welfare responsibilities not taken over by states or markets. Welfare provision is not just a state concern, then, but a characteristic blend of responsibilities allocated to states, markets, and families. A society's particular pattern of these features tells us a great deal about its institutional organization and the distribution of welfare-providing tasks within its domain. Countries like the United States, for instance, favor individual responsibility for welfare but maintain relatively well-developed markets in which many services can be purchased. Many continental European countries, in contrast, allocate a substantial part of welfare provision to families, maintaining wage and tax laws that discourage outsourcing of such responsibilities to the market. Scandinavian countries tend to centralize more welfare functions in the state, displacing markets while simultaneously reducing the responsibilities borne by families.

Given such important variations in welfare provision, it would be analytically misleading to focus only on functions directly performed by the state. Esping-Andersen maintains a broader focus, using the term "welfare regime" to refer to the welfare-providing complex of states, markets, and families. A welfare regime is the entire set of institutional arrangements that promote welfare. These arrangements include systems of social policy instituted by governments, markets in welfare-providing services, and work done by families to maintain the health and well-being of their members.[3] Using this notion as an analytic framework for comparison, Esping-Andersen departs from the assumption that the state is merely a superstructure appended to an economic base. Conversely, he also argues that it is a mistake to discuss only the political, "public" aspects of welfare while ignoring the important interconnections between government policies and the "private," economic and familial domains. To focus solely on either the state or the economy as a prime mover in society creates an artificial division that could characterize only a state-socialist or laissez-faire liberal state. A central aim of Esping-Andersen's analysis is to show precisely the opposite: that state policy is dynamically interrelated with markets and families, and that the welfare-providing functions of any of these cannot be understood without reference to the others.

The most celebrated feature of Esping-Andersen's work is his typology of welfare regimes. His so-called three worlds of welfare are three sets of family resemblances among contemporary welfare states. He names them liberal, conservative, and social-democratic to indicate the dominant political philosophy shaping each type. Liberal regimes are predominantly descendants of the British Empire. They industrialized early under the influence of a strong capitalist class. Not surprisingly, their social policy and market structure tends to be oriented towards economic performance and efficiency. Conservative regimes, in contrast, industrialized late. Their social policy adapted already existing traditions of service provision by craft and professional guilds. Countries like Italy and Germany, for example, still award many pensions and other benefits based on a person's occupation. Such regimes are called conservative because they tend to reproduce traditional status distinctions. It is no surprise, then, that conservative regimes also tend to be the most strongly "familialistic," providing welfare through family-wage, (male) breadwinner jobs, encouraging women to stay at home, and shifting care responsibilities into the family. Finally, social-democratic regimes were largely formed during the postwar welfare state expansion. They tend to award benefits universally on the basis of citizenship. This provides workers with more comprehensive protection from market forces and decreases emphasis on the family unit in favor of provision to individuals. The Scandinavian countries are classic models of this regime-type.

The notion of welfare regimes allows Esping-Andersen to compare the freedom that workers have from paid labor in various regime-types. His particular focus is on the relative bargaining position of employers and workers. When the market places employers in a better bargaining position than workers, it gives them an unfair advantage and allows them to extract wage and benefit concessions. Employers gain an advantage due to market conditions structured by law and public policy. Periodic variations in labor supply and demand restrict workers' ability to change jobs. They are at a particular disadvantage during labor-market gluts, because they cannot stockpile their labor-power to wait for better prices like other commodity sellers can. In such circumstances people without jobs are forced to bid against each other for unacceptably low wages, while those who are employed must be careful not to jeopardize the job they already have. Thus labor market cycles make people looking for jobs vulnerable to prospective employers because they are forced to conclude contracts from disadvantaged bargaining positions. These cycles also reduce the market mobility of those already employed. As the economic system goes through cycles of expansion and contraction, it systematically places workers at a disadvantage, weakening their ability to negotiate fair labor contracts and preventing them from leaving unacceptable jobs.

In actual fact, however, no labor market is unregulated. The relative vulnerability of workers is determined by labor market regulations and by the alternatives to wage labor that welfare policy provides. Esping-Andersen refers to this feature of social policy as the decommodification of labor.[4] Social policy decommodifies labor by providing workers with alternative sources of income, giving them a better bargaining position in wage negotiations and shielding them from the uncertainties of the labor market. Labor is not literally taken out of circulation as a commodity in this view. Rather, its value is increased by changing the conditions under which it is bought and sold.

Esping-Andersen's three welfare regime-types take quite different approaches to decommodification. Conservative regimes were historically formed in reaction to the growing dominance of capitalism in modern Europe. As such, they draw on traditional conceptions of patronage to gain the loyalty of workers. These welfare states tend to be fairly decommodifying. However, their benefits also tend to be conditional on loyalty or conforming to moral norms. Conservative regimes thus decommodify labor in order to assert other forms of obligation and control, typically in relation to the state, religious institutions, and social groups. Historically this logic can be seen in the Papal Encyclicals *Rerum Novarum* (1891) and *Quadragesimo Anno* (1931), and in the Bismarckean welfare state of the 1880s and 90s.[5]

Liberal regimes are the most strongly dedicated to reinforcing the logic of the market. Therefore they promote the commodification of labor most heavily. This includes reliance on means-testing and less-eligibility rules, and a general ethos of self-reliance, independent initiative, and moving people "off of welfare into work." Not surprisingly, this regime-type is most clearly characteristic of former parts of the British Empire, led by Australia and the United States.

Finally, social-democratic regimes emphasize decommodification most heavily. They tend to award benefits without regard to employment status or contribution. They have fairly generous pension, medical, and leave programs. In general, they provide workers with alternatives to paid labor and with greater means of independence in both the workplace and the labor market. The Scandinavian countries and the Netherlands provide the best examples of this type.

Although the comparative approach permits a great deal of analytical sophistication in studying labor markets, it has a more difficult time enunciating what is good or bad about them. It is not surprising that the normative capacities of the comparative approach are not well developed. This approach is designed to be descriptive rather than normative. It thus devotes little attention to accounting for the values and norms its puts forward as goals for the welfare state. It is not designed to accomplish this kind of philosophical task.

This is not to say, however, that the comparative approach is not normative. Normativity is frequently implied by the choice of methodology and subject matter. Investigating patterns of labor-market mobility implies an understated indictment of labor-market dependency. Decommodification gives workers freedom to move in and out of paid employment, preventing vulnerability and balancing power between workers and employers. It counterbalances the unfairnesses of capitalist labor markets by making the bargaining positions of the parties more symmetrical. Such policies ensure that labor contracts are more truly consensual by giving workers meaningful alternatives to the labor market. Value judgments are indeed present in the comparative approach, then. They tend to be values that are broadly agreed-on aspects of our common background culture, largely norms of autonomy, equality, and freedom. These values provide an unenunciated agenda for research and an implicit schema for interpreting its results.

Such implicit normativity has both drawbacks and advantages. The lack of carefully worked-out normative values deprives comparison of some of its rigor. It is not clear, for instance, exactly what is objectionable about bargaining asymmetries between capitalists and workers. Is the asymmetry itself objectionable, in the sense that we expect people to enter a contract on equal footing? Or is the objection against the implicit power that comes with such an asymmetry, the fact that it could provide employers an advantage over workers? More radically, would such an advantage be objectionable only when it forced workers into employment out of desperation or fear for their life? Or is the objection that asymmetries in bargaining power allow employers to profit from the labor of workers? These are important questions; answering them allows us to decide at exactly what point an intervention should be made into the labor market. Without clarifying its normative concerns, the comparative approach risks formulating a welfare state that corrects the wrong problem. Any theory that implies normativity rather than arguing for it runs this risk.

On the positive side, the fact that the comparative approach is not tied a priori to any particular values provides it with an admirable flexibility. Comparative investigations of the economy can be connected with many different normative bases. These connections require justification, of course, but their very contingency allows an investigator a great deal of leeway in identifying the unique problems of a particular situation. Rather than viewing the economy solely through the lens of, say, exploitation, one could talk about a broader range of problems like wage differentials, differences in control and self-direction,[6] and the insecurities people face when economic risk increases.[7] Normativity in this approach is open ended and pluralistic, and therefore in some sense more robust. As I have said, though, this open-endedness can also be a liability. The more pluralistic a value system is, the less precisely targeted it is as well.

In sum, the comparative approach gives us a finely drawn analysis of the market conditions that undercut workers' independence and place them under the power of employers. This analysis is formulated in terms of the dependence or independence of labor: its degree of decommodification. This approach charges the welfare state with regulating markets, both through legal means and by providing extramarket alternatives to paid labor. The tasks of the state, in this scenario, are to promote economic autonomy by counterbalancing the dependency-creating force of the market.

## 2.2 The Structural Approach

While the labor market paradigm as a whole benefits greatly from the analytical sophistication of Esping-Andersen's work, it needs a stronger basis for enunciating the acceptable limits of market vulnerability. A second strand of the labor market paradigm provides one such view by developing a normative indictment of exploitation. I will call this the *structural approach* because it focuses on structural features of markets rather than the particular forces that act within them. Here the market's constitutive rules, particularly property laws, enable exploitation. The strongest version of this view has been developed by John Roemer. Roemer's theory is built on a notion of class as a set of structural positions in the capitalist economy. This allows him to discern the interests of capitalists and workers, allowing a similarly clear analysis of how they are opposed to one another. This vision of conflicting class interests in turn grounds a sharply focused critique of capitalism.

Roemer defines class in terms of the ownership of productive resources. Owning productive resources makes one a capitalist; not owning them makes one a wage-laborer. Unlike the classic Marxist theory of exploitation,[8] however, Roemer's does not rely on the idea that surplus value is taken from workers in the production process itself. He locates capitalism's unfairness more generally in the causal connections between the fortunes of workers and capitalists. If one person's fortunes improve at the expense of another's, then on Roemer's account the former is exploiting the latter. The actual mechanism of exploitation is not at issue, then, only its result. Roemer formalizes these ideas in the following manner. Exploitation occurs when: (1) The exploited would be better off if they withdrew from the society, taking their per capita share of productive, alienable assets with them. (2) The exploiters would be worse off if they withdrew with their per capita share of productive, alienable assets. (3) The exploiters gain from the labor of the exploited.[9] This schema draws on an implicit suggestion that the exploited cannot "withdraw from the society" for particular reasons. Roemer makes this assumption explicit in other parts of his work, referring to it as domination.[10] This implicit premise is needed because the moral force of exploitation relies on the fact that the exploited are forced to benefit the exploiters. If they did so voluntarily, we would call it not exploitation but generosity.

Although this view does not rely on an account of how exploitation occurs, Roemer tends to interpret it in terms of labor transfers that result from inequalities in private property. In his analysis, price equilibrium in a market economy systematically favors people who own productive assets. Consensual trading between people who have less capital and people who have more will result in transfers of labor from the former to the latter. Exploitation in this technical sense, then, emerges as a result of trade between people who own different amounts of the means of production. People with more productive assets than they themselves can use will always be able to charge people without productive assets who desire their use. This is a general property of price equilibrium rather than the result of any specific market conditions. Thus exploiters do not have to gain from the labor of the exploited by directly appropriating the products of their labor. It can occur through trade in the marketplace instead.

Roemer's conception of class structure produces an elegant analysis of conflicting material interests. It shows a clear correlation between one's class identity—defined as one's relation to the means of production—and economic interaction. People who own productive resources will fare better than those who do not. More important, they will fare better *at the expense of* those who do not. This reveals a direct antagonism within the productive relations structuring the capitalist economy.

Two features of the market are crucial to Roemer's account of exploitation: private ownership of productive assets and some kind of domination holding the system in place. Unequal ownership of productive assets creates the market conditions in which capitalists gain from the labor of workers. Unequal ownership itself is not normatively bad, however. If no economic system more advantageous to workers is possible in current technical, economic, and social conditions, then domination is not necessary to hold the present system in place. An exploitative system is bad, on Roemer's account, only when there *is* a viable alternative that is blocked by the domination of one class over the other. In capitalist societies this domination is not typically overt, though in the last instance it does depend on police power and the state legal apparatus. Rather, it can be found in the system of property rights that allows unequal ownership of the means of production. The form of domination undergirding the capitalist economy is a subtle one, then: it lies in the laws determining ownership and control. Capitalist property rights enable exploitation by creating classes of owners and workers, and they entrench it by fixing the system of ownership in place.

The structural approach produces a normative diagnosis competing with that of the comparative approach. It is not based on conceptions of reciprocity in bargaining or equal freedom in the market. Rather, this approach centers on the structures of the market and the system of domination that holds them in place. For the structural approach, labor market conditions are irrelevant. According to Roemer, regulating markets may shift wage equilibria in one direction or the other, but it will not change the fact that capitalists gain from their disproportionate share of productive assets whenever labor is commodified. Changes in market conditions may change the *rate* of exploitation—the relative proportion of workers' wages to capitalists' profit—but not the fact that exploitation *exists*. From this perspective, the comparative approach seems to be fussing over details rather than addressing basic questions. Structural theorists would claim that market regulation only gives workers more power in bargaining for exploitative wages, whereas the structural approach circumvents the entire issue by ending exploitation.

Because the structural approach locates the problems of labor markets deep in the structures of the economy, it tends to focus on restructuring the economy rather than ameliorating conditions of workers within it. This perspective focuses above all on equalizing the possession of productive assets. As a result, it develops a forceful argument for full-blown market socialism, giving us a distinctive vision of an economy in which markets are retained but productive resources are socialized. The structural approach is correspondingly dismissive of any welfare regime not dedicated to rearticulating property relations. A combination of welfare state plus capitalist property rights, for instance, would be an insufficient compromise. A redistributive welfare state might improve the plight of workers to an extent, but it would leave the sources of class conflict in place. In this picture, middle paths incorporating elements of capitalism and welfare could be temporary stopping points in some grander transformation, but they are not free-standing solutions to the problems of the market.

Although the structural approach makes strong claims about the function and justification of the welfare state, these claims are limited by its narrow range of view. The structural approach is based on a conception of identity defined by the ownership of productive assets. Within this framework, a person's identity is either worker or capitalist. Actual people, of course, fit into many different positions in society. They are not only workers or employers but also spouses, consumers, parents, members of racial and ethnic groups, and so on. Their identity is defined not only by their place in relations of production but also in terms of consumption habits, social status, relations of power and domination, organization and club membership, citizenship, belief, age, race, ethnicity, religion, and gender. The structural approach thus excludes many other possible axes of social differentiation, or at most it includes them as elements subsidiary to a primary distinction between capitalists and workers.

The structural approach does not claim to portray the entire social world in one model, of course. Its claim is more modest: to have identified a deeply structured faultline within the capitalist economy, around which actually existing social conflicts would likely form. In this picture, the objective interests of the working and capitalist classes are the interests of classes in-themselves, abstract entities defined strictly in terms of asset ownership. Any person occupying either of these positions would, in this view, have interests dictated by her place within economic relations.

The structural approach's restrictive definition of identity creates normative problems, however. It is difficult to sustain its core claim that people's interests can be specified solely with reference to their class identity. The structural approach's assessment of interests focuses narrowly on the processes generating and distributing wealth. It thereby ignores important social and cultural factors in economic life. Access to economic opportunities is regulated in subtle ways by group membership, racial identity, spatial and geographic location, and gender. Interests cannot be read narrowly off of one axis of social identity, then, nor can they be seen as deriving directly from social position in a culturally unmediated sense.

Consider, for example, the hypothetical case of an African-American male capitalist. There is a sense in which the capitalist's interests are best described by his class. He has an interest in exploiting workers of any identity, so long as they produce profit. Taken as a group, capitalists all share material interests in the exploitative efficiency of capitalism. On the other hand, the interests of this capitalist are shaped in a different way by race. In a racialized, Anglo-dominated business world, racial identity diminishes his access to business connections and markets more open to European-American colleagues. It can also lead to disrespect and "misrecognition" that decreases his overall well-being.[11] The African-American capitalist would benefit materially, then, from measures ending stigmatization and bias. In this sense, African-Americans taken as a group share material interests that can be said to conflict in important ways with those of European-Americans. This example shows that culture and class intertwine to shape a person's interests. If we tried to theorize the African-American capitalist's interests solely based on his class, we would misunderstand important aspects of the structural milieu in which he acts.

Similarly, the interests of women are related to those of men in complicated ways. A woman in a traditional male-breadwinner, female-caregiver family shares the material interests of her husband to the extent that his pay satisfies their material needs. If his interests are harmed by exploitation, so are hers; if his are advanced by owning the means of production, so are hers. However, her interests are not determined purely by her relation to the means of production: they also depend importantly on social, cultural, legal, and economic structures of family life, her own hypothetical market mobility, and other social and cultural determinants of material well-being. In our present system of social norms, women perform unwaged domestic labor much more frequently than men.[12] This holds whether a woman is employed outside the home or not. In either case, her interests are undermined by the inequitable distribution of household labor, by social norms limiting women's mobility into paid employment, and by inequitable control of resources within the family. Men and children are the beneficiaries of these inequities. To this extent, a woman's interests are structurally opposed to those of her husband.

Unwaged domestic labor does not fit well with the structural approach in general. The worker of the structural approach is a waged worker who labors in the economic sphere. This definition of labor excludes uncommodified household and caring labor because it is not a wage relation between workers and capitalists. Unwaged labor does not fit the class definition of exploitation because it does not involve the transfer of labor between those owning productive assets and those who do not. Caring labor is a necessary component of the productive process, however. It reproduces the laborer himself, providing him with the material means to sell labor in the marketplace.[13] A gendered division is typically drawn between domestic and wage labor. Wage labor has traditionally been a male-dominated domain, while unwaged caregiving labor has been a predominantly female domain. By ignoring this vital dimension of labor, the structural approach is in principle unable to theorize the gender dimensions of its division, or even take unwaged labor into account as an additional form of exploitation.

Similarly, women's vulnerability to violence, harassment, rape, and abuse has an important effect on their material interests. This vulnerability has economic bases, to be sure: a woman is more vulnerable to the extent that she lacks the labor market mobility to leave any given job or household. Lack of mobility, however, is largely based on the gendered character of markets. In addition, both a woman's vulnerability to violence and her actual experience of it are determined by largely non-economic factors: gendered laws and political spheres as well as gendered habits, attitudes, and practices. Again we find that a woman's material interests are culturally mediated and socially complex. They cannot be reduced in any simple sense to her relation to the means of production.

Overall, the material interests of caregiving women are thus a complex mix of class and gender considerations, including their relation to the means of production, relation to other individuals, market mobility, status as legal and economic actors, and vulnerability to gender-based forms of violence. Interests are not given simply in class relations here, but in the mixture of elements composing a person's identity.

Both race and gender furnish examples of interests determined jointly by economic class and other identity criteria. This shows that class is not a sufficient descriptor of material interests: actual people have complex and sometimes conflicting interests. Within our present system of racial norms, for example, the African-American capitalist shares interests with racial compatriots, on one hand, and with fellow capitalists, on the other. His interests are divided in a very important sense: his capitalist interests are clouded by commonality with similarly raced workers, while his racial interests are complicated by his place within the structure of economic exploitation. Similarly, women in our current culture have interests that are determined by their own relation to the gendered economic sphere, by gendered economic relations mediated through spouses and other family members, and by sociocultural threats to material well-being. Culture, social relations, and economy converge to shape material interests in complex and contradictory ways. In particular, the conditions of domination that make exploitation possible are rarely just differences in productive assets. It is thus normatively problematic and analytically limiting to claim that material interests deduced purely with reference to class identity provide a sufficient basis for evaluating capitalism. By extension, we cannot go directly from this analysis to a wholesale dismissal of the welfare state.

## 2.3 The Moral-Theoretic Approach

Robert Goodin provides alternate foundations for the labor market paradigm. His work parallels Roemer's but operates through considerably different methods. Like Roemer, Goodin develops a normative perspective on the labor market by criticizing exploitation. Like Roemer, he bases his criticism on an analysis of the conditions that make exploitation possible. Unlike Roemer, however, Goodin's conception of exploitation is based on a moral assessment of our responsibilities to protect vulnerable people. In this *moral-theoretic approach,* exploitation is a special case of what goes wrong when the vulnerable are not protected.

Goodin builds a case for a general moral principle requiring protection of vulnerable people. This norm, based on the idea of not allowing harm to come to the vulnerable, is allied with a stronger one forbidding us to harm them directly.[14] These closely related norms, he claims, are the source of our judgments about many social relations and practices: about intimate relations like friendship, marriage, and the treatment of elderly parents and children; about fiduciary relations between professionals and their clients; and even about promises and contracts. Goodin argues that many of the specific norms governing our treatment of such others are actually founded on norms about vulnerability.

Moral norms requiring us to protect vulnerable people also extend to the economy. Goodin claims that market-generated vulnerabilities are morally problematic because they leave people open to harm and being taken advantage of. Such vulnerabilities are, in short, exploitable. Goodin clarifies the moral logic of exploitable vulnerabilities using four criteria. A vulnerability is exploitable when: (1) the relationship between two parties is asymmetrical; (2) the subordinate person needs the resource provided by this relationship; (3) the relationship is the subordinate person's only source for such resources; and (4) the superordinate person has discretionary control over the resource.[15] In this account the superordinate person abuses his superior position to take unfair advantage of the subordinate. Market conditions that give someone a bargaining advantage also obligate him not to use this advantage to others' harm.

A capitalist market economy is prone to creating vulnerabilities that would undercut its own bases if left unchecked. Goodin identifies three of these, each of which requires the correcting influence of some kind of welfare state.[16] The first arises as a threat to property rights. Private property is one of the fundamental features of a capitalist economy. Correspondingly, property rights are the defining legal characteristic of capitalism because they allow people to own productive assets, invest them, and own the proceeds of their investment. Goodin notes, though, that property rights can be jeopardized by the market at the same time that they are its presupposition. When the economy fails to provide all people with resources sufficient to meet their basic needs, some will be forced either to steal or die. Those who choose to steal will be *morally justified* in doing so because the economy itself places them in a vulnerable position. If stealing is moral, however, the normative basis of property rights is undermined. The market systematically undercuts itself, then, by destroying the moral and social conditions of its own survival.

A second class of vulnerabilities would arise by universalizing the logic of the market. This would happen if everything were considered fungible and all needs were to be met by the market. Not everything can be marketed, however. Some goods and services must be supplied outside the market, and some people cannot be dealt with on a market basis. Every constitutional democracy has a core set of rights, for instance, that are nonfungible. One is not allowed to sell one's vote or sell oneself into slavery. Vulnerable people constitute such a case as well. Their vulnerability cannot be protected by market forces, say by the emergence of a market in vulnerability protection. If people are vulnerable because they are poor and starving, then they would have no money to purchase vulnerability insurance. Markets in this case are the source of the problem, so they cannot also be its solution. The vulnerable must therefore be protected outside of the market. Universalizing the market's logic by commodifying everything would leave the vulnerable open to exploitation, causing us to default on our moral duties.

A third class of vulnerabilities arises as a threat to people's independence in the market. People need to be independent so their buying and selling decisions result in optimal allocations of resources. Dependencies of various kinds distort the market's coordinating ability. The exclusive seller of a needed good, for instance, is in a privileged position to demand a much higher price than a perfectly competitive market would allow. Similarly, any buyer who will die without a given good is forced to pay any price simply to stay alive. Such a price reflects demand governed by desperation, rather than the buyer's estimation of the value of the good relative to other preferences. Lack of independence creates functional problems in the market, but more importantly, it allows the exploitation of vulnerable people by those in a position to supply what they need. Ultimately, then, such vulnerabilities create moral problems for the economy producing them.

A welfare state is necessary to prevent such vulnerabilities from being exploited. It functions as a means to eliminate both functional and moral contradictions in the economy. In the case of morality, the welfare state is the institutional mechanism we use to discharge our collective responsibilities to protect vulnerable others. Our collective responsibilities thus determine the character of the mechanism in a straightforward way. Here Goodin's definition of exploitable vulnerability is very useful. The connection between exploitation and vulnerability can be cut by disrupting any one of the features outlined above. Goodin's own preferred point of attack is on (3) and (4). To foil condition (3), the welfare state must stand alongside the market as a provider of needed resources. It thus serves as an escape route for people who would otherwise be exploited. A potential danger of such an arrangement, of course, is that people will simply depend on the state instead of the market. To prevent this, Goodin argues that administrative discretion must be minimized to foil condition (4). Welfare rights could serve this function in a decently approximate way. More important, though, are rules obligating bureaucrats to award particular benefits to particular kinds of people.[17] This, Goodin claims, is where the real work of discretion narrowing is done.

The core function of the welfare state, according to Goodin, is to serve as a safety net against exploitable vulnerabilities. The shape and size of the resulting welfare state would be determined by the conditions creating vulnerability. The greater the extent of exploitable vulnerabilities, the more substantial would be the measures required to counteract them. Crucial here is determining the threshold of exploitation. This, Goodin notes, is a contextual standard—the list of things that a person can "reasonably do without" before opening herself to exploitation depends on culturally embedded notions of need.[18]

Goodin's work combines a fine-grained analysis of market conditions with a subtle dissection of the moral norms constraining them. Its careful exposition of moral norms provides a persuasive account of the conditions under which we would claim that the state ought to intervene in the labor market. Moreover, this approach is pitched at the right level of generality to be normatively flexible. It does not depend on a particular definition of social relations or a particular structure of exploitation. It is not, in other words, tied to a conception of class defined by the ownership of productive assets. Instead it relies on basic intuitions about the conditions in which it is inappropriate to press one's advantage.

This analysis thus applies to a variety of vulnerability-producing situations. It could apply, for instance, to norms of domesticity that make husbands the sole, discretionary providers of food, clothing, and shelter. It could equally well apply to discriminatory cultures in which people of particular identities are frozen out of all but the most poorly paid jobs. Here racist employers become sole, discretionary providers of income. In general, this account can accommodate a multitude of intersecting concerns at the same time because it is based in a description of the social conditions permitting exploitation. It provides us with means to say, for instance, whether the African-American capitalist ought to be protected as a vulnerable person. This judgment would hinge on the way social conditions affect his relation to needed resources and their suppliers, rather than his relation to the means of production. This account could provide the basis for deciding whether people of similar identities in different locations are entitled to different levels of protection, or whether people of similar identities with different job skills or different education might fare considerably differently in the same labor market. Because the framework itself is flexible, the possibilities for its employment are many.

The moral-theoretic approach is normatively subtle as well. It is not a full frontal attack on the capitalist economy but a more abstract description of the conditions under which social relations are morally impermissible. As such, it can operate within the horizon of a capitalist economy, drawing a meaningful distinction between interdependence and exploitation. It could comment insightfully on varieties of socialism as well. Here it would suggest, for instance, that if the state becomes a monopoly supplier of goods, it must not have discretion in distributing those goods. Across each of these economic formations, the moral-theoretic approach allows a subtle dissection of social problems, permitting a finely calibrated response to them.

Although the moral-theoretic approach is quite robust, there are limits on its normative reach. This analysis is premised on de facto acceptance of moral norms protecting the vulnerable. Such norms draw their force from their general acceptance as rules that members of a given culture ought to obey. The more culturally universal, ubiquitous, and taken-for-granted such norms are, and the more deeply they are embedded in a communal code of conduct or moral background culture, the greater their force. Such norms need not be consciously embraced by every individual. They bind a person's conduct equally well when they are upheld by a group that the person views as an arbiter of right and wrong. Such groups can enforce norms of behavior by exerting moral sanctions over their members. In either case, however, actual people must embrace a given norm for it to govern their conduct. This form of de facto acceptance is required for the norm to have normative force.

This point can be seen more clearly by considering the situation from the opposite side, one of moral conflict rather than consensus. Take, for example, Robert Nozick's example of person who negotiates with a drowning millionaire over the cost of his rescue.[19] If one were to suggest to the prospective rescuer that it was immoral to drive a bargain in such circumstances, the rescuer could conceivably respond, "You're right, I hadn't thought of that." Here he could realize that there is a background consensus on this point. Or, failing that, he could be persuaded by the argument one marshals for this idea, an argument likely drawing on other norms that he recognizes as binding in his culture. In either case we could hold him normatively accountable for acting on this principle.

A different kind of response is also possible, however. The prospective rescuer could reply, "You're wrong; there is nothing immoral in my acts. Any arrangement the millionaire and I negotiate is just as long as we both consent to its terms." In this case he denies that norms against desperation bargaining apply. This may be a statement about his own convictions, or it may be a broader denial that there is a moral consensus about such a point in present circumstances. In this situation neither person is clearly right or wrong. Rather, the situation shows lack of moral consensus on the point in question.

Absent a clear background consensus one way or the other, the only way out of this impasse is to persuade the prospective rescuer that driving a hard bargain in such circumstances is immoral. We could try to convince him that there is in fact a normative consensus on this point in a background culture that we both recognize as binding on our conduct. Or failing that, we could try to persuade him that there ought to be such a consensus. There is no obvious way to win this argument. It simply relies on the formation of a new consensus about the values governing such situations. This is a dialogical process of forming agreements about rules, norms, and values. Dialogue, then, is needed to achieve de facto agreement when it is not already present.

Such problems of value pluralism are magnified when we move from talking about face-to-face interactions to discussing the norms regulating social institutions and practices. When the issue is assessing the conditions under which labor contracts are arrived at, many conflicting moral norms come into play. Counterposed to norms of protecting the vulnerable are those claiming that a party's consent to an agreement invalidates any criticism we could make of the agreement. People upholding such norms might say that vulnerability does not jeopardize a person's rational ability to consent. Or that the vulnerable deserve our sympathy but not our protection. Or they might make a distinction between, say, the intimate sphere, where we have responsibilities to protect the vulnerable, and the economic sphere, which (they say) is a realm of strategic interaction in which moral norms do not apply.

This shows the limitations of relying on the de facto acceptance of a moral norm as a kind of justification. That justification is limited to the sphere in which the given norm is consensually accepted. If a given norm is not consensually accepted, then one cannot necessarily rely on it to settle difficult normative issues. In conditions of value pluralism, there will likely be many such points of incomplete agreement about right and wrong. There will be correspondingly few norms that enjoy agreement in modern cultures. My point is not that this invalidates the idea of protecting the vulnerable, however. Rather, it shows the risks of relying on the de facto acceptance of moral norms in modernized, rationalized societies. In such circumstances, the idea of protecting the vulnerable has normative force primarily among those who accept it as a valid norm. To employ this norm on a broader scale, we need additional means to shore up the consensus underlying it and widen its sphere of acceptance.

The problem that the moral-theoretic approach encounters, I believe, lies in drawing too direct a connection between morality and public policy. Such a connection could be made in a small, traditional community with strict enforcement of ethical unanimity. Value pluralism is strongly discouraged in such communities, and collective endeavors can be explicitly formulated along the lines of group morality. In such communities all "institutions" are permeated by morality because a shared moral ethos can function as a taken-for-granted truth about daily life. In modernized societies, however, the value consensus required for such a translation is lacking. Here there must be some mediation between morality and public policy.

Under modern conditions, moral consensus is *politically* achieved. Consensus over norms and values is formed through processes of political deliberation. Politics, then, is the means for creating the de facto acceptance of norms in complex societies. As such, politics is also the means to translate moral norms into a form in which they can govern collective conduct and shape our institutions.

Ideally we would like a justification for the welfare state that is not tied to any particular ethical community. This would be a more universalistic justification, one capable of binding the conduct of those who do *not* think the vulnerable ought to be protected. A focus on political processes provides a way to extend the reach of a moral justification of the welfare state. It solidifies such a justification by expanding the acceptance of the principles on which it is based. This kind of investigation would complement and extend the moral-theoretic approach by describing how de facto acceptance of moral norms protecting the vulnerable could be achieved.

## 2.4   Three Worlds of Labor Market Criticism?

Although the three approaches I have just surveyed travel separate paths, they maintain many points of contact and can be combined into one robust perspective. I will assemble this overall position by identifying its core features and problems.

The various strands of the labor market paradigm are united in their focus on exploitation, but they differ in their respective assessments of exactly what is wrong with it. The comparative approach, I have noted, is relatively silent on this subject. It richly contrasts different state–market combinations, identifying the complex social effects produced when economy and social policy meet. Although this approach establishes clear standards for characterizing different types of labor market conditions, it does not develop the means to discriminate between their preferable and objectionable forms.

The structural approach also has normative problems. It is based on a conception of material interests narrowly defined in terms of the ownership of productive assets. This approach claims to show that conflicts between capitalists and workers are inherent and endemic. It is objectivistic in the sense that it aims to assess human interests independently of anyone's actual preferences or opinions. The structural approach evaluates our interests, in theory, more correctly than we may understand them ourselves. Such a theory has a large responsibility to account for its own objectivity and truth. I have argued, however, that the structural approach fails in this ambitious undertaking. A person's interests cannot be isolated from other aspects of identity. Thus those interests are characterized by multiple, crisscrossing agendas, conflicts, and allegiances. Because each person's interests are so complex, there is no single, fundamental axis of social conflict. An analysis founded on the ownership of productive assets only captures a small part of this and formulates the concept of interest in a way that prevents it from being connected with other concerns. The structural approach, then, does not produce a normatively satisfactory indictment of the problems of the labor market.

The moral-theoretic approach, in contrast, deals well with complex interests and identities and provides a persuasive indictment of the problems of the labor market. Because it is based on an analysis of moral norms governing our treatment of others, it does not rely on interests in a normative sense. Instead of searching for objectivistic grounds for criticism, this approach draws on *intersubjective* assessments. These are our moral judgments about human relations. The moral-theoretic approach thus bears a much lighter burden of justification. It draws on our own assessments as a community of people generating standards for our collective conduct. It thus appeals to actually existing moral norms rather than idealized theoretical projections. As such, the moral-theoretic approach inherits none of the demanding burdens of justification carried by the structural approach.

In sum, the moral-theoretic approach is easier to justify, more robust, and more flexible. I believe, then, that the normative commitments of the labor market paradigm are best theorized along these lines. As I have said, however, an approach relying on moral norms commits itself to a kind of realism about them. Justification here ultimately terminates in the question whether a given norm really does exist in a form comprehensive enough to ground public conceptions of law and policy. To ensure that this strategy works, we need additional resources to promote moral and political consensus. As I will argue shortly, this is not an impossible task. The welfare state is in fact the perfect institutional complement to such a dialogical process.

Although the normative bases of the structural approach are problematic, it does contribute several valuable insights to our understanding of exploitation. It highlights the extent to which laws and institutions structure the conditions within which economic interaction occurs. Further, it shows that such structures only create exploitable vulnerabilities when they are held in place by domination. This is not the direct domination of specific workers by specific capitalists. Rather, it results from the political disenfranchisement of people who could benefit from other economic arrangements. This insight is important for the labor market paradigm as a whole. Regardless of how we characterize the problems of the labor market, they are relational problems that arise within a legally structured environment. The laws can be structured to benefit some people rather than others. This is one of the chief ways that exploitable vulnerabilities can be created and sustained: by establishing a system that makes them unavoidable.

In sum, the labor market paradigm identifies two important problems. One is the creation of exploitable vulnerabilities within the market economy. The second is the political domination of people disadvantaged by the economy. Both of these make exploitation possible: the first by reproducing its social preconditions; the second by reproducing the structures within which it occurs.

The view of the welfare state that arises from this analysis is one dedicated to protecting the vulnerable. It is targeted at the kinds of vulnerabilities that put people in a position to be exploited in the labor market. When we consider the institutional features of such a conception, we can see a broad harmony between the comparative and moral-theoretic approaches. The comparative approach's contrasting analyses of decommodification in ideal types of welfare regime show how people can best be provided with independence from the imperatives of the labor market. As such, it provides one way to think about how vulnerabilities can be shielded from exploitation. Decommodifying labor enhances worker's agency vis-à-vis employers. In Goodin's terms, it makes the relation between the two groups more symmetrical (cf. criterion 1 in section 2.3 above). It also ensures that employers are not collectively the only source of needed resources like incomes (cf. criterion 3). Decommodifying welfare policy thus helps to decouple vulnerability and exploitation at at least two points.

Goodin himself suggests an additional means to render vulnerabilities not exploitable. This is statutory attribution of duties and obligations to welfare state administrators. Statutory obligations limit the discretion administrators have in awarding benefits. This ensures that welfare states do not adopt the logic of the market and reproduce exploitation by preserving workers' vulnerability (cf. criterion 4). A legal strategy of this kind supports and supplements direct market interventions like Esping-Andersen's. Of the four criteria Goodin outlines, then, the only one the welfare state cannot address is the question of what resources people actually need (cf. criterion 2). This consideration is biologically and culturally determined and is not easily amenable to intervention.

A welfare state that protects the vulnerable is a flexible instrument for solving complex labor market problems. It need not be targeted solely at protecting workers. This vision has the potential—not yet fully explored—to contrast the relative effects of complex socioeconomic identities and dynamic processes of social differentiation. It has the means to discern the relative vulnerabilities of various groups and understand what welfare policy can do to eliminate them. As such it has the ability to develop a complex and far-reaching conception of exploitable vulnerability, one consistent with much contemporary work on race, gender, ethnicity, and other identitarian concerns.

## 2.5 Dynamics of Exit and Voice

The central characteristic of the labor market view, shared by all of its strands, is a focus on ending exploitation. As I have said, however, this concern requires additional normative support. I will now outline the beginnings of such an approach, though it will take the rest of the book to fill in the details.

One way to think about the conditions facilitating exploitation is to use Albert Hirschman's celebrated distinction between exit and voice. In Hirschman's characterization, exit and voice are two parallel strategies for effecting change.[20] The strategy of exit, typically associated with economics and markets, allows a person to express disapproval with a situation by voting with her feet. The strategy of voice, typically associated with politics and participatory governance, allows her to demand change instead of leaving. In most situations, one, the other, or both of these strategies can be employed to solve problems. Choosing between them largely depends on circumstance, including the extent to which a person has exit options, the extent to which she can expect to bring about change, the relative costs of protest versus leaving, and the extent to which she feels committed to changing the institution instead of just moving on.

The labor market paradigm focuses on exit when theorizing the problems of market economies. The dependence of a subordinate person on the exclusive supplier of a needed resource is a case of blocked exit. Exploitation is made possible in such situations because it is not possible to shift one's dependence to some other supplier. Similarly, decommodification is based on the idea of exit. It allows workers to exit and enter the labor force more easily, providing them with better bargaining power in the process. In a general sense, exploitation is made possible when a person's exit options are curtailed.

Exit cannot stand alone as the basis of an indictment of the labor market, however. People are not vulnerable to exploitation simply because social conditions prevent them from exiting and entering the labor market at will. In some cases, the very structure of the market makes exploitation unavoidable. The laws establishing the market can arbitrarily put some at an advantage over others. In these cases, changing the structure of the market is necessary because leaving is not an option. In such situations *voice* provides unique benefits that exit cannot.

Exit and voice are both forms of communication. Each expresses disapproval with a given state of affairs. Exit is nonverbal, unilateral, and communicates a meager amount of information. It states disapproval without specifying the exact nature of the problem, nor does it provide opportunities for correcting the problem. As a form of communication, it is not very specific and aims only at protest rather than consensus. This is why, for instance, marketing executives resort to opinion polls and focus groups when their sales start to drop. Knowing *that* a product is not selling well is not as informative as knowing *why* it is not selling well. Voice is in many ways the functional opposite of exit. It communicates a rich amount of information bidirectionally. It provides means, if both parties wish to use them, for renegotiating a set of arrangements to produce a mutually satisfactory result. It is multilateral rather than unilateral, and deliberative rather than declarative. Market research on consumer satisfaction, to continue the example, solicits voice from consumers to prevent their exit before it is too late.

Understanding labor market problems in terms of exit and voice produces a number of advantages. Most strikingly, the addition of voice to exit solves many of the normative problems outlined above. Moral norms, I noted, are universalized and translated into policy through discursive means. To achieve widespread acceptance, they must be the object of political deliberation. Choices between conflicting norms are also carried out in public deliberation, and their application requires a contextual understanding of how to translate abstract principles into concrete policy. The moral norms that ground public policy draw from many sources, but in the end these must all be translated into political terms. Voice provides the means to do this. It describes the conditions under which people can enter into deliberations producing moral norms and public policies. Exit and voice thus work in tandem to eliminate exploitation. Voice provides a standard for the conditions under which people are free to deliberate about moral norms and public policies, while exit provides a standard for their freedom in the market.

In a general sense, voice allows people to raise claims about moral norms and argue for their adoption. It thus provides the needed means to strengthen the normative bases of the labor market paradigm. Voice is needed, for instance, to secure consensus on the very norms that classify blocked exit as bad. Full and adequate voice allows people to convince others that it is unfair to take advantage of vulnerable people. Because consensus on moral norms is a public, deliberative process, it is important that all people have a voice in that process. In order to achieve the widest possible acceptance for moral norms governing the economy, the greatest number of people must be able to deliberate and be convinced of their validity.

Within public deliberation, the idea of protecting the vulnerable is a claim about social justice. Exploitation, from this perspective, is not first and foremost a theoretical assessment of the problems of the labor market, but a claim that people make about their treatment by others. To achieve consensus on such a claim, vulnerable people and those sympathetic to them must argue that particular kinds of behavior and particular social conditions should be considered unjust. These are actual claims raised in political contexts, inviting negotiation over the meaning of exploitation and the conditions under which it can be said to exist. There is no script for establishing the acceptance of such claims as moral norms. Instead they rely on the quality and persuasiveness of the arguments that can be made on their behalf. This process is discursive to the core. In this view, a secure background consensus on important values requires vigorous public deliberation. It requires, in other words, the widest possible employment of voice.

Voice has a number of other valuable uses as well. The interplay between exit and voice allows them to function as mutually reinforcing strategies for eliminating exploitable vulnerabilities. The labor market paradigm takes a one-sided approach to foiling exploitation. It focuses on promoting exit options to ensure that people's vulnerabilities are not exploitable. Enhancing voice, however, has a similar function. A worker who is vulnerable to exploitation actually has two options: quitting (exit) or complaining (voice). Exit is a viable possibility when she can find other means of support, such as another job or an income-replacing welfare benefit. Voice is possible when legal guarantees are in place to ensure that all claims are heard, to facilitate settling complaints, and to prevent retaliation. Because labor is legally structured and politically regulated, workplaces can be set up to institutionalize formal mechanisms for protest and/or participatory decision making.[21] Worker grievance boards, governance councils, and laws protecting whistleblowers are examples of institutionalized channels for voice.

Voice allows people to register claims about many levels and dimensions of economic justice, from mundane claims about local labor market conditions to challenges to capitalism itself. It could entail that the basic structures of the economy should be open to periodic political review and that groups should be able to contest the fairness of such basic structures in cases where their interests are systematically disadvantaged. This could be the basis for far-reaching deliberation about the legal and regulatory bases of the economy.

Interestingly, measures increasing exit options in these situations also benefit voice. In a tight labor market, employers are forced to listen more attentively to the demands of workers because ignored workers could simply leave. Unionization, which collectivizes the power of exit by organizing mass exits from a given firm, is not typically oriented at helping workers actually leave their jobs. Its function is in fact to improve working conditions by strengthening voice. Similarly, welfare measures enhancing workers' exit options also increase their ability to negotiate and protest rather than leave. The threat of exit, in this case, amplifies workers' voice in renegotiating the conditions under which they work.

Because of the dynamic interrelation between exit and voice, an adequate labor market paradigm must consider them in tandem. The vulnerability of workers can arise either through lack of exit, lack of voice, or some combination of the two. Workers are made vulnerable to exploitation by both their inability to exit paid employment and their lack of voice in political and workplace decision making. Their lack of self-determination takes two forms, then: blocked exit options and stifled voice.

## 2.6 A Political Turn in Political Economy

We can now better see how the strands of the labor market paradigm gain strength by being twisted together. The revision that I have outlined provides a more solid conception of exploitation. It draws on both the analytic richness of the comparative approach and the normative insights of the structural and moral-theoretic approaches.

This view of exploitation moves away from a reliance on class and the distribution of productive assets. Rather, exploitation is seen as taking unfair advantage of exploitable vulnerability. This view is multidimensional because exploitation is made possible by many kinds of vulnerability. These potentially include not only lack of productive assets, but also various other economic differences in market position and bargaining power. They would equally include important social and cultural differences with economic effects, like gender, race, ethnicity, age, and social status.

This view extends the analytical abilities of the labor market paradigm beyond the bounds of labor markets proper. Vulnerabilities of gender, race, ethnicity, age, and social status can make exploitation possible outside of the labor market. The vulnerability of women to men in the household, created by economic dependency, social norms, and differences of power, is one example. Another is the vulnerability of poor people and non-whites to businesses, banks, insurance firms, mortgage lenders, credit companies, and other service providers. Racial identity and demographics often create vulnerabilities that limit people's access to goods and services or make them more expensive. In the end, then, the notion of economic exploitation developed in the labor market paradigm serves as the basis for a more general critique of exploitable vulnerability.

Exit and voice are connected in this view. Vulnerability to exploitation is produced by unequal agency. Whereas the labor market paradigm theorizes this in narrowly economic terms, I have argued that it must construe agency more broadly. People are vulnerable to exploitation either when they cannot exit to a better situation or when they cannot change the present one. Exploitable vulnerability, then, has two interconnected dimensions: lack of exit and lack of voice. This analytical framework considerably broadens the range of vulnerabilities that count as important. Rather than limiting our analysis to the kinds that show up as asymmetrical bargaining positions, we must also investigate the ways people are rendered vulnerable by silence.

An expanded critique of exploitation necessitates improving options for either exit or voice, depending on the kind of exploitation and the particular circumstances involved. In some situations, exit makes more sense than voice. Individuals who are vulnerable to family members in the household, for example, could be provided with better exit options. Alternative sources of support like the so-called citizen's wage would enhance people's independence from the family and decouple vulnerability from exploitation. Voice would be hard to institutionalize in such settings. On the other hand, some kinds of exploitable vulnerability cannot be well addressed by exit. Racism, for example, creates exploitable vulnerabilities but is not something from which one can "exit." Here voice is more important, taking the form of rights to legal recourse in fighting discrimination, and more generally, rights to participate as an equal in the processes that govern economic norms and practices.

Adding voice to exit expands our notion of economic agency. Proposals to partially decommodify labor and proposals for greater worker management are interconnected in basic ways. Each seeks to increase the economic agency of workers relative to employers. The difference between them is a matter of strategy. One emphasizes exit while the other focuses on voice, but each is unnecessarily limited without the other. To make this more sophisticated notion of economic agency possible, the labor market paradigm requires supplementation. In particular, it needs a thoughtful elaboration of the concept of voice equal to its sophistication about exit.

Beyond strategizing about economic agency, voice has an even more crucial role to play in synthesizing the norms that underlie the economy and the welfare state. It provides the means to develop guidelines for the fairness of economic interaction. Such a conception focuses on the discursive, deliberative, political bases of norms for the economy. In the coming chapters, I will argue that economic arrangements are illegitimate if fair and equal political participation is not first guaranteed. A legitimate economic system, from this perspective, would be one in which all participants consented to the basic legal structures of economic interaction. By providing the basis for such a view, voice takes normative priority over exit. It allows citizens to establish the meaning and boundaries of the norms governing their cooperative activities.

Although voice takes normative priority over exit, the two must still function very much in tandem. If people are to have the freedom to participate in workplace governance or the official political sphere, their degree of economic vulnerability and deprivation must be limited. Political agency and economic agency are thus deeply interconnected. The welfare state's task is to ensure that the two function smoothly together, so that economic norms can be politically developed under fair conditions. The state is thus charged with functionally necessary tasks like tilling the soil of democracy, for example, ensuring that all claims are heard and maintaining a level playing field for public discourse. This, in turn, makes possible a fair and balanced exercise of voice in articulating claims about economic problems and finding their solutions.

The normative priority of voice changes our view of the labor market paradigm at a normative level while leaving many practical matters as they were before. It sustains the paradigm's attention to issues of vulnerability and market freedom. It does this, however, under the banner of promoting the discursive conditions necessary to develop political agreement about the economy. The welfare state is first and foremost charged with ensuring the material bases of equal voice by supporting the kinds of agency needed for democratic equality. How it does this is likely to involve both classically political measures and classically economic ones. Political equality, as we will see, is also a joint product of exit and voice.

This kind of political turn raises a host of new problems, however, even as it solves many old ones. As greater emphasis is placed upon voice, we must pay more attention to the economic, political, and cultural conditions under which it can be fairly and freely articulated. The equality and fairness of public deliberation is now of prime concern. People must be equally able to participate in the processes of decision making that govern their lives. The success of the view I have outlined hinges on the richness and equality of such participation. We must investigate what forms of political equality are needed to fairly develop new norms, laws, and policies. Similarly, we will need a much clearer idea of political agency and its connection with various other material and social conditions. What all of this means and how the welfare state can best promote it is, however, a very complicated question.

# 3

# Recognizing Gender, Redistributing Labor

In any measure of social policy in which regard is had to facts, the great majority of married women must be regarded as occupied on work which is vital though unpaid, without which their husbands could not do their paid work and without which the nation could not continue.

—*Sir William Beveridge*[1]

Much has been said in recent years about the limitations of the politics of class. What we need instead, the new consensus claims, is something combining at least race, class, and gender into one picture. The refrain "race, class, gender" is not simply academic fashion, however. It reflects much deeper social and cultural currents in the developed democracies. Chief among these are political gains made by women and minorities during recent decades. Political mobilization has expanded our notion of the social problems welfare should countenance, at the same time highlighting the state's complicity in creating such problems or rendering them invisible. This shift also reveals the increasing anachronism of the old industrial order of economic relations. Many manufacturing jobs of the old economy have been exported to the developing world, while immigration, gender, and race issues highlight the extent to which political economy provides only a partial description of social problems. As a result, the classic worker-capitalist picture structuring the labor market paradigm must be broadened to take account of a wider range of concerns. I have argued that the labor market paradigm is compatible with such changes, and that if suitably revised, it has much to teach us about economically driven sociocultural problems. This revision requires a broader articulation of identity in our understanding of the welfare state, one capable of subtly combining class politics with other axes of social differentiation. Such an understanding correspondingly forces us to expand our view of the functions of welfare. In this broader view, welfare takes on significance not only for redistributing labor, but for addressing a wider array of contemporary social problems.

Feminist welfare research has been a driving force behind such a reconsideration of the labor market paradigm. Starting from the insight that welfare regimes are inherently gendered, feminists have shown how gender relations are reproduced through labor markets, social policy, and domestic economies, at the same time that all of these are patterned by gender. Their work demonstrates the limits of the politics of class and shows that welfare cannot be conceptualized purely in terms of production, possession, and the official, waged economy. It broadens our analytic focus to include reproduction, gendered forms of labor, threats to women's welfare, and the broader cultural milieu surrounding welfare regimes. Feminist welfare research has also made significant strides toward visualizing a new gender order in recent years. Feminists have identified ways to redistribute caregiving labor and shelter women from vulnerability and domination. At the same time, they have suggested means to erode the boundaries between gender norms, rendering roles and identities more fluid. In these senses, their work shows the limits of a purely labor-centered picture and provides resources for going beyond it.

In this chapter, I will examine the logic of gender in the welfare state, outlining a *feminist paradigm*. This work brings much-needed modifications to the labor market paradigm. In particular, it provides sophisticated ways of thinking about identity, culture, and politics in the welfare state. Feminists theorize the effects of welfare across a number of identity categories: not simply class nor simply gender, but a unique fusion whose complexity goes well beyond what one would get simply by adding them together. This conception opens up important horizons in our thinking about welfare, providing means to theorize labor and class in the same frame with welfare's cultural and political aspects. This is particularly true of the promising synthesis that Nancy Fraser calls the universal caregiver model.

While the feminist paradigm has great potential to resolve economic, social, and cultural problems of gender, I believe that it also has hidden pitfalls. I will draw some of these out by focusing on Fraser's exemplary work. The universal caregiver model, I will claim, does not take adequate account of the broader cultural milieu within which welfare regimes are situated. Enculturation has a strong effect on the choices people make. In the case of gender, people's actions, practices, and choices often reproduce the gender norms of their own socialization. I claim that this holds true for gender-progressive welfare regimes as well. Social policies designed to recognize gender and redistribute labor are limited by their beneficiaries' culturally rooted choices. When enculturation is patriarchal, men will tend to choose and act in characteristically male ways and women will tend to choose and act in characteristically female ones. As a result, culture and choice will work together to foil a social policy's progressive effects.

To resolve this problem, I will claim that we need to take much greater consideration of the connections between cultural norms and welfare institutions. The circular relation between culture and choice can best be broken, I believe, by further developing the insights on voice discussed in the previous chapter. Here voice takes the form of guaranteeing the equal cultural agency of all citizens. To make sense of this idea, I will draw on Amartya Sen's work to develop a notion of "cultural capability." When the welfare state ensures that women have equal capabilities to influence the formation of gender norms, it also provides them with the means to challenge and rearticulate disadvantageous conceptions of gender. This conception of cultural agency helps us to rethink the meaning of gender equity and the notion of equality implicit in universal citizenship. It also requires us to combine pragmatic considerations of policy analysis and institutional architecture with more abstract cultural concerns. The best way to address problems of gender through welfare, I will claim, is by targeting the cultural entrenchment of gender itself. Such an approach has immediate consequences for the politics of gender, but also provides us with broader insights into the political and cultural significance of voice.

## 3.1 After the Family Wage

Feminists have made great strides in broadening the analytical scope of the labor market paradigm. They have shown that welfare structures much more than labor markets and income distribution. Each regime encodes gender norms that extend more generally to the economy, families, and the state itself. This includes various normative assumptions about family structure and the distribution of labor and resources. For many years the conceptual linchpin of this gendered economic order was the idea of a "family wage"—the amount of money sufficient for a (male) wage-earner to support a dependent wife and children. The family wage provided a yardstick of sufficiency for wages and welfare and was thus a hard-won victory for early labor movements. At the same time, it also normalized a gender order built around a fairly stark distinction between male breadwinners and female caregivers. In this vision wages and work were distributed along gender lines, and relations of dependence and independence followed suit.

Labor was divided into two separate categories in the gender order of the family wage. "Productive labor" was waged, sold on the labor market, conducted in the public, economic realm, and socially respected as a valuable contribution to society. "Caring labor," in contrast, was unwaged, uncommodified, and conducted in the private, domestic realm. It was typically not valued as highly as productive labor, save perhaps in romanticized notions of motherhood and apple pie. This division of labor in turn defined two separate work roles: the "breadwinner," whose existence was public and economic, and the "caregiver," whose existence was private and domestic.

The family wage has largely passed away in recent decades, due chiefly to economic globalization and decreasing real earnings. The hearty male solo breadwinner is increasingly replaced by double wage-earner couples in the postindustrial economy. The line between breadwinning and caregiving has correspondingly blurred. Many people do some of each. In addition, family leave allowances, commercial daycare, and eldercare facilities combine the two roles into one, providing breadwinning jobs that commodify caregiving.[2] This is not to say that the gender order centered around the family wage has disappeared, however. Women's wages and economic opportunities are still unequal to men's. Their labor market participation is less constant, more likely to be interrupted by periods of childcare and care of other family members. Women are more likely to shoulder the burden of household labor, even when they are also working for wages. Inequitable gender norms and material conditions still conspire to make women more vulnerable to harassment, intimidation, and violence. The character of women's entry into the workforce, their predominant involvement in family responsibilities, a second shift of unpaid housework, and gendered threats to safety and well-being all show the residues of the old system of gender relations. They belie an incomplete transition away from the gender order of the family wage. The social and cultural dislocations brought about by these changes also suggest a lack of direction towards some workable alternative. Although labor is now distributed less strictly along gender lines, we have not made a clear transition to some new, postindustrial set of gender relations.

Given the ambiguity of the current situation, it is all the more important to maintain an analytic distinction between breadwinning and caregiving. Such a distinction allows us to compare formations of gender in various welfare regimes.

Considered purely as abstract definitions of identity, these roles can be embodied in various ways by various people. Prior to the commodification of labor, for instance, most people participated in each without distinguishing carefully between them. One's daily tasks consisted of both labor bringing cash or barter into the household and labor reproducing life and the household itself. With the development of the capitalist labor contract, however, a de jure distinction was made between time in which commodified labor is delivered to its purchaser and time in which people are free to pursue their own ends. Employees contractually agreed to devote their time to productive labor, leaving reproductive tasks for the off-hours. The conditions of the labor contract brought about a factual separation of domestic and economic roles that were only analytically separable before.

In spite of the legal separation of waged and household work, it is still quite possible for one person to occupy both breadwinner and caregiver roles. An employed single parent, for instance, functions as a breadwinner during working hours and a caregiver when cooking, cleaning, and caring for others. The case of such a single parent is not typical, of course, though increasingly common. More typically, these abstractly defined roles have a long history of cultural association with specific gender identities. Contemporary gender norms associate the caregiver role with feminine identity and the breadwinner role with masculine identity. This identification has been more or less strong throughout the past century. During the time of the family-wage system, the association of gender and the division of labor was so strong as to be almost completely naturalized. Gender division of labor, in other words, was a taken-for-granted feature of social life. Feminist politics has problematized the naturalness of this division, of course. Today it is seen as less natural and more the product of choice within a particular economic and social environment. For instance, it is often seen as simply more "rational" for a married woman to give up breadwinning for caregiving, given the costs of daycare and her smaller wage-earning potential relative to her husband. This is not to say that all androcentric norms have been entirely outed, however. Informal, unrecognized norms still govern choices about the distribution of caregiving and the relative importance of men's and women's careers, allocating a second shift of caregiving labor to breadwinning women. Although gender roles are only contingently associated with the division of labor, that association seems to be culturally deep-rooted and tenacious.

Present-day inequities in gender roles can largely be attributed to the fact that the breadwinner role has been degendered much more thoroughly than the caregiver role. It is much more acceptable now than it used to be for women to seek autonomy and self-fulfillment in the official economic sphere. "Bread-winner" has not been completely degendered, of course. Women's labor is still not valued equally to men's, many men still expect to earn more than their spouse, and women are still expected to sacrifice career for care responsibilities. Nonetheless, substantial changes in the gendering of the breadwinner role have occurred during the past forty years. This is not nearly as true of the caregiver role. Caregiving, both waged and unwaged, is still predominantly thought of as a female task. Carework conducted in the home is still thought not to require a wage. And the home is still ideologically framed as a private, domestic sphere distinct from the public, economic sphere of paid labor. The infamous second shift comes about, then, precisely from the differential degendering of bread-winner and caregiver roles. "Breadwinner" is not as strictly male-linked as it was before, whereas "caregiver" is still heavily female-linked. Thus breadwinning tasks are associated with both masculinity and femininity, but caregiving is associated only with femininity.

To envision a more equitable gender order, feminist welfare research has focused on the normative question of how states, markets, and families could be acceptably gendered. For the most part, answers to this question have taken their conceptual starting point from the politics of class articulated in the labor market paradigm. Feminists have criticized the relatively undifferentiated analyses of labor market theorists.[3] They have highlighted this paradigm's economic one-sidedness and criticized its tendency to ignore the gender division of labor. They have shown the extent to which resources are unequally distributed within the family and the extent to which labor market theorists focus on distribution of resources to wage-earners but not to other family members.[4] They have identified unwaged, caregiving labor as an important omission from analyses otherwise focused on labor. Feminists have also broadened the notions of autonomy and independence standing at the heart of the labor market paradigm, noting that dependence on family members and state agencies is as real and important as dependence on an employer.[5] They have traced welfare's influence on both family structures and gender roles, noting the ways it shapes the distribution of tasks and resources within the family, as well as predominant definitions of masculinity and femininity themselves.

Conversely, feminists have also identified ways that existing gender norms pattern states, markets, and families. Prevailing notions of autonomy, independence, citizenship, and entitlement are frequently masculine in at least an implicit sense, privileging traditionally masculine activities while marginalizing traditionally feminine ones. As a result, issues vital to women's autonomy and well-being are excluded from the state's agenda. Violence against women, for instance, is not typically seen as pertinent to the welfare state, while concerns about women's unequal labor market participation have been more easily incorporated into existing (masculine) agendas focused on labor.[6] Implicitly masculine notions of labor equity "make sense" and receive quicker uptake in ways that issues of violence do not. Feminists thus show the limitations of a critical focus on labor and the need for a further-reaching, more deeply cultural analysis of the gendered character of welfare provision.

In sum, feminists have shown with great analytic acuity how states, markets, and families produce gender norms, at the same time that states, markets, and families are structured by those very norms. Their work rearticulates many concerns of the labor market paradigm, but simultaneously goes well beyond it to show that some important issues of women's well-being cannot be theorized solely in terms of labor and economy.

The question remains, though, how an equitable system of gender norms can be developed within and through reconfigured welfare regimes. Nancy Fraser's essay "After the Family Wage: A Post-Industrial Thought Experiment" stands out among the many attempts to answer this question.[7] This influential piece synthesizes many insights of other feminist work on the welfare state and sets a new agenda for further theorizing. Fraser starts from the observation that our present system of gender relations allows a substantial amount of male free-riding on women's domestic labor. Women's increasing labor market participation has combined with culturally rooted gender norms to produce substantial inequality in the distribution of household tasks. To the extent that the welfare state promotes women's labor-market autonomy without addressing the gender roles that create "domesticity," it facilitates a massive moral-hazard problem.[8] An adequate welfare regime, in Fraser's analysis, must move to counteract men's free-riding on women's labor. It must encourage a more equitable distribution of caregiving and breadwinning, simultaneously supporting caregiving and labor market mobility for both men and women. To do this, however, such a policy must also address the underlying causes of gender differentiation and the gender division of labor.

Fraser outlines a "universal caregiver" model designed to accomplish this task. This model attempts to reshuffle the association between gender norms and work roles. It supports both work-enabling policies and policies supporting release time for caregiving. These are designed to encourage flexible transitions between informal care and the official economy, providing people with the means to move back and forth without regard to gender. The universal caregiver model thus facilitates caregiving and breadwinning for both men and women. It aims to universalize the bundle of roles that women already perform, splitting their time between waged work, informal, unwaged "domestic" work, and informal, unwaged participatory work in volunteer organizations and civic groups. The idea is not to universalize caregiving simpliciter, but to universalize the complex role definition of those whose current responsibilities predominantly include care. As such, no tasks would be strictly associated with gender. Rather, state policy would make it possible for any individual to choose the mix of caregiving and breadwinning that best suits her or him. By breaking down barriers between labor markets and "domesticity," this regime-type aims to erode the border between male and female definitions of appropriate work activity. Such a policy tears out some important institutional roots of the gender division of labor and destabilizes cultural norms more broadly as well.

Fraser's universal caregiver regime combines the perspectives on social justice that she elsewhere describes as "recognition" and "redistribution."[9] In the language of that work, two analytically distinct perspectives can be taken on problems of gender equity. The perspective of recognition surveys society in paradigmatically cultural terms, viewing problems of gender in terms of the construction, coding, and valuation of norms and identities. Seen from this perspective, the problem of gender in the welfare state is one of the denigration of women's work, the cultural linkage of gender and work roles, the construction of male labor as more important than female labor, the marginalization of gendered issues of vulnerability, harassment, and violence, and a background system of norms, institutions, and practices undermining women's status and well-being. Unequal respect is the diagnosis that one obtains from this point of view. The perspective of redistribution, in contrast, surveys society in paradigmatically economic terms. Viewed from this perspective, the problem of gender in the welfare state is one of the unequal distribution of labor and resources. Income, leisure time, and household resources are inequitably distributed in most marriages and between men and women generally. Unfair distribution is the diagnosis one obtains from this point of view.

Recognition and redistribution are merely analytic perspectives, of course. None of the problems the universal caregiver regime is designed to address is purely cultural nor purely economic. Women's poverty, for instance, is clearly an issue of economic justice that can effectively be viewed through the lens of redistribution. Redistributing income—or even better, restructuring the economy—would significantly alleviate problems of poverty faced by many women. This issue also has an irreducibly cultural dimension, however, which is analytically separable from redistribution per se. Women's poverty is importantly conditioned by notions of the value of women's labor, the naturalness of women's responsibility for children after divorce, and by interruptions to women's careers during caregiving. To resolve this problem we need to face both its economic and cultural dimensions. A truly effective solution—one that would not result in contradictions between economy and culture[10]—would have to redistribute income at the same time that it restructures cultural assumptions about gender and deconstructs the border between "domesticity" and the official economy. Women's poverty must therefore be viewed from two analytically distinct perspectives, shedding light on one complex problem from two separate angles. Most of the universal caregiver regime's beneficial effects mix redistribution and recognition in similar ways. This model focuses our attention simultaneously on *recognizing gender* and *redistributing labor* within the same set of social relations and practices.

One of the prime virtues of Fraser's approach, then, is its integration of cultural politics with more traditional, distributive concerns. It provides a way of thinking about classically economic issues in relation to the cultural norms embedded in institutions and practices. This approach recognizes that welfare regimes are never purely distributive institutions. The mundane details of each regime encode a vision of society. The New Poor Law of 1834, for instance, envisioned a society oriented around economic markets and the discipline of work. Similarly, the Bismarckean welfare state of the 1890s visualized a state-centered society in which workers' loyalty to the state was modeled on the loyalty and discipline of soldiers. The minute details of welfare policy not only structure life in subtle ways, they also naturalize particular social structures, visions of society, and even different types of person.[11]

The universal caregiver regime is specifically sensitive to the symbolic effects of welfare. It avoids gender typing altogether, developing instead a conception of universal citizenship that enables both caregiving and breadwinning. As such, the universal caregiver model portrays these tasks as elements of a whole life or as tasks that any citizen could undertake, regardless of identity. Here reshuffling tasks not only foils the association of gender with particular work tracks, it also undermines the naturalism of their association. When breadwinning and caregiving are portrayed as gender-neutral aspects of a complete life, the norms that connect gender with the division of labor are undermined. Thus social policy has broader cultural effects, reshaping conceptions of gender roles, promoting equal respect, and decreasing stigmatization.

Because of its unique form of universalism and its epistemological sophistication, the universal caregiver model would be a significant improvement over any existing welfare state. It subtly combines cultural and economic elements of egalitarianism and moves our thinking about the cultural aspects of welfare to a new level. In particular, this model integrates issues of identity with issues of labor, providing a powerful solution to some of the problems I have identified in the labor market paradigm. It goes well beyond concerns about labor, however, by destabilizing gender norms and eroding some of the cultural bases of women's subordination to men and their vulnerability to male power and violence. In this sense it helps to promote women's equality, agency, and well-being beyond the bounds of the labor market. The question that needs to be examined, however, is how well the model completes its task. As a post-industrial thought experiment, does the universal caregiver regime tell us everything we need to know about the logic of gender equity in the welfare state? Would a policy supporting both caregiving and market labor take us far enough in the direction of gender equity? Could this welfare regime end male free-riding on women's labor? Could it go further to undermine the conditions that promote women's vulnerability and subordination?

## 3.2   The Two-Track Paradox

If my sympathetic reconstruction is accurate, I believe that the universal caregiver model is incomplete and requires extension in certain ways. In order to correct the gender shortcomings of the labor market paradigm, we need to think in more detail about gender equity as a normative goal and about the ways the welfare state can enact it. We should not only ask how the welfare state can improve women's lives directly, but also how it can advance the cause of gender equity in a more broadly cultural sense. The two issues are linked: if we do not view the welfare state as part of a larger context of gender norms, we risk undermining its gender-progressive effects. In order to pursue gender equity through welfare policy, then, we need to take a step back from policy analysis per se, looking at the welfare state in its broader cultural milieu.

Let us continue the post-industrial thought-experiment initiated by Fraser. Suppose we establish a welfare regime supporting a mix of market labor, caring labor conducted within various institutions of civil society, and caring labor at home. It is, in Fraser's terms, a universal caregiver policy. In this scenario, citizenship entitles an individual to a combination of market-labor-enabling benefits and care-enabling benefits. This policy renders the border between paid and informal work more fluid, enabling citizens of all genders to cross back and forth between the labor market and less public, structured forms of work. It thus collapses many customary distinctions between waged and unwaged labor, between domestic and market labor, and between caregiving and the "official" economy of waged employment. In so doing, it cuts rigid, tracked connections between gender roles and the division of labor. People are no longer confined to one of two labor tracks, so the two-track paradox of gendered labor that characterized the family wage system is presumably undone.

Disconnecting gender norms from the division of labor via welfare policy does not fully separate them, however. In the broader system of norms that pervades our current society, it is still seen as natural for men to choose paid employment over caregiving. It also remains natural for women to take on caring responsibilities regardless of their employment status. Furthermore, various career tracks are gender coded. The industrial heavy-lifting occupations and many technical jobs still tend to be coded masculine, whereas so-called pink collar and caring occupations remain overwhelmingly feminine. The oxymoronic dissonance of an expression like "male nurse," for example, is testament to the ongoing force of these associations. There are, in other words, informal norms that gender labor and many other aspects of our current social life.

The naturalness, pervasiveness, and persistence of gender norms pose a problem for any feminist conception of welfare. The universal caregiver model would presumably be institutionalized in a broadly democratic political system of some sort,[12] particularly if it is oriented toward making the kind of political turn I outlined in chapter 2. *Choice* is a key element of such a system. In a general sense, democrats see the state as a choice-promoting institution, one that opens up a wide variety of life options for its citizens rather than dictating particular forms of life to them.[13] Any such state would have to countenance a certain amount of choice in the benefits people receive. For instance, the universal caregiver model would presumably permit people to choose their own mix of caregiving labor, other forms of labor, and leisure. Presumably it would allow people to choose whether their caregiving takes the form of official economic work or informal work. And presumably it would permit people to decide the extent to which their informal, unwaged labor involves caring for friends and relatives, to what extent it involves voluntary community activities, and to what extent it pursues completely different ends like education or job training. These forms of choice are indeed key aspects of the social fluidity that the universal caregiver model is designed to promote.

Because of its centrality to political ideals of freedom and participation, choice is an important comparative characteristic of welfare regimes. Regimes vary in the leeway they allow individual action within legal and policy structures. They also differ considerably in the extent to which they see choice as an endogenous property of individual free will versus a socially embedded activity supported and structured by the state. Liberal regimes tend to view choice as a free sphere of individual responsibility from which the state should remain distant. More purely social-democratic regimes, in contrast, narrow the range of choice to an extent by removing some goods from market provision and maintaining higher tax rates. They are correspondingly more likely, however, to see social policy as providing important material bases for choice. From this perspective, policy both structures choices and supports them.

Regimes also differ considerably in the way they *distribute* choices. The options opened up to different groups of people are determined by many individual characteristics as well as by their relation to social policy regimes, markets, and domestic life. The liberal conception of choice, for instance, accords the greatest range of options to those with the best market position—largely men, whites, professionals, and people without children. Choice is more egalitarian and universal in social-democratic regimes. Universalist conceptions of citizenship tend to equalize people's range of choices and support choices for many who could not obtain them through the market alone. Because of such characteristic differences between regimes, choice is a valuable category for comparative research.[14] By extension, the mix of choices that a regime provides and the way it distributes them should be the object of careful normative consideration.

Of course, choice is a political concept that must be treated with caution. On one hand, it is central to the idea of popular sovereignty and is thus basic to our political tradition. On the other, however, it has been used to draw an ideological line between private and public life that is highly problematic for women. Private life, in this construction, is a protected realm of unencumbered choice that contrasts with the compromises inherent in public, political life. In such a scheme, the distribution of domestic labor and resources is "private" and cannot be second-guessed by others. In this case, however, the idea of free, private choice veils male power from scrutiny and obscures the extent to which female consent is not entirely free.[15] Choice has been used for similarly ideological purposes in demonizing the behavior of women as welfare recipients.[16] The choices of poor women have been unfairly derided as immoral and lazy, fueling public objections to welfare, justifying punitive rules, and rationalizing many cutbacks in recent years.

Although liberal regimes in particular tend to portray choices as free expressions of individual preference, this characterization is also ideological to an extent. Choices are socially and culturally embedded and strongly conditioned by various aspects of a person's life and environment. Materially anchored norms are an important part of the background against which people formulate their preferences and tastes. As Pierre Bourdieu shows, people express group identity as well as individual freedom when making choices.[17] In a largely unconscious way, what one should want is importantly conditioned by who one takes oneself to be. Choices, in other words, are importantly influenced by social position and the norms that attach to particular social identities.

The norms governing choices about careers, domestic tasks, and the use of social services are all pervasively gendered. Pursuing success in the job market is most closely associated with male identity. Other things being equal, this increases male predisposition to use policies assisting employment rather than policies enabling caregiving. Employment-enabling benefits are thus, in at least a weak sense, masculine. Similarly, nurturing and caregiving are more closely associated with female identity. Ceteris paribus, this increases female propensity to choose caregiving over paid employment, though in a weaker sense than male preference for paid labor. Care-enabling benefits are thus, in a much stronger sense, feminine. This increases the likelihood of women including more caregiving assistance in their bundle of benefits relative to men. Against our current cultural background, then, men are more likely to use employment-enabling benefits and less likely to use care-enabling benefits, while women are more likely to use care-enabling benefits regardless of their use of employment-enabling benefits. In exercising choice, men and women reflect the dominant norms of their own socialization.

Choices are complex, of course, and socialization is not the only factor acting on them. Structural and institutional considerations also shape people's decisions in important ways, as does economic instrumentality. To gauge the effects of gender norms on choice, then, it would be useful to have some idea—however rough—of the extent to which enculturation really matters in the choices people make about welfare usage. Fortunately, an instructive case study is available. Sweden has tried (with only partial success) to pursue goals very similar to those of the universal caregiver model. As such, it is a valuable laboratory for examining the dynamics of culture and choice in something like a universal caregiver regime. This case study gives us a way to test the universal caregiver model's ability to counteract the effects of deeply rooted gender norms. It also shows how tenaciously gendered patterns of choice can persist in the face of policy measures designed to eliminate them.

Sweden has tried for several decades to develop care-enabling policies that promote shared caregiving between men and women. It was recognized as early as the mid-1950s that women's freedom to pursue activities outside the home was partly premised on men's willingness to adopt caregiving responsibilities. This insight shaped the 1974 Parental Insurance Act, a parenting policy designed to support caregiving labor for both men and women.[18] It includes long-term leave benefits as well as short-term leave after the birth of a child, for care of a sick child, or for helping a child start daycare or school. Importantly, these benefits are attached to parenthood in general, not just to motherhood. They are thus designed to promote the redistribution of domestic labor and to change traditional gender norms. Moreover, this policy contains provisions designed to neutralize the effects of economic rationality that entrench traditional gender roles. Both fathers and mothers were compensated for 90 percent of their earnings during leave until 1995, when the rate was dropped to 75 percent.[19] A high wage replacement rate presumably helps neutralize the extent to which a person feels the need to choose work over caregiving for economic reasons. To further encourage equal participation, a portion of parental leave days are reserved for men—the so-called daddy month.[20] Under this policy, a couple has to divide leave time between them to take maximum advantage of it.

In spite of extraordinarily generous leave benefits, and even though Swedish culture is highly egalitarian, Swedish men have been remarkably intransigent in adopting caregiving responsibilities.[21] Men's use of parental leave grew steadily from the beginning of the program in 1974 until 1978. From 1978 to 1987, though, men's leave participation plateaued at about 23 percent. In other words, of those men eligible to take parental leave at 90 percent of their full pay with a guaranteed return to work at their present seniority level, only one quarter chose to do so. Only 5–8 percent of total leave days were taken by men during the first fourteen years of the program. At the peak in 1994, men took 11.4 percent of all leave days and their participation has declined since.[22] Even more dramatically, in 1986 only 1 percent of couples surveyed shared parental leave time more or less equally.[23] It was only after the government increased family leave to fifteen months, reserved ninety days for men, and conducted a sustained (and rather clever) advertising campaign that male participation rose to a higher level. Between 1985 and 1989 the percentage of men taking some leave increased from 22 percent to its current level around 40 percent.[24] Even though the plateau of male participation shifted significantly following the reforms of the late 1980s, it only underscores the striking fact that less than half of eligible men make any use of their parental leave benefits.

A broad range of factors seem to influence leave-taking decisions. During the 1970s and 1980s when Parental Leave Insurance was taking shape, Swedish women entered the workforce in previously unseen numbers. Their labor force participation was largely gendered, however. Women were predominantly employed in the lower-paid, frequently part-time social service jobs of the welfare state itself, whereas men largely occupied full-time, better-paid positions in the commercial sector. This new regime of gender relations recoded the old division between the private home and the public political and economic sphere, creating a gendered split between public sector and private sector employment. The liberating effects of welfare policy were thus partly subverted by a resegregation of women and men and a rearticulation of traditional ideas of femininity and masculinity.[25] In this case women were delegated roles in the social, careproviding sphere, while men continued to occupy profit-making and decision-making roles. This segregation has in turn affected men's and women's relative willingness to use parental leave because the private sector puts more informal pressure on men not to take parental leave than does the public sector.[26] As a result, the gendering of the labor market also genders choices about leave taking.

Gender norms also play a significant role in men's use of leave time. Haas's 1986 study[27] found that the less men believed that women were naturally better suited for parenting than men, the more likely they were to take parental leave. Similarly, egalitarian attitudes toward role sharing increase a man's likelihood of choosing to take parental leave: a positive attitude toward role sharing was the factor most strongly correlated with a man's taking more leave time. Anecdotally, every study participant cited traditional values as the leading reason that men do not take parental leave.[28] Men were also more likely to take leave time when they perceived society and friends as supporting it. Women in the study were found to be significantly less traditional in their attitudes toward gender and parenting than men. Nonetheless, women's attitudes also exercised a strong effect on the decision about men's leave taking. When women had been exposed to nontraditional ideas about gender in childhood, they were more likely to have a partner who took leave time and more likely to share that leave time equally. Similarly, a woman was more likely to support leave taking when she had a job that had high status, was not traditionally female, and paid well. Thus women's attitudes toward gender norms and their labor-market position both seem strongly related to equality in leave taking.

To be sure, economic instrumentality plays a role in leave-taking decisions as well. Men tend to earn higher wages in Sweden; when wages are replaced only as a fraction of income, the overall loss to a family is greater if the higher wage earner stays home. This seems to be confirmed by the fact that fathers' leave taking began to decrease in 1995, when the wage replacement rate was dropped from 90 percent to 75 percent.[29] It is also borne out by Haas's finding that people reported income as a factor in their decisions about leave taking. It was seen as less important, however, than considerations about the man's work situation or the woman's desire to take more or less leave.

In sum, a complicated mix of factors determines the gendering of policy use in Sweden. Structural barriers, cultural norms, and economic disincentives intertwine to undermine some of the progressive effects of family leave insurance. In order to achieve gender equity in contemporary Swedish society, each of these would have to be overcome. This insight provides a valuable template for testing the effectiveness of the universal caregiver model. Suppose we could institute a full-blown universal caregiver regime, rather than a rough approximation, in Sweden. Would this rearticulate gender norms in a more equitable way?

A universal caregiver regime would go a long way toward removing some of Sweden's barriers to gender equity. It would, ex hypothesi, eliminate the public–private split between men's and women's labor market participation or at least neutralize its effects. To do this, it would have to eliminate structural distinctions between public and private sector jobs. This would include equalizing the rate of wage replacement for leave time and reducing the gap in wages between public and private employment. Such a regime would also, ex hypothesi, close the more general gap between men's and women's wages. In so doing, it would eliminate the economic incentives that make it more "rational" for men to stay in the wage force while women take leave. It would thus eliminate the most potent structural roots of gendering in Sweden's current labor market.

In spite of these progressive effects, the universal caregiver regime would not completely resolve the gender problems seen in Sweden. The structural and economic bases of gendering are intertwined with a number of informal, cultural factors. Men and women have been sorted into private and public sector jobs not simply by the coincidence of women's entry into the workforce with the expansion of the public sector. Existing ideas about the gender differences between caring labor and commerce have also played an important role.[30] These norms continue to undermine Sweden's current efforts to desegregate the labor market.[31] Similarly, both the current Swedish state and the universal caregiver model allow couples to decide how to mix care and other labor. Once the universal caregiver regime has neutralized economic and structural influences, these choices will still partly be governed by existing social norms and various aspects of personality and character. Because dispositions are patterned by gender, men and women will to some extent reproduce the cultural background of their socialization. The choices they make, in other words, will express not only what is rational in a self-interested sense, but equally importantly, what it means to be a man or woman in their society.

Even though the Swedish welfare state is an imperfect approximation of the universal caregiver regime, it reveals an important limitation of this ideal-typical model. A full-blown universal caregiver regime would solve many of the problems that Swedish family leave policy has encountered. It does not have the means, however, to foil the effects of persistent gender norms lodged in the background culture. This restriction on the reach of the universal caregiver regime threatens its effectiveness, as the Swedish case shows. When the background culture is not effectively problematized, gender norms are not destabilized so much as reinforced through use.

The problem encountered by the universal caregiver model is caused by a circular relation between choice and cultural background norms. Cultural norms about gender influence people's choices when they are confronted with an array of options between market employment and caregiving work. The structure of employment and caregiving in turn reproduces gender norms and socializes people into them. People's choices in these circumstances further naturalize the image of women as carers and men as market-laborers. Insofar as they make differential use of their benefits, men and women perpetuate cultural conceptions of gender roles.

The circular relation between choice and culture can be viewed as a circularity between forms of redistribution and recognition. The problem in this case is not a classic redistribution-recognition dilemma of the kind Fraser describes.[32] The logic of the universal caregiver model is well calibrated to avoid internal conflicts between redistribution and recognition. It circumvents the dilemmas faced by other models because it actively deconstructs gender boundaries and gendered identities within its domain of action. As I have shown, though, the internal logic of this model can be isolated only for analytical purposes. Any democratic welfare state will be inextricably entangled with its cultural, economic, and social milieu. In this case the bidimensionally transformative effects of the universal caregiver regime, seen from the perspectives of both recognition and redistribution, must be actively chosen by ordinary citizens. Citizens, however, often embody traditional norms and values. Progressive public policy thus faces a circularity problem. The very choices and cultural norms it hopes to reconstruct are the ones that enact and legitimate it. The transformative dynamics of redistribution and recognition in the universal caregiver state are potentially short-circuited by the intrusion of recognition problems "from outside." The universal caregiver regime is susceptible to these outside influences because of the cumbersome but necessary presence of individual choice. Considered as a whole regime, then, and not simply as a welfare state, the universal caregiver regime is open to conflicts between redistribution and recognition. The problem in this case is not a dilemma in the classic sense. It is rather one of cultural inertia and the need to achieve a degree of cultural change in order to make cultural change possible.

To be sure, a universal caregiver regime disrupts this unfortunate dynamic to some extent. Its various recognition effects—anti-androcentrism, equal respect, and so on—help eliminate the explicit tendency of social policy to normalize and enforce gender roles. Such a regime uproots important anchors in the construction of gender and blurs the symbolic lines between male- and female-differentiated roles. The universal caregiver model thus has cultural effects outside the boundaries of welfare provision per se. In a pervasively gendered society, however, the welfare state is only one structuring influence among many. Reforming welfare tears out one root of the current gender order, leaving many more. Other areas of social life remain subject to the dynamic of norm reproduction I have already described. This, I believe, is the crux of the problem encountered in Sweden. Policies designed to encourage male participation in caregiving fight an uphill battle against broader forces of male (and to some extent female) socialization.

What is needed, clearly, is some leverage against the broader normative context of gender socialization. The most direct option would be to circumvent it completely by eliminating choice itself. If the progressive effects of the universal caregiver regime were not subject to choice, it would not be vulnerable to drag and inertia from its environment. The regime could then institute gender-progressive policies without interference. It could, for instance, constrain the choices available to men and push them into the care track, say, by shortening the work week and taxing overtime at a higher rate. Such a policy would provide an economic incentive for men to do less paid work and more informal caregiving. This solution would be problematic, however, because it would discriminate against wage earners relative to salary earners. A man on an annual salary could easily avoid the state's system of costs and incentives simply because his work hours are contractually open ended and his salary is fixed. It would be very difficult to make him go home and do domestic chores, legally speaking, if the length of his day is informally determined by his duties.

Another proposal would radicalize the daddy month, stipulating a particular distribution of benefits for care and market labor. It would be possible, for instance, to constrain the mix of benefits each member of a couple could claim: not 100 percent caregiving nor 100 percent breadwinning, but a more rigidly specified mix of the two. This would give each an incentive to engage in both caregiving and breadwinning because only such a mixed work regime would allow them to claim full benefits. This scheme promotes task sharing by subsidizing it to the fullest extent only when it is evenly divided. At the limit, however, such a policy introduces a substantial amount of paternalism into welfare, stipulating social relations in a way that welfare theorists find quite problematic in other contexts. This plan would also discriminate along the axis of class. The burden of gender equalization falls, in this case, on those needing subsidies for market mobility and childcare. The incentives and burdens of the policy fall disproportionately on those who most need support.

These proposals share a common problem. By using economic incentives to promote gender equity, those who have the most to gain or lose from social policy are disproportionately affected. Conversely, those who can afford to avoid the corrective influences of social policy are allowed to escape. In either case, solutions are circumscribed by their economic character and by their entanglement in issues of class. They pursue gender equity by modifying the structural circumstances in which people act. They do not, however, directly modify the social and cultural bases of choice in the use of social services. Because the welfare state is not a complete institution in Foucault's sense,[33] its effect on the norms that govern choice is relatively constrained. Here we see the deep interconnection between the key concern of the labor market paradigm—labor market mobility—and its feminist corrective. In this case, the feminist paradigm shows that labor market mobility in itself is not enough. In spite of well-intentioned policies to equalize labor market access, gender norms reproduce themselves through other means: not through the formal tracking of occupational categories but through informal effects on freely chosen work activities. We cut the policy connection between gender and labor only to discover the salience of informal dispositions and naturalized worldviews. The result is a two-track paradox of a different sort, one driven by the unfortunate conjunction of culture and choice. The universal caregiver regime does not resolve the two-track paradox, then, but merely translates it into the cultural realm.

## 3.3 Renegotiating Gender Norms

How can a feminist welfare state escape the two-track paradox? The solution must be a relatively ambitious strategy of rearticulating gender norms, one that breaks the circular relation between gender and choice. To do this, we need to take seriously the symbolic component of welfare policies. We must do this not simply in the negative sense of asking how gender is structured within such policies but more broadly by asking how the welfare state can help restructure gender norms in other areas of life as well. Here it is useful to return to the idea of voice. We can ask both how the welfare state helps promote or hinder the voice of various of its constituents, and how voice can be deployed in a symbolic, cultural-political sense to influence the reproduction of gender norms.

As we have seen, gender norms function as an unseen, unthematized background for people's choices about labor, leisure, and domestic life. They are part of a society's taken-for-granted cultural milieu. Although gender norms permeate daily life and structure institutions and bodily comportment, such norms are rarely recognized as normative or even extant. Rather, they are reproduced through discourse, representation, and practice within the minutiae of everyday life.

To change such norms, people must be able to identify them as constructions and argue for their alteration. This requires critical abilities to unmask the contingent character of such norms and understand how they are fixed in place by social practice. It also requires abilities to articulate and argue for different norms, either by means of representation, discourse, or institutional reform. A person's ability to change such norms ultimately depends, then, on being able to influence the construction of the social world. I will refer to an individual's ability to renegotiate social norms as her "cultural agency."[34] Cultural agency consists of the critical, cognitive, and discursive abilities to act as an agent in defining the terms through which oneself and one's society are understood. As such, it is a gauge of a person's capacity to alter gender norms and similarly constructed aspects of social life. It is one aspect of a broader, political, and cultural conception of voice.

I take cultural agency to be a genre of what Amartya Sen calls a capability.[35] Sen defines a capability as a "potential to achieve some functioning." In this sense, a capability describes a person's real opportunity to undertake some activity or to be a particular kind of person. It is the combination of traits, circumstances, and resources necessary to create some possibility of action or existence. Sen claims that capabilities are forms of freedom because they create realizable possibilities in a person's life. In the context of his work on development economics, for instance, Sen notes the difference between a person who is hungry because he has no choice to eat—say because he is living in famine conditions— and a person who is equally hungry because she refuses to eat to make a political statement. Although neither person eats, one has opportunities for action not open to the other. In Sen's terms, we would say that the latter person has capabilities that the former lacks—the freedom to choose between eating and not eating. "Capability," then, gives us a rich conception of the actual opportunities open to a person or group.

My use of capability is more abstract than such tangible examples as whether one can choose to eat. This conception focuses on what we could call a person's epistemic and discursive opportunities—her actual opportunities to act as an agent in processes of knowledge construction. My claim is that biased or discriminatory gender norms are prima facie evidence of unequal capabilities used in their construction. Women, in other words, live within a system of gender norms that systematically disadvantages them because they have not had an equal seat at the table in the formation of such norms. As feminists have repeatedly shown, the Western cultural and intellectual tradition is one in which dominant paradigms of thought took shape hand in hand with women's silence, marginalization, and exclusion. These forms of blocked and unequal participation can be theorized as capability deficits in Sen's sense. They describe ways in which women's freedom to participate in the construction of truths about gender and social identity has been impaired. Capability deficits provide us with an explanation for the formation of such biased and damaging gender norms. They describe the ways in which women have not been equal participants in defining the dominant cultural images of this society. That the cultural and epistemological output of such marginalization disadvantages women is no surprise.

Saying that women have historically had capability deficits sounds potentially tendentious and derogatory. My claim is actually more mundane, though, and its potential for offense is based on a misunderstanding of what a capability is. Capability, as I use the term, has two aspects. The first is what I call the "agent-rooted aspect."[36] This is the sense in which a capability depends on a person's own skills and competencies. The capability to ride a bicycle, for instance, is in part a learned skill acquired through practice. One's capability depends, in this sense, on mastering certain challenges of balance and coordination. In Sen's vocabulary, these are "achieved functionings" that confer further capabilities. A person's capabilities also depend upon a second aspect, however, which I call the "structural and institutional aspect." If a person knows how to ride a bicycle but lives in a dense forest with no roads, then she does not have a real opportunity to ride. Similarly, a person too poor to rent, borrow, or buy a bicycle has no capability to ride one. In both cases, the person may have some kind of *hypothetical* opportunity: she *could* ride, if only the jungle were cleared, if only she had access to a bicycle, and so on. In neither case does the person have a capability to ride, however, because capabilities describe actual opportunities to function rather than hypothetical ones. In other words, if I am to be truly free to do something in Sen's sense, choice must be the only factor determining whether or not I do it. For this to be the case, a person must have both the requisite abilities and favorable circumstances. Capabilities, which are actual opportunities, thus depend on one's personal characteristics and one's social, material, and institutional milieu. The claim that women have suffered from unequal cultural capabilities is no insult, then. It is, rather, an indictment of a social system privileging certain kinds of voices over others. One could equally well claim, in this sense, that men have benefited from capability surpluses relative to women.

To say that a disadvantageous system of gender norms is evidence of unequal cultural agency posits that women would articulate a less disadvantageous system of norms if their cultural agency were equal to men's. This inference works backwards, from the evident disadvantage in which women are placed by the current system of norms to the supposition that things would be otherwise if they could be. This inference is silent on the nature of the inequality, however. It could be that women understand the disadvantage in which they have been placed but are fighting an uphill battle against an entrenched system of male privilege. Or it could be that the nature of the disadvantage is ideologically mystified and unrecognized. Each of these is surely the case in different ways. In each scenario, different forms of cultural agency are implicated and different capabilities are called for. The first chiefly requires capabilities for renegotiating cultural norms themselves—the abilities to rewrite laws, reshape institutions, renegotiate informal labor and living arrangements, alter structures of systematic disadvantage like gendered wage and lending discrimination, contest damaging forms of representation, and participate in discourse as an equal, capable of articulating fairer ideas of gender. The second scenario requires all of this plus critical capabilities to recognize the fact and sources of disadvantage in the first place. It requires the kinds of organic critical praxis that used to be called consciousness raising.

In sum, cultural agency is a capability concept that describes people's opportunities to act as participants in the cultural affairs of their society. As such, its value is both critical and normative. This notion is critical in the sense that it provides us with the means to identify some of the crucial underpinnings of men's advantage and women's disadvantage. They are conditions of unequal cultural agency. The notion is normative in the sense that it provides grounds to say that a given system of gender norms is unjust. The fact that the symbolic understandings of our social world are formed under conditions of inequality, and the fact that these inequalities create additional inequalities and disadvantages, gives us a fulcrum for criticizing such norms. This normative perspective is based on a notion of what it would mean for a society to be culturally fair. Such a society would be one in which people had an equal chance to influence the formation of background norms and values in their society.[37] Cultural fairness thus calls for equal cultural agency. Equal cultural agency in turn provides a standard for evaluating the relative capabilities of people to articulate the norms and labels applied to them.

Now we can return to the case of gender norms and the welfare state with additional critical armament. The universal caregiver model envisions a society in which market labor and caregiving are degendered. I have argued, though, that measures designed to facilitate this within the boundaries of welfare policy are not enough. They run into a two-track paradox of a cultural sort—even though they do away with the explicit tracking of labor into gender categories, they do not escape the informal, cultural effects of gender on life choices. To fix this problem, we need an additional basis for criticizing the cultural background that genders people's choices. The ideas of cultural capabilities, cultural agency, and a culturally fair society provide the conceptual tools for doing this. They give us the critical and normative means to identify situations in which women are less able to challenge androcentric norms that disadvantage them. By extension, they provide means to help us break the circular relation between gender and choice.

## 3.4 Cultural Agency as an Analytic Perspective

At first blush, the idea of cultural agency seems an awkward addition to the literature on the welfare state. One could charge that it is a hopelessly abstract notion, quite foreign to the pragmatic, concrete, policy-oriented character of most feminist welfare theorizing. Its talk about intangible things like "participation in culture" is in sharp contrast to the relatively more concrete standards of discussion in most welfare literature. The same accusation could be made of my proposal to graft an idea like cultural agency onto the universal caregiver model. A messy, abstract construction of this kind bears little resemblance to the clean logic of Fraser's discussion. One might well ask how well it sits with her more concrete post-Marxist materialism.

Although I can see some basis for such a charge, it misunderstands the critical dimensions of the project. The idea of equal cultural capability takes a step back from the level at which feminist work on the welfare state is usually conducted. Rather than ask how gender equity can best be institutionalized or what dimensions of it are most important, this conception questions the content of the ideal itself. In this spirit, I claim that cultural agency is a necessary component of gender equity, one that cannot be left out of a welfare state claiming to promote gender equity in any meaningful way. By extension, then, the feminist project of rethinking the labor market paradigm cannot succeed without taking such concerns into account. This argument operates at a normative level, one that is consistent with a wide range of policy proposals. Its prime virtue, in fact, lies in allowing us to leave policy questions underdetermined from a theoretical point of view. This conception puts us in a fairly flexible position by providing critical and normative means to identify the most progressive alternatives from among a broad array of options.

To make this point clearer, it is worth providing a more careful exposition of what cultural agency is supposed to do for the feminist discussion of welfare. Cultural agency—or more properly, *equal* cultural agency—functions as a critical principle under the rubric of distributive justice. It frames a notion of equality that is, I believe, a necessary component of gender equity in the welfare state. This critical principle functions as an analytical perspective from which we can evaluate actual welfare regimes and their social, cultural, and institutional milieu. To speak precisely, it should be described as evaluating institutions and practices "from the perspective of cultural agency." Such an analysis could in principle be applied to any set of material conditions—not only those of the welfare state but in other areas of life as well. The question posed by this concept is whether a given set of arrangements puts women in a better position to renegotiate the norms applied to them, regardless of what those arrangements are or how they would be institutionalized.

Equal cultural agency aims at an essentially political form of equality, at least in the broadest sense of politics. To put women in a better position to renegotiate gender norms, it must describe the conditions under which cultural politics can proceed in a fair manner. This critical principle establishes baseline conditions of political equality in its particular domain. It focuses above all on equal *voice*, and is thus a crucial component for a political turn in the welfare state.

To see how cultural agency functions as a component of the political turn, it is worth discussing the renegotiation of gender norms in greater detail. In a general sense, gender norms are the set of behaviors and practices that are expected of the two conventionalized genres of people. Men are expected to behave as men, and women are expected to behave as women. Gender-differentiated norms thus create distinct sets of stereotypical practices for men and women. The question we must ask, then, is how norms governing the division of these particular practices can be degendered?

Schematically, the connection between gender norms and practices can be undermined in at least five ways. (1) First, the identity groups to which practices are attached—particular genders—can be *dissolved* or *dedifferentiated*. If male and female stopped being meaningful concepts, practices could not be parceled out by gender. Less strongly, as the lines between masculine and feminine roles are blurred, the basis for gendering practices is also blurred. This kind of gender deconstruction is the ultimate goal of Fraser's universal caregiver state. De-differentiating gender is, however, a profound and difficult task, one that is likely the aggregate outcome of many smaller forms of social change.

(2) Second, the *signification* of a practice can be changed. A practice's cultural connotations—how it is best done, what doing it signifies, who can properly perform it—can be changed through several means. Some norms are cognitively available to us. We can articulate certain rules of behavior and argue about their

justification. When norms are explicitly thematized in this way, they can be *rene-gotiated* through discourse. We can ask why a practice is performed in a certain way and what would be at stake in performing it differently. A couple's argument about the domestic responsibilities allocated to one of them (as a man) versus the other (as a woman) is a good example of this.

(3) Alternatively, norms sometimes circulate in an unthematized fashion as "natural" representations of the social world. Images in the media and our observations of others' behavior have important symbolic effects on what we see as obvious, natural, and right. When norms circulate in this way, they can be *resymbolized* through representation. American children of the 1970s, for instance, may well remember massive football player Rosey Grier talking about his love for needlepoint and singing "it's all right to cry" on a popular children's album.[38] Grier's obvious sensitivity clashed with his equally obvious masculinity to challenge many children's ideas of what it meant to be male.

(4) Some norms are embedded in daily life as habitual, obligatory actions.[39] Table manners and the subtleties of interpersonal communication are examples of such deeply embedded norms. The idea that one ought to reciprocate the friendly greeting of an acquaintance, for example, is so habitual that it is obeyed without thinking.[40] Similarly, women are often normatively expected to perform the bulk of worrying and coordination work in the household—"what kind of mother wouldn't care how her child was dressed in the morning?"—and this embodied habit is often quite difficult to break. Changing such norms typically requires *changing habits* themselves.

(5) Finally, some norms are lodged in a society's institutional structure. The family wage, for instance, institutionalized a division of labor in which one member of a couple would serve as breadwinner while the other served as caregiver. More directly, the common law doctrine of coverture institutionalized a particular set of gender norms.[41] Restoring the legal status of married women undermined these androcentric norms to an extent by tearing out their institutional roots. In today's era of formal equality, many gender norms are informally structured into institutions. Many of the norms underlying the current Swedish gender contract, for instance, seem to be lodged in workplaces and labor markets. Although many men express interest in child rearing when surveyed as fathers, they act on quite different conceptions of gender in their roles as corporate decision makers.[42] Here male workers are seen as more valuable, more loyal, and less expendable. Women, correspondingly, are frequently seen as liabilities and productivity problems. Thus, even though many Swedish corporations express an

official openness to leave taking, actual corporate culture can reflect quite different attitudes.[43]

Similar institutional gendering can be seen in the state itself. Gender norms are informally reproduced, for instance, by state silence on violence against women. A state's failure to recognize such issues establishes a zone of "privacy" within which women are vulnerable to male domination. Gender norms are not patterned by the state directly, but by its seeming neutrality towards actions and choices that reproduce male power and female subordination. Dislodging these institutional anchors requires laws preventing violence against women and shelters to protect them when it occurs.[44] In general, then, altering the normative context within which people act often requires us to *restructure institutions*.

Increasing women's capabilities to challenge norms in any of these ways would increase their cultural agency. To see how this works in actual institutional settings, it is instructive to consider two contrasting types of policies that fit the normative guidelines I have laid out. The first is what we might consider a classically cultural policy. Sweden's national school curriculum mandates teaching *jämställdhet*, the Swedish doctrine of gender equality.[45] Two components of this are the goals of equal economic independence for men and women and equal parenthood between men and women. Since 1969, the school curriculum is mandated to promote equality between the sexes in these ways, including countering "the traditional attitudes to sex roles and stimulating pupils to question the differences between men and women with respect to influence, work assignments and wages that exist in many sectors of society."[46] Because this policy challenges traditional attitudes through education, it fits squarely within the normative bounds I have laid out. A welfare regime including such an education policy would make many inroads against the two-track paradox because it thematizes traditional gender norms and opens them to discursive negotiation (cf. item 2 above). Further, insofar as such a policy succeeds in "stimulating pupils to question the differences between men and women" in a broader sense, it may actually contribute to dedifferentiating genders themselves (cf. item 1).

We could imagine broadening such a policy to include the teaching of critical analytical skills in a more general sense. These would focus on identifying taken-for-granted aspects of knowledge and representation. Students would be taught to see the ways in which gender norms are constructed by means of discourse (cf. item 2), representation (cf. item 3), or habit formation (cf. item 4). Such an education would not only help to equalize the cultural capabilities of boys and girls from an early age; it would also likely increase their level of sociocultural insight in general. Teaching such basic critical skills could have many spillover benefits, helping children see through the ideological effects of advertising or political discourse, for instance. In this sense, basic critical capabilities could even be seen as a necessary educational component of equal political citizenship.

A gender-progressive welfare regime need not focus directly on promoting agent-rooted capabilities in its citizens, however. As I have noted, capabilities are also importantly structural in character. Consider, then, a classically redistributive proposal. Barbara Hobson makes elegant use of Albert Hirschman's work to argue that exit and voice are importantly interconnected in the domestic sphere.[47] The relative bargaining position of men and women within the family—their relative voice—is determined in large part by the exit options available to each. The more dependent women are on men, the less voice they have. Increasing women's labor market options and earning potential is thus equivalent to increasing their voice.[48] Conversely, forcing men to bear a greater part of domestic burdens decreases the subsidized labor market mobility they have long enjoyed and brings their exit and voice options more into line with women's. Equalizing voice in turn gives women a better bargaining position in negotiations over who does what work, who will make career sacrifices, and so on.

Renegotiating the household division of labor is tantamount to renegotiating gender roles because articulating a different understanding of who does what articulates a new notion of what it means to be a man or a woman in a given household (cf. item 2).[49] At the same time, reallocating domestic labor changes a couple's daily routines and responsibilities. It thus ingrains new habits, changing people's perceptions about the expectations placed on their conduct (cf. item 4). Finally, increased exit and voice place women on a more equal footing with men, resymbolizing their relative power and agency (cf. item 3). For all of these reasons, Hobson's analysis fits squarely within the normative program I have outlined. When greater exit and voice allow women to rearticulate gender norms, it improves their cultural agency in a very real sense. Policies that allow women to negotiate more freely and build a life more to their own advantage have cultural effects. It follows that policies equalizing wages or providing greater labor market mobility for women will also give them cultural capabilities. The kinds of mobility-enhancing policies favored by the labor market paradigm are helpful in this regard, as long as they are formulated in a gender- and culture-sensitive way. The same would hold of policies facilitating exit for women, such as battered women's shelters or subsidized day care. Because of their perhaps unexpected cultural side effects, these policies would promote equal cultural agency.

Given the deeply structural, institutional, and legal character of many gender norms, it is important not to forget the *official-political* dimensions of cultural agency. Gender norms are deeply structured into the institutional fabric of society. The norms underlying marriage, divorce, rape, sexual harassment, violence against women, sex discrimination, the public–private split, and corporate compliance with family leave are all legally encoded in important ways. Many of these issues have been identified only because women achieved enough political agency to put them on the political agenda as gender problems.[50] Any account of cultural agency must include an official-political dimension, then, if it is going to foil the reproduction of such norms. Women must be able to take equal part in forming the laws that encode and reproduce gender norms. Similarly, they need the ability to politicize new issues, identify areas of gender blindness in state policy, and redefine what a welfare state is for.

When we talk about cultural and political agency, it is important to be clear not only about the connections but also the differences between them. I take agency to be a capability concept that describes capabilities for doing particular kinds of things. We can evaluate such capabilities from different perspectives: their utility for promoting agency in the renegotiation of norms and meanings, for instance, or their utility for promoting agency in the official-political sphere. These assessments are perspectival because they are not mutually exclusive. Sometimes a capability to redefine cultural meanings will also confer agency in a more formal political sense. This would be the case for someone of unusually good rhetorical skills, for instance. Moreover, the activities in which agency is expressed are often not separate. Strengthening laws against rape is both an act within the official-political sphere *and* one with important cultural manifestations. Further, many different kinds of things count as improving a person's capabilities. Some of these are beneficial as seen from the perspective of culture, others as seen from the perspective of politics. Many things will increase capability as seen from both perspectives. Finally, it is important to realize that the abilities and structural circumstances that promote agency can be qualitatively quite different from the forms of agency they support. In our society, for instance, money enhances agency in many spheres, including both culture and politics. For all of these reasons, assessments of a person's cultural and political capabilities are always a perspectival assessment of the different kinds of opportunities open to her.

An analytical distinction between political and cultural agency allows us to see better how the two frequently go hand in hand. Pragmatically, any policy increasing women's political agency in an official sense would give them greater means to restructure the institutional anchors of gender norms (cf. item 5).[51] More generally, the political presence of women[52] would increase their voice as a group, representing women as capable citizens (cf. item 3) and bringing issues of women's identity more strongly to the fore in the public sphere (cf. item 2). Greater political participation for women could also help to change habitual norms of discourse between men and women (cf. item 4)—norms of female deference and male discursive privilege that pervade both public discourse and intimate relations. Thus women's political participation could have salutary symbolic and cultural effects as well as improving the representation of their interests in the classic sense.

What is ultimately important about these examples is the fact that they exemplify the same normative aims. Each increases the actual agency of women in a cultural sense. Equal cultural agency provides an umbrella justification for each example, as well as setting a standard for the effect they are supposed to achieve. Once this normative benchmark is established, the door is opened for pragmatic experimentation to see what policy measures could most effectively promote equal agency. Although the normative standard itself is abstract, the measures enacting it are very concrete.

There is another sense in which the capability view I have outlined could be seen as hopelessly abstract, however. If thought of as a critical notion, particularly with a distributive valence, it seems that cultural agency would need to be equalized for each and every person. This argument seems to suggest that a society is culturally fair only when each person has the same ability to contribute to its cultural background. That would be absurd, though. It would require some Harrison Bergeron view of equality in which draconian measures are needed to impose equality on an inherently diverse population.[53]

Luckily, literal, individual equality is not the only option. Cultural agency is most profitably thought of as a property of groups. This is easily seen when we consider how social norms work. In their most general deployment, norms attach social expectations to the behavior of all members of a society. In other words, most norms are naturalized and universalized in practice—they are thought to be obligatory for all people as such. Those who employ and reproduce them think that "this is simply how one ought to behave." Small, daily rituals like table manners and customs of politeness are often used in this way. They create obligatory behavioral expectations for people as such, and deviations from them are seen as rude or ill mannered regardless of what kind of person one is. Even members of other cultures are expected to obey the daily manners of their hosts. In many Western cultures, for example, chewing with one's mouth open or failing to shake an extended hand is interpreted as a violation of social norms, regardless of the cultural background of the person violating them.

Some norms, however, are group differentiated. They apply to people by virtue of perceived membership in a group, typically as defined by various ascribed characteristics. Gender norms, as their etymological connection with "genre" shows, are examples of this. They apply behavioral expectations to people by type. Masculine norms apply only to those sexed as male, while feminine norms properly apply to those sexed as female.[54] Men are typically disapproved of if they follow feminine norms of dress and comportment; similarly, though less strongly, women invite disapproval by adopting masculine dress and behavior.

We must follow the same lines of group differentiation in asking questions about cultural agency. Because gender norms are group differentiated, it is not important to ask whether any *individual* person has the capability to renegotiate the meaning of the norms applied to her. It is significant, on the other hand, to ask whether the members of her group, on average, possess these capabilities relative to the members of other groups. Although cultural capabilities are individually exercised, individual acts of symbolic definition become significant only in a broader context of group action. If the norms that apply to a particular identity group seem to place that group at a disadvantage, that is prima facie evidence that the members of the group, on average, have less cultural agency than others. So when we ask questions about the fairness and equality of gender norms, we are asking about the relation between males as a group and females as a group.

Throughout this discussion, the tasks and goals attributed to the state seem to fit less and less well within the ideological boundaries of American political discourse. The idea of the state intervening in cultural affairs is profoundly unsettling to the American imagination. The United States is a country built around the ideal of the religious neutrality of the state. It is also one in which culture wars have been a significant controversy in recent years, including prominent disputes over the government's role in funding allegedly dysfunctional behavior among welfare recipients, particularly among poor, single women. It could be asked, then, whether a welfare regime promoting cultural agency isn't exactly the kind of paternalistic nightmare envisioned by neoconservatives. Isn't this the equivalent of government endorsement of a sectarian set of values, one particular vision of "the good life"?

The ideal of equal cultural agency is not in fact an example of picking winners and losers. It is instead part of a conception of equality that identifies culture as a source of injustice, both directly, in the sense of misrecognition, and indirectly, in the sense of maldistribution. As such, the welfare state intervenes only to maintain background conditions of equality. The key insight guiding the standard I have outlined is not one of cultural intervention, then, but of upholding basic social commitments to equal opportunity. It is not legislating culture but providing a fair and equal basis for its formation.

Similarly, this is not a paternalistic conception of the state. The regime I have described promotes gender equity while countenancing a wide array of choices for individual citizens. It does this by ensuring fair and equitable *grounds* for choice while placing few restrictions on actual choices themselves. It is thus consistent with both liberal commitments to individual autonomy and social-democratic commitments to equality and universalism. This conception also avoids paternalism because it does not view the state as the organizational center of society, nor does it privilege its progressive capacities over those of individuals. Here the state is charged only with leveling the playing field on which individuals negotiate norms and structure institutions. It is not the primary vector of social progress nor even the most important one. Rather, it is given the considerably more mundane task of maintaining an environment of equal opportunity for the action of its citizens. The state functions largely as backdrop in this picture, whereas individuals, groups, and the discursive contexts of voluntary associations, civil society, and daily life occupy center stage.

In this sense, equal cultural agency is a component of a universalist conception of citizenship. To achieve gender equity, according to this standard, we must go beyond the routine redistributive tasks on which the welfare state usually focuses. A more robust conception of equal cultural participation is additionally required to live up to the ideal of equal citizenship.

### 3.5 From a Politics of Class to a Politics of Culture

The feminist paradigm that I have described starts from some of the basic presuppositions of the labor market paradigm. It views labor markets both as problematic institutions and as sources of freedom. It diagnoses social problems in familiar terms of inequality, exit, voice, and freedom. And it sees the welfare state as a potential source of enablement. What is different, however, is the set of challenges the feminist paradigm poses for the welfare state. Feminists point to the pervasively gendered and gendering character of states, markets, and families, the undervaluing of caregiving labor, the unequal distribution of labor and resources in the family, the ideological construction of "domesticity" in opposition to the "official" economy, and threats to women's welfare through violence and domination that are often marginalized from the welfare state's agenda. By highlighting these features of welfare regimes, feminists paint a very different picture of society and thus of the challenges faced by the welfare state.

The primary goal of the feminist paradigm, as I have outlined it, is to pursue gender equity through welfare policy. It interprets gender equity as a complicated blend of *recognizing gender* and *redistributing labor.* This requires substantial forms of redistribution to equalize income, wealth, labor, leisure, safety, and opportunity between the sexes. It also entails a politics of recognition to revalue and rearticulate women's and men's identities. I have claimed, though, that the transformative project of redistributing labor and recognizing gender has hidden points of paradox. If we try to degender welfare regimes by focusing primarily on issues of labor, we will be fighting an uphill battle against norms governing other areas of social life. Redistribution and recognition are intertwined in the welfare state in ways requiring us to think beyond the boundaries of a narrowly labor-oriented view. The capability model I have outlined provides the means to do that.

Ultimately, feminism must go beyond interrogating the structures of gender within welfare policy itself. In a democratic political system and a patriarchal culture, gender equity will be subverted by the conjunction of choice and tradition. The best alternative is for feminists to go on the offensive. A normative feminist argument can be made for taking the logic of equal citizenship in a cultural direction. This vision expands the politics of the welfare state to include cultural concerns. Here politics functions as a solvent fusing class and other aspects of identity into one coherent picture.

Although the feminist paradigm considerably broadens the notion of politics underlying the welfare state, this view is not simply created by adding gender to class to get gender-plus-class. Culture and economy meet in messy ways, so that recognizing gender has complicated relations with redistributing labor. Taking culture into account requires us to consider the economic bases of cultural agency. It reciprocally requires us to consider the cultural character of economic institutions and practices. On the whole, this double shift in perspective entails a substantial rearticulation of the tasks with which the welfare state is charged. We move from a welfare state construed primarily as a counterweight to the market economy to a welfare state charged with enabling its citizens in a political, cultural, and economic sense. The feminist paradigm thus expands the notion of voice outlined in chapter 2. An adequate notion of voice cannot focus narrowly on electoral politics nor the politics of daily life. It must include both at once.

In sum, the feminist paradigm reveals important limitations in the labor market paradigm and provides means to expand its range of concerns. Feminists argue persuasively that issues of identity sit at the heart of the welfare state. I have tried to show that addressing such issues requires equal cultural agency for women. To address problems of women's labor-market position, domestic subordination, and vulnerability to violence, we must support women's political agency in a distinctively cultural sense. This means ensuring that women have capability equal to men in articulating gender norms, particularly those encoded in laws and policies. This proposal sets an additional normative standard for the welfare state: any adequate regime must promote equal cultural and political capabilities for its citizens.

This chapter has focused above all on describing norms of equal voice. I have made some programmatic remarks about various avenues for accomplishing this. There is much more to be said about this topic, however. In order to promote gender equity in the welfare state, we need a more detailed conception of the kinds of political participation required. We also need a better idea of what equality—equal voice in the sense of equal cultural agency—would mean in this context. This requires a more carefully worked out conception of politics and political agency in a broad sense. In particular, we must trace the ways the welfare state promotes, foils, and depends upon such forms of equality. That will be our next topic.

# 4

# Democracy, Rights, and Citizenship

In the previous two chapters I have sketched the beginnings of a new approach to the welfare state. It shifts from a focus on labor market agency, or exit, to political agency, or voice. Voice has many advantages over exit as a strategy for dealing with economic problems in particular and social problems in general. It provides people with freedom to make claims about values and social norms in a broad sense. It gives them formal means to change practices and institutions that they find objectionable. By enhancing political and cultural agency, voice cuts the connection between vulnerability and exploitation in a different and more powerful way.

Voice is an imprecise metaphor, of course. It is a placeholder for ideas about political and cultural participation that must be articulated in greater detail if they are going to bear any weight. In this chapter I provide a more detailed rendering of voice, one designed to parallel and supplement the labor market paradigm's conception of exit. Voice, not surprisingly, is best thought of as a form of democracy in a broad sense. In this chapter I will outline some of the considerations that must inform voice-as-democracy. Starting with a preliminary sketch, I will pass through three progressive layers of refinement. These draw not only on Albert Hirschman's concepts of exit and voice, but also on T. H. Marshall's canonic conception of citizenship and its elaboration by Jürgen Habermas. The final result is a conception of constitutional rights connecting politics and welfare, a view that I will call the *deliberative-democratic paradigm*. This paradigm will eventually allow us to dispense with metaphorical talk of exit and voice to focus more concretely on the complex interrelations between political and material inequality.

## 4.1   A Political Turn

The political turn I have outlined in the past several chapters is a normative one. It is the idea that the goals and ideals underlying the welfare state should be politically, rather than theoretically, determined. The normative bases of particular regimes would thus rest squarely on the shoulders of actual citizens, rather than on speculative theoretical arguments. The challenge, from this perspective, is to make sure that politics is up to the task. Normativity can come from politics only when political processes themselves pass philosophical muster. To make the political turn I have outlined, then, careful attention must be given to the circumstances under which we would say that a society's politics can perform the functions we would normally reserve for the most refined moral theorizing.

The most comprehensive response to this challenge would specify a complete, normatively correct form of democracy. Such a view would settle a great many unanswered questions in the history of political thought, but it is both unnecessary and undesirable in the present circumstances. The view I am outlining in this book is intended to apply to a whole class of democratic, constitutional welfare states. An overly specific conception of democracy would unduly narrow the scope of the argument. To preserve conceptual generality, then, I will limit this discussion to describing the conditions under which issues central to the welfare state can be politically adjudicated.

As I argued in chapter 2, one of the fundamental motivations for a political turn is to promote dialogue over the values underlying particular welfare regimes. Such a political process would be able to take over the burden of formulating and justifying social norms. It would thus clarify the animating values of such regimes: Should they shelter people from vulnerability? Should they block exploitation? Should they promote economic equality or gender equity? Such norms are discursively reproduced, gaining acceptance through everyday conversation in everyday social contexts. A conception of politics for the welfare state must have the ability to process these kinds of concerns and forge agreement on them. It must therefore include the processes of communication and argumentation through which such norms are produced.

As we have seen in chapter 3, some norms create types of people and affix various values and expectations to them. Such identity politics lies at the heart of the welfare state. Feminists show well how welfare regimes articulate gender norms at the same time that gender norms shape welfare regimes. Similarly, feminists make clear how the action of the welfare state can enable or block women's voice. They thus highlight the artificiality of the boundary between culture and politics. By attacking the gendered distinction between a male public sphere and a female domestic one, they show that issues of identity permeate and even structure political life. Cultural ideas about gender are inherently political, and gender is one of the constitutive elements of the political realm. As such, politics is inextricably tied to cultural systems of signification, valuation, and differentiation. By drawing connections between gender and politics, feminists undermine attempts to sideline cultural issues and reify the public/private distinction. They thus foil the claim that gender is a private, domestic concern separate from a gender-neutral public realm. More broadly, they show that identity is inherently political. Feminists thus demonstrate that political deployments of voice have inherently cultural effects as well. The politics of everyday life cannot be separated from traditionally "public" concerns. Therefore a conception of voice for the welfare state must include both elements. It must be political in a broad sense that includes symbolic and cultural aspects of identity.

Social norms are not simply cultural in an abstract sense, however. They are materialized in laws and policies. Gender norms, for instance, are inscribed in family leave policies, tax law, marriage and divorce regulations, domestic violence statutes, and welfare benefits. The law structures many other aspects of identity as well. It defines citizenship and determines the benefits and norms attached to it. It sets ages of maturity and retirement, defining a minimum age for political participation and a maximum age for economic participation. Law and policy naturalize heterosexuality to an important extent, forbidding certain kinds of marriage and defining permissible forms of sexuality.[1] Because social norms are so thoroughly rooted in a society's legal and policy apparatus, any politics focusing on norms must focus on laws and policies as well.

Voice about norms, laws, and policies is not a complete list of desiderata for a political conception of the welfare state. It provides only a minimum standard for the project I have outlined. This standard is quite useful, however, because it identifies some key tasks that such a view must accomplish. Considering these features as desiderata will allow me to trace the outlines of a political turn. Above all, such a vision must show how political discourse can be considered fair and normatively valid. It must include some conception of what fair outcomes would look like and how they could be produced. What follows is a first attempt to fill in such a vision.

To begin this task, we must determine to what extent the conceptions of politics I have already examined fit the bill. The labor market paradigm has implicit political resources, located in the interconnection of exit and voice. Decommodifying policies provide people with economic agency: freedom to exit and reenter paid employment. Moreover, as Albert Hirschman insightfully demonstrates, economic agency is connected with political and cultural agency in complex ways. Exit, as he says, can enable voice. An examination of exit and voice reveals both complex interconnections and disjunctions between them. This dynamic gives us good insight into the material basis of politics.

Exit and voice are paradigmatically connected in small-scale settings where economic vulnerability translates directly into silenced voice. They tend to be localized spheres of discourse and decision making in which one's economic autonomy and one's ability to speak are tightly conjoined. These are largely characteristic of informal, face-to-face situations. Workplaces are the archetypal example because market mobility is a defining feature of a worker's relation to his employer. Exit enhances the worker's knowledge of his own value, thus his willingness to speak out assertively. His employer's knowledge of these same features determines her willingness to listen and make concessions. The calculations involved rely on relatively concrete knowledge of the opposing party's situation. This is even more characteristic of domestic situations. The allocation of household resources and the relative size of salaries determines the exit options available to each party, but their *perception* of these options determines how exit translates into voice. Confidence to speak and willingness to listen are both products of intimate, face-to-face knowledge of the other person's situation.

Exit and voice are not always so closely conjoined, however. They are often uncoupled in large-scale, anonymous settings. Voting is a paradigmatic example. Ballots are an anonymous form of voice. Because they are anonymous, they are not subject to reprisal. Thus exit options per se have no effect on one's ability to vote. Similarly, volunteering for a political campaign or issue organization is not likely to affect one's employment status. It is unlikely that one's employer would ever be aware of such political activities. In the formal political sphere, then, exit is not importantly related to voice. A person's political agency is instead determined by legal entitlements to participate—political rights—as well as by possession of the skills and material resources needed for effective participation. Economy and politics are still very much interconnected in the formal political sphere, but that connection is not primarily through the labor market.

By tracing both connections and disjunctions, an analysis of exit and voice provides a rich picture of the relations between politics and markets. The crucial question for present purposes, though, is whether exit and voice provide a sufficient picture of participatory decision making in a welfare state. Does decommodification protect voice to the necessary extent? Does decreasing economic uncertainty sufficiently promote the kinds of voice I have outlined?

Unfortunately, exit and voice are uncoupled in areas of concern vital to the welfare state. The normative bases of the welfare state are political in a way that extends beyond small-scale, localized situations. Consider again the case of gender. While many gender norms are informal, deeply cultural, and reproduced in everyday domestic life, others are importantly rooted in the formal political sphere. Welfare laws and policies materialize gender norms on a society-wide scale. They are created through formal political processes. The kind of informal, indirect guarantees of agency produced by exit are insufficient to guarantee participatory equality in this realm. Although a person sheltered from economic insecurity may feel freer to participate in such processes, mere freedom from insecurity does not guarantee that she will be heard. Exit is not enough by itself to guarantee the necessary dimensions of voice.

Voice must therefore extend beyond informal, localized contexts in which it can be protected by exit. It must be drawn out as a free-standing theme and incorporated into a conception of formal political processes. When institutionalized in a formal sense, voice would allow citizens to make claims about the kind of welfare state they want, integrating economic, political, and cultural preferences with other goals and values. It would also provide citizens with a forum for institutionalizing the norms that they clarify through less formal means. Voice, then, must go beyond abstract, informal deliberation to formulate laws and policies in a classic, democratic sense.

The feminist paradigm does a better job than the labor market paradigm of bridging the gap between informal and formal politics. To promote fairer, nonstigmatizing gender norms, it lays out a broad agenda for political action. This ranges from critical practices attempting to dissolve or change identity categories to more formal political practices focusing on laws and policies. Feminists do an admirable job of showing the lines of continuity between these various elements. They show both that the personal is political *and* that the political is personal.

These insights provide a solid basis for the more general project I have begun to outline. A conception of politics for the welfare state must extend from the immediate, local contexts of everyday life to formalized processes of democratic decision making. Voice cannot be guaranteed by focusing only on the localized and interstitial domains of politics. These domains are crucial and often over-looked by political theory, but they cannot stand alone. Similarly, political equality cannot be supported merely through guarantees of income security or cultural agency. Freedom from economic risk may well be a necessary precondition for political agency, but it is not a sufficient one. It says nothing about the abilities people have to participate in politics, about the material bases of participation, nor about the processes structuring it. To fill in these gaps, we must focus more precisely on the kinds of political agency needed by citizens and on the procedures that can provide it. Only then can we adequately conceptualize the interrelations between the global and the local, between society-wide deliberation and claims about one's immediate circumstances, between institutionalized, legally binding employment of voice and the politics of everyday life. Only by moving voice more firmly to center stage can we reflect back on the relations between political and material inequality, knitting the two together into one conception of the welfare state.

## 4.2 The Participatory Ideal

The conception of voice that I have outlined so far is a vision of politics *sensu lato*. It spans a wide range of political practices from formally structured legislative procedures to informal deliberation about values, identities, and interests. It is thus a broadly democratic conception, encompassing both the institutionalized democratic participation of citizens and the everyday politics in which cultural norms and values develop. For ease of reference I will call this view the *participatory ideal*.

Beyond general insights about participation, it is not immediately clear which political norms should apply in this case. Two groups of issues need to be resolved. The first concerns the demands that the welfare state imposes upon democracy. What norms and procedures would be necessary to institutionalize voice in a welfare state? What kind of democracy? How rich a conception of participation? How egalitarian? The second group concerns the demands that democracy imposes upon the welfare state. What forms of material equality are needed for democratic equality? Does democracy place any qualitative limits on the kind of welfare regime one could have? These questions are central to a more detailed conception of voice. It is clear that they are interrelated. It is equally clear that they draw important connections between democracy and the welfare state, in the first case from welfare to democracy, in the second case from democracy to welfare. In what follows I will begin to frame some answers to them. As we will see, the juxtaposition of these two sets of issues has a great bearing on what one can say by way of response to them.

The conception of politics appropriate for the welfare state is a broadly deliberative one. Norm formation requires people to justify and reevaluate their beliefs. This in turn requires content-rich forms of political communication, both because of the subject matter and the claims raised about it. Conflicting values and preferences can best be translated into common agreements when they are transformed rather than simply aggregated.[2] This process requires a communicatively rich form of politics, a trait maximized when political decision making is conducted via linguistic means rather than the ballot. Voice must be taken literally, then, as a form of politics aimed at persuading others and synthesizing common understanding. It connotes not just politics in a general sense, but specifically a kind of *discursive* and *deliberative* politics.

If norms, laws, and policies are genuinely said to be shared by a given society, their formation must be rooted in equality. The idea that a decision is going to be made that is binding on a group implies a starting point of equality: the group must decide by what modality its decision will be made.[3] The default starting point in this process is one in which everyone has a say in determining the extent of their participation. Equality is therefore implicit in the very idea of developing a set of shared norms.

Because equality is implicit in the discursive processes giving rise to norms, their participants must be equally capable of making arguments and expressing their own points of view.[4] Equal political agency is thus a very important part of the political processes formulating the welfare state. If discursive participants are not equal in this way, decisions about values, identities, and interests are not truly representative. The result would be a systematically biased, nonconsensual system of belief, rather than a shared system of social values. Equal political agency is thus an important normative limitation on the kind of political process consistent with the welfare state.

Because of its commitments to equal political agency, the participatory ideal must recognize the likelihood of gaps between democratic ideals and actual social reality. As such, it must stand for the notion that opportunities for participation be *actually* rather than formally equal. Deliberative equality could not be maintained if economic or social inequalities undermined people's abilities to use their political rights. Citizens must actually be capable of participating in public affairs in addition to being formally allowed to do so. Thus their capabilities to participate must be equal in certain senses. Equal opportunity can be guaranteed only when people are sufficiently equal in the abilities and resources that enable participation. Only such a rich sense of equal opportunity can properly capture the sense of democratic equality put forward by the participatory ideal.

In addition to its egalitarian commitments, the participatory ideal must also embrace some notion of *sufficiency*. Citizens must not only be able to participate as equals with one another, they must also be able to participate in a significant and binding way.[5] It would not be enough, from this perspective, to provide everyone with the same minimal, low-level participatory opportunities and no others. One could imagine a situation, for instance, in which citizens were given an opportunity to choose between competing party platforms every several years, but were formally excluded from feedback on the content or implementation of those platforms. Such a least-common-denominator form of participation would fulfill the demands of equality because each citizen would have an equal vote. It would not count as sufficiently participatory, however. To meet this criterion, the participatory ideal requires that citizens have an official role in drawing up the agenda, participating in deliberation, and making legally binding decisions. Participation must be substantive and meaningful, not simply a yes-or-no choice on programs formulated by others.

Standards of sufficiency run orthogonal to those of equality. In the situation I have just described, for instance, standards of equality are met without sufficient participation. All citizens participate equally, but at the same unsatisfactory level. Similarly, it is possible for standards of sufficiency to be met without equality. Imagine, for instance, a situation in which citizens have full rights to participate in forming the values, norms, and laws under which they live. Furthermore, each of them has the minimal skills and opportunities to do so. Nonetheless, some people have greater participatory capabilities than others, either because of different abilities or different structural circumstances. All citizens participate sufficiently in this case, but not equally. Sufficient opportunities and equal opportunities are thus independent aspects of the participatory ideal. Each much be achieved for the ideal to be met.

Because of its commitments to equality and sufficiency, the participatory ideal puts a high premium on promoting citizens' participatory agency. It puts forward, as a normative desideratum, the idea that certain dimensions of agency must be maintained. Those dimensions are specified directly by the procedures regulating political interaction. Here we see an important point of connection between democracy and the welfare state: certain equalizing measures are integral to political procedure itself. In this vision, the welfare state is seen as an *enabling* institution, one that maintains participatory equality in conditions that would otherwise undermine it. The welfare state is charged with equalizing the skills and resources necessary for participatory equality. It promotes equal and sufficient opportunities for participation and acts against marginality and exclusion.

We are now in a much better position to characterize the conception of politics needed for a political turn in the welfare state. This conception, the participatory ideal, can be summed up in the notion that *citizens should have sufficient and equal opportunities to participate in formulating the norms, laws, and policies under which they live.* This view captures the meaning of democracy for a welfare state wishing to institutionalize voice as a partner to exit. The participatory ideal enables people to have an equal and sufficient voice in the norms, laws, and policies affecting them.

Commitments to equality, sufficiency, and participatory agency put the participatory ideal squarely within the historical tradition of progressive, populist democratic theories. Such views have traditionally supported a universal franchise, universal education, voluntary associations that fertilize the grounds of civil society, and greater economic equality so that differences in wealth do not undermine citizens' equal participation. This rubric broadly connects Rousseau and Mill with many contemporary political theorists.[6] It valorizes consent, dialogue, and direct citizen involvement in public affairs.

It is important to note the underdetermination of sufficiency and equality in the definition of the participatory ideal I have just given. When we say that citizens should have "sufficient and equal opportunities," no particular standard is given for either sufficiency or equality. The participatory ideal sets out a framework or generalized schema for a political turn, but does not dictate precise limits on political processes. The only conclusion that can be drawn so far is that *some measure* of equality and *some level* of sufficiency are necessary to create a normatively sound political process. I have not advanced an argument capable of determining these levels; nor do I think such an argument is possible. This is an epistemological limitation. Levels of equality and sufficiency are largely determined by the peculiarities of individual situations. Exactly which discursive capacities, what level of material equality, or how much citizen control is needed cannot be set from a purely theoretical perspective. Because of this limitation, theory would significantly overstep its bounds if it specified such levels. These decisions require the information, perspective, and deliberation of the people most directly connected to them. They must be determined democratically, then, rather than through some kind of academic inquiry.

Beyond epistemological limitations, democratic deliberation over the meaning of equality and sufficiency is the only consistent position for the participatory ideal. Strong commitments to participation preclude any paternalism in the measures designed to support it. If welfare measures are used to promote equal participation, for example, it would be inconsistent and self-defeating to *impose* them on their intended beneficiaries. Forcing people to be free is an idea with striking rhetorical force, but that force derives from daring self-contradiction. If the goal is to encourage people to participate in the processes governing their lives, then it is directly self-contradictory to impose a governmental regime on them. Since the central goal of the participatory ideal is to promote participation, a policy apparatus that denies participation goes directly against the normative intentions on which it is established. Because of this deep-seated commitment, the participatory ideal must be institutionalized through participatory means. It must extend its participatory commitments, in other words, to its own enactment. The political processes fostering participation are best constructed by their beneficiaries, then. They are best formulated through participation itself.

The preceding argument shows that two moments are implicit in the participatory ideal. On one hand, the participatory ideal is dedicated to the basic principle of participation itself. It holds that citizens should have equal opportunities to participate in the affairs of their society. This principle goes beyond formal equality: it holds that some policy measures be put in place to ensure actual, substantive equality in the political realm. This thoroughgoing conception of participatory equality is a response to the first group of questions posed above. It specifies limitations that the welfare state imposes on democracy. The welfare state, in this case, requires a fairly rich, thoroughgoing sense of democratic participation. On the other hand, and quite consistently with this, the participatory ideal also stipulates that the measures necessary to ensure participatory inclusion should be the outcome of participation. This is a limitation that democracy imposes on the welfare state. Such a rich form of democracy requires equality-promoting measures and also stipulates that they be democratically formulated.

The participatory ideal thus maintains two core commitments: the idea of using agency-supporting policies to *promote* participation, and the idea that agency-supporting policies should *result* from participation. In this sense the policies it proposes are doubly democratic. They both safeguard democratic equality and they are its product. The participatory ideal makes a commitment that the welfare state should result from equal participation and a commitment to using the welfare state to promote participatory equality. The enabling functions of the welfare state, in other words, should be democratically formulated by those who benefit from them.

## 4.3 Rights and Citizenship

The participatory ideal, as I have outlined it, is a comprehensive and idealized conception of democracy. One could get the impression that this is intended to be the last word on the welfare state. Once the participatory ideal is institutionalized, citizens would be able to decide what norms, laws, and policies they want, and theorists would have correspondingly rendered themselves obsolete. Things are much more complicated, however. The interlocking character of democracy and welfare provides some hint of this. Even when citizens do all the hard work of justification, theorists still have many important things to say about a political turn in the welfare state.

To draw out the theoretical aspects of a political turn, it is useful to think more carefully about the relations between welfare and democracy. T. H. Marshall provides a classic view of this relation.[7] He sees the two as components of a broader developmental path of citizenship. According to Marshall, citizenship is composed of civil, political, and social elements. Each element is encoded as a particular kind of right. Civil rights are protections like the freedom to own private property or freedom from arbitrary arrest. Political rights consist of formal entitlements to vote or hold office. Social rights compensate for the effects of political and legal inequality and generally ensure equal status and a minimal level of well-being. Marshall claims that these general categories were originally fused in early states. Each type was differentiated out to solve particular problems characteristic of a given stage in the evolution of constitutional democracy. As civil and political rights were differentiated out of the primordial institutional order, the social support mechanisms that used to accompany them were left behind. Civil and political rights became more abstractly formal, allowing substantive inequalities in their actual use. Social rights, in Marshall's analysis, were invented to compensate for this problem. They take up the slack caused by differences between people, allowing the less fortunate to make use of their rights as effectively as the more affluent.

The most important lesson we learn from Marshall is that citizenship is a collection of functionally differentiated statuses. A regime of citizenship specifies the kinds of equality and difference that will obtain between its members. These are defined in specific functional areas: private life, political decision making, and legal-political agency. The rights that correspond to these areas specify what it means to be a citizen in each domain. Civil rights establish equal citizenship in the domain of private life. The current U.S. conception of citizenship, for instance, stipulates that decisions about contraception are private but third-trimester abortion are not. Similarly, political rights define equal citizenship in the public, political sphere. The Nineteenth Amendment to the U.S. Constitution, for example, dramatically changed the prevailing definition of political equality by enfranchising women. Finally, social rights establish equality for what Marshall calls defending and asserting one's other rights. In the United States, the public education system primarily fulfills this function.

It is important to note how Marshall defines social rights. His readers usually interpret them as simple redistributive measures. In this reading social rights have a purely economic function. They guarantee a particular measure of economic equality, typically in the form of redistributive cash payments. Marshall is much more subtle than this, however. He writes very clearly that "The extension of social services is not primarily a means of equalizing incomes."[8] Social rights are not defined by the form they take, but by their purpose. This purpose is to guarantee "the right to defend and assert all one's rights on terms of equality with others and by due process of law."[9] Social rights are thus rights to *agency*, particularly to the kinds of agency needed to guarantee equality of civil and political rights. They are entitlements to the opportunity to act as a political and legal equal. Correspondingly, they are not simply redistributive transfer payments, but guarantees to the resources and skills needed for political and legal agency. It is no accident, then, that universal education is Marshall's archetypal example of a measure fulfilling social rights. Education actively promotes agency, whereas cash redistribution would have a much less direct effect.

Marshall's insights about agency provide a vital connection between politics and welfare. In his account the two are linked via the functional connection between social rights, on one hand, and civil and political rights, on the other. Social rights are instrumental for the actual realization of civil and political rights. By drawing this connection, Marshall provides means to think in finer detail about some of the issues I have outlined above. Social rights are defined and given content by deficits in the realization of other rights. They fill the gap between formal guarantees of civil and political freedom and their actual realization. Marshall's conception of social rights thus aims at exactly the kind of equal participatory agency lying at the center of the participatory ideal.

More broadly, Marshall's notion of citizenship is very useful for discussing the kinds of equality and sufficiency with which citizens should be provided. He ably ties together the themes of rights and equality, in the sense that rights are the concrete expression of the forms of equality granted to citizens. The question of how equal people should be is thus transmuted into the question of what rights they should have. A question of abstract values therefore becomes a much more tractable politico-legal concern.

Although Marshall provides an excellent analytic framework for thinking about the relations between politics and welfare, his analysis is not normatively rich. He traces historical relations between citizenship's elements and notes a tendency towards increasingly comprehensive conceptions of equal status. He does not, however, provide an explanation of the extent to which people *should* have equal status or the kinds of rights they ought to have. Marshall supplies the conceptual architecture for such a view, but his work lacks the resources to undertake the project itself.

Jürgen Habermas, in contrast, has developed a conception of citizenship that combines civil, political, and social rights in a powerful way. He rethinks the idea from the ground up, moving beyond Marshall's preliminary formulation to a persuasive account of the interrelations between various kinds of rights. Particularly noteworthy is Habermas's account of voice—in this case, democratic politics—as an element of citizenship. His insights provide many valuable resources for the project I have outlined.

## 4.4   The Interdependence of Autonomy and Rights

Like T. H. Marshall, Habermas centers his notion of citizenship around the idea of equal status. He improves on Marshall's work, however, by developing a normative conception, one that explains the grounds of equality. Habermas argues persuasively that citizenship must be seen first and foremost as a status that citizens confer upon one another. Citizens thus have equal status from the start. Citizenship, in his conception, is above all oriented toward promoting the autonomy of its bearers. This emphasis on autonomy provides a valuable entry point for thinking about the state as an enabling institution, rather than as one that simply redistributes goods. Habermas particularly emphasizes the dynamic sense in which citizens are simultaneously authors of a particular constitutional order and subject to it. He thus draws attention to the political aspects of citizenship, providing an important basis for the view that I will outline in subsequent chapters.

According to Habermas, citizenship is a status that people grant one another to enable their mutual participation in a politically organized society. Citizens must recognize one another as equals, he claims, and institutionalize this equality in the basic framework of a constitutional state.[10] This is done by granting one another autonomy, specifically the "private autonomy" that provides citizens with the freedom to define and pursue their own goals and the "public autonomy" that enables them to participate in processes of collective self-determination. For Habermas such commitments are basic presuppositions of equal citizenship itself, particularly when people see one another as fellow citizens in the joint project of creating a democratic body of laws.

Habermas claims that public and private autonomy presuppose one another. In order to be publicly autonomous, which is to say politically and discursively competent, citizens require freedoms of life, liberty, property, conscience, and so on—civil liberties, in short. The absence of basic civil liberties would undercut a person's freedom to speak her mind in public by denying her equal status as a citizen and depriving her of the freedom necessary to function as an autonomous agent. Reciprocally, the particular combination of private liberties that citizens accord one another must be negotiated through public discourse. If public political deliberation were not securely institutionalized, it would be impossible for people to develop a system of laws to ensure their private freedom. Habermas concludes, then, that public and private autonomy are "co-original"—neither is possible without the other.[11]

Public and private autonomy can best be guaranteed, Habermas believes, through a system of constitutionally anchored rights. A legal system guaranteeing public and private autonomy would do so through political and civil rights. Each of these categories of rights is necessary to institutionalize each dimension of autonomy. Thus public autonomy requires a functioning system of civil *and* political rights; the same is true of private autonomy.[12] Citizens cannot function as citizens until they have granted one another all of the necessary rights to undergird citizenship itself.

More crucial for present purposes, however, Habermas recognizes the potential for a gap between the formal guarantees provided by civil and political rights and their actual realization. Public and private autonomy must be realized in actual political contexts, and they are thus at the mercy of empirical circumstance to some extent. Citizens must be well-enough fed, housed, and educated to be capable of equal participation, they must have sufficient access to media of communication to influence public opinion, and they must have the necessary status and respect to be taken seriously in public deliberation. Material and social considerations thus have a primary importance in realizing autonomy.

In this case, the tension between the abstract ideals of citizenship and its worldly realization requires Habermas to stipulate a set of conditions to ensure the fairness and rationality of public dialogue. To meet these conditions, he introduces a category of "social and ecological rights," describing them as "basic rights to the provision of living conditions that are socially, technologically, and ecologically safeguarded, insofar as the current circumstances make this necessary if citizens are to have equal opportunities to utilize the civil [and political] rights [described above]."[13] Thus Habermas connects the realization of public and private autonomy with a contingent, relative justification for certain social rights. He conceives of these rights as providing the material preconditions for autonomous political participation and a secure private life. Any democratic state faced with inequalities in the political or legal capabilities of its citizens, he claims, would have to institutionalize some system of social rights to make fair deliberation possible and guarantee the true worth of civil rights.

Habermas's conception of rights and citizenship clearly harkens back to T. H. Marshall's, both in its functional definition of rights and in its instrumentalization of social rights to guarantee the equal realization of civil and political ones. Beyond Marshall's work, this view also follows an established tradition of concern about the material basis of public political life. Fear of material inequality was the source of pessimism about the universal franchise for both Hegel and Mill. Marx enunciated the idea in a more positive sense when he claimed that political emancipation requires economic emancipation. John Rawls also draws a connection between democracy and its material basis, which he parses as a gap between formal liberties and their actual worth. Frank Michelman develops this idea more fully, tracing out penumbral arguments for the social rights necessary to realize constitutionally guaranteed liberties.[14] Habermas thus follows an established tradition in noting that something beyond civil and political liberties is needed to guarantee the autonomy of citizens.

Two features of Habermas's formulation are unique, however. First, he is much clearer than his predecessors about the exact status of social rights within the *justification* of a system of rights. He shows that civil and political rights have a mutual, "internal" relation to one another, so that each justifies the existence of the other in a circular relationship. These categories of rights are justified as what Habermas calls *formal-pragmatic presuppositions* of the democratic rule of law.[15] Habermas sees such rights, in other words, as features that citizens would have to include when creating a constitutionally organized, democratic society. Citizens would have to devise some way to protect each other's autonomy both in the public sphere and the private one; something functionally equivalent to civil and political rights would be their eventual solution to this problem. Civil and political rights are thus presupposed in a pragmatic, problem-solving sense by the actual law-forming practices of citizens. They therefore function as necessary, formal elements of the practices in question.

Social rights, in contrast, are not part of this idealized mutual implication. They are contingent and subsidiary, dependent upon the complex empirical relations between autonomy, on one hand, and income distribution, class, status, personal abilities, and other factors that influence autonomy's development, on the other. Social rights can thus be justified *only* if material or social deprivation produces systematic inequalities in the worth of civil or political liberties. They serve as functional adjuncts for the achievement of autonomy, and thus do not have the free-standing status of civil and political rights. If there are no significant disparities in the autonomy of citizens, then social rights are not justified, at least not on grounds of promoting autonomy.

The second striking feature of Habermas's discussion is the attention it devotes to the *legitimation* of social rights. The social rights that are justified as functional adjuncts of autonomy must be given specific form by the people they are designed to benefit. The functional requirements of autonomy in general—not just social rights, but also civil and political ones—must be institutionalized through the will of the people.[16] This takes the form of an ongoing constitution-building process, through which the public understanding of what is needed for fair and equal political participation is continually refined and updated to match changing conditions. Because such processes of democratic deliberation are crucial for social rights in Habermas's view, they merit much more detailed examination.

Habermas emphasizes the decentered nature of deliberation in his democratic theory. Public opinion is formed in diffuse, largely unregulated, and loosely interconnected public spheres. The political will of legislatures and parliaments is based upon this relatively free-floating public opinion, but only after it has been processed in a more procedurally regulated sphere of public argumentation. The "weak" public realm of deliberation thus provides reasons and arguments that serve as the basis for the binding political decisions formed in "strong," official spheres of representation.[17] Habermas claims that this system expands the state's ability to use and respond to important information. It places universalistic limits on the kinds of reasons that can be used to justify political decisions, but it also allows far-flung, "home-grown," and relatively inchoate claims to find their way into public dialogue. Public opinion thus provides information sensors to detect social problems. Data is passed from periphery to center, so that legitimate decisions can be made at the center representing the interests of the periphery.[18]

Because procedurally regulated public discourse is Habermas's criterion of legitimacy, actual systems of social rights must be democratically formulated. Through this process, the formal-pragmatic requirements of democracy are realized in particular social and political contexts, ensuring that the constitutional order expresses the values of the society in which it was formed.[19] Actual public discourse is thus crucial in fleshing out the constitutional essentials of a welfare state. It regulates the use of state power, identifies problem areas in society, and develops and authorizes legislation. Proceduralized popular sovereignty is required not only to run the reformulated welfare state, but to create it in the first place. This theory relies heavily on the rationality of deliberative participation and thus must place a high value on the rationality of the procedures regulating it and the people participating in it.[20]

Habermas's work is a particularly good example of what I have called the participatory ideal. It displays both of the ideal's two moments. The first moment can be seen in Habermas's strong commitment to deliberation, participation, and democracy. He believes that citizens must develop their own system of laws and democratic procedures. In so doing, they must guarantee one another forms of autonomy that are comprehensive enough to promote a vigorous public sphere and a secure private life. In Habermas's view, democracy extends from the informal, unregulated interstices of daily life to the formal political sphere. Moreover, this carefully proceduralized notion of democracy provides a criterion of legitimacy for norms, laws, and policies. Democratic participation forms the basis for a democratic constitutional state from start to finish in this view.

The second moment of the participatory ideal is seen in Habermas's treatment of participatory inequalities. He realizes that autonomy requires state support in some circumstances. Habermas thus adopts T. H. Marshall's insights about the need to guarantee the realization of civil and political rights. As a result, he puts forward a category of social rights designed to bridge the gap between formal and substantive equality. Because social rights are measures enacted by the welfare state, the state becomes the basis for maintaining equality of democratic participation. Habermas thus draws together the two moments of the participatory ideal: he claims both that democracy should be supported by the welfare state *and* that the welfare state should be democratic.

Habermas also fills some of the normative lacunae in T. H. Marshall's conception of citizenship. Marshall offers no explanation of why citizens *should* think of one another as equals. Habermas addresses this important question. His notion of autonomy establishes a relatively abstract standard of equality. This standard is particularly useful for thinking about equal status, the issue that Marshall located at the heart of citizenship. Because citizens must see one another as equals in the project of creating a democratic-constitutional state, a conception of equal status in built into the democratic rule of law from the start.

Habermas's double notion of autonomy also provides a standard of equality for systems of rights. Citizens must grant one another the equal rights needed to maintain public and private autonomy. Rights should thus be oriented toward maintaining equal agency in public and private life. Again, this view provides greater specificity about rights than Marshall was able to muster. It details functional tasks for rights to perform, while leaving their actual formulation to citizens themselves. Habermas thus adopts Marshall's basic architectonic, but adds a strong normative element to it.

Finally, the specificity of Habermas's view filters down to his conception of democracy itself. The formal presuppositions of autonomy are the basis for the democratic procedures I outlined above. Habermas argues that it would be inconsistent for citizens to found a democratic-constitutional state without robust notions of democratic inclusion. I will discuss this genre of argument in detail in chapters 7 and 8. For the moment, it is sufficient to note that Habermas provides a basis for a free-standing conception of politics—one going beyond market conditions and moving politics and political agency to center stage. He thus moves us much closer to accomplishing the task I outlined at the beginning of this chapter: developing a conception of politics that can provide a normative basis for the welfare state. In Habermas's work, welfare is instrumentalized to promote equality in politics and law. This justifies welfare by shifting the normative burden to political and legal equality.

## 4.5 Politics Beyond the Market

I have passed through four successively narrower approximations of a political turn in the welfare state. In the ensemble, these describe what I will call the deliberative-democratic paradigm. That view is a free-standing conception of politics, one that is normatively prior to the market logic of the labor market paradigm. This conception spans formal and informal domains of politics, including abstractly cultural concerns about values and identities as well as more concrete, legally binding deliberation over laws and policies. I have built this conception up in layers, from a core notion of participatory equality to fundamental ideas about citizenship to more specific conceptions of rights to an account of the relations between different kinds of rights. This finally leads us to a point where we can talk in much more concrete terms about those rights and their interrelationships. On the side of political rights, this will take the form of a conception of democracy; on the side of social rights it will be a conception of welfare. My elaboration of the deliberative-democratic paradigm is not finished, then. This chapter is only propaedeutic to a more involved and complex discussion.

Because of its normative sophistication and rich detail, Habermas's work furnishes a particularly instructive model for the deliberative-democratic paradigm. I will adopt many of its insights as I develop the paradigm further. Habermas's contributions are not without problems, however. In what follows I will identify some of the limitations of his view. The deliberative-democratic paradigm will continue to take much of its inspiration from Habermas's work, though in considerably modified form.

At the beginning of this book, I proposed to change the division of normative labor in our understanding of the welfare state. Rather than relying on the kinds of values that Max Weber witheringly referred to as "emotionally colored ethical postulates," we should allocate such tasks to the political participation of citizens themselves. The conception of voice I have outlined so far provides the means to do that. It taps the normativity implicit in everyday life.

The deliberative-democratic paradigm implies a shift from thinking directly about the norms underlying the welfare state to thinking about the political processes through which such norms are formed. It thus moves from a direct specification of norms to an indirect, second-order consideration of the conditions under which they can be fairly developed. The considerations about voice that I have just outlined should be viewed in this light. They describe a conception of politics that could allow citizens themselves to create and justify conceptions of welfare. Theory is allocated the more minimal task of making sure that the norms arising in this way are developed fairly.

Such a view considerably redefines the tasks of the welfare state. It does not bind the state a priori to particular conceptions of human needs or social justice. Rather, the state is only required to maintain the conditions under which the sovereignty of citizens can be fairly and accurately translated into law. It must enact the background presuppositions of public deliberation, providing a rich, egalitarian environment for democratic decision making. In such an environment, citizens are both equally and sufficiently able to take part in determining under what norms, laws, and policies they will live. Basic guarantees of equality and sufficiency allow them to decide which needs they will mutually satisfy, adding additional tasks to the state's duty roster as they see fit.

This kind of view marks a paradigm shift in our thinking about the welfare state. It draws upon ideals central to modern societies: democracy, participatory equality, freedom, equal opportunity. Such ideals enjoy broad consensus in most societies, and even when they are thwarted in practice, they serve as the broader basis for our political and economic interactions. Rejecting them, I will argue in chapters 7 and 8, would be tantamount to rejecting some of our most cherished institutions and practices. As such, the political turn provides a solid starting point for justifying welfare regimes.

Although the preceding discussion answers many of the questions I posed at the beginning of this chapter, some important ones remain unanswered. The participatory ideal stipulates that citizens must have equal and sufficient opportunities for political participation. Even this relatively rich notion of political agency is substantially underdetermined, however. It does not specify exactly what equality or sufficiency means. The discussion so far cannot answer that question beyond saying that equality and sufficiency would be functional to the demands of political agency. As I have said, there is no clear way to determine these criteria more precisely from a theoretical perspective. Unfortunately, this leaves the connection between politics and welfare vague and undetermined.

Matters stand similarly with autonomy and rights. Habermas bases his conception of rights on the functional requirements of autonomy. Autonomy is in turn a status that citizens grant one another in forming a democratic body of laws. From this point of view, there is little that a theorist can say about its dimensions or extent. That is a contextually specific decision that must be made by citizens. Similarly, we cannot say exactly what content civil, political, or social rights should have, so we cannot determine precisely what connection would obtain between politics and the welfare state. According to the participatory ideal, this would depend on decisions made by citizens granting such rights to one another.

These questions indicate a lack of determination in the argument so far, raising an important concern that must be dealt with in coming chapters. The deliberative-democratic paradigm might seem to reduce the welfare state completely to democracy, to the point where theorists cannot say anything useful about it. From this perspective, the paradigm seems to be a retreat from normativity, a frank admission of the powerlessness of theory. The proposal I have been outlining, then, might seem like an attempt to save face by proclaiming the sovereignty of the people while folding camp and stealing quietly off into the bush.

More conceptually, this proposal could be read as a retreat to a kind of straightforward legal positivism. This sort of position would decline to say anything about the content of the law, only specifying a minimal opinion about who should be entitled to make laws. Once citizens are handed this task, their decisions would by definition be legitimate. Such a view would provide only a minimal and negative conception of the welfare state. It would completely abandon any attempt to justify welfare, merely affirming the sovereignty of those entitled to make decisions about it while abdicating any ability to pass judgment on their decisions.

In a similar sense, the proposal I have outlined could also be accused of emphasizing the liberties of the ancients at the expense of the liberties of the moderns.[21] It puts great stock in citizen participation, championing democracy as the preferred means for citizens to articulate common values, needs, and interests. It thus seems correspondingly inattentive to individual rights and benefits. It appears to give up the normative high ground of distributive justice in favor of open-ended democratization and politicization. It could thus provide room for political domination, power politics, and welfare backlash as well as the more egalitarian aims I have outlined.

A political turn in the welfare state is not a retreat from normativity, however. Nor does it result in a kind of norm-free legal positivism or a democratic free-for-all. In coming chapters I will argue that a careful analysis of the politics of welfare specifies fairly narrow parameters for democratic procedure. These procedures are required to make good on the normative commitments of the participatory ideal. This ideal is not a reversion to the unstructured democracy of the ancients, but a careful democratic proceduralism with safeguards to protect the liberties of the moderns. These safeguards go a long way towards limiting what can be democratically decided and specifying a view of the welfare state. Significant political or economic inequalities or bureaucratic domination will be out of bounds to democratic decision makers in this view. A political turn is not so much a retreat from the welfare state, then, as a concrete normative basis for justifying it. To turn questions about the welfare state over to democratic deliberation, I will claim, is in large part to *answer* those questions.

To redeem this claim, I will next examine some of the paradoxes implicit in the deliberative-democratic paradigm. With an eye toward similar problems, T. H. Marshall famously declared that "A human society can make a square meal out of a stew of paradox without getting indigestion. . . ." In the next chapter I will call Marshall's bluff, arguing that indigestion inevitably catches up with a society whose system of laws is inherently paradoxical. Identifying and resolving those problems will force us to specify more precisely the relationship between democracy and welfare. It will thus narrow the scope of issues that actual citizens need to debate, providing a tighter explication of the deliberative-democratic paradigm in the process.

# 5

## The Paradox of Enablement

"—at least for quite a long time." So T. H. Marshall qualifies his assertion that "a human society can make a square meal out of a stew of paradox without getting indigestion. . . ."[1] This qualification is an important one, particularly since it occurs in *the* canonic text on welfare state citizenship. Here Marshall boldly asserts, then quietly retracts, the idea that conflicts between economic inequality and status equality can persist indefinitely. Stews of paradox impose their own costs in the end, even if they seem to make a square meal at first.

Many lessons can be learned from the welfare state's paradoxes. In the present chapter I return to the deliberative-democratic paradigm to explore some important aspects of the relation between democracy and material inequality. I will identify an important tension within this paradigm, arguing that it fails to make an adequate connection between the political aspects of citizenship and their material bases. As a result, the deliberative-democratic paradigm becomes entangled in contradictions and cannot ensure equal and sufficient participation for all citizens. When material inequalities create political inequalities among citizens, the procedural legitimacy of democracy is jeopardized. In this case, democratic citizenship founders on problems of welfare rather than resolving them. The stew of paradox is, in the end, indigestible.

This problem is an object lesson in the relationship between democracy and welfare. It shows how important welfare is for ensuring actual equality of democratic citizenship. More broadly, this problem prompts questions about the extent to which capitalism undermines democracy, about the kind of distributive justice appropriate in modern welfare states, and about the conception of politics appropriate to the welfare state itself. It forces us to ask how well the welfare state reconciles norms of democratic deliberation with facts of social inequality and material disadvantage.

To resolve the problems of the deliberative-democratic paradigm, I will outline a firmer justification for welfare rights. This view forges strong connections between democracy and welfare. At the same time, I claim that we should resist the idea of subordinating material, distributive concerns to questions of political equality. Instead, I outline a conception of citizenship that includes a more solidly justified notion of welfare rights from the start. This results in a deliberative-democratic paradigm rooted firmly in the idea that welfare and democracy are symbiotic and intertwined at the deepest level. That insight will serve as the cornerstone for the rest of this book.

## 5.1 A Stew of Paradox

In chapter 4 I took pains to show that a principal strength of the deliberative-democratic paradigm is its thoroughgoing commitment to participatory democracy. Participation shows up in two distinct ways—two moments, as I said in section 4.2. The first of these is a strong commitment to deliberation and political equality. The participatory ideal requires deliberative decision making in both formal politics and daily life. It lays down standards of equality and sufficiency for deliberation. These standards are substantive ones: they hold that people must have equal capabilities to participate. The participatory ideal thus stipulates that a democratic state should include measures to ensure some equality among its citizens. The second moment is an extension of the first. It holds that the policy apparatus of the state should be democratically formulated. This follows directly from the participatory ideal itself, which states that people should be able to participate in forming the norms, laws, and policies under which they live. "Policies," in this case, includes policies supporting political agency itself. The participatory ideal thus maintains two core commitments: on one hand, to policies *promoting* the participatory agency of its citizens, and on the other, to policies *resulting from* citizens' participation.

Unfortunately such strong commitments to participation come at a price. The two moments of the participatory ideal create a paradox. On one hand, participation is needed to promote equal political and cultural agency; on the other, participation depends on it. The participatory ideal is thus circular. It depends on exactly the same processes it is designed to safeguard. This circularity is not accidental. It is deeply structured into the participatory ideal itself. Consider the situation from the following perspective. When we try to uphold the participatory ideal, we are also committed to making sure that conditions of participatory equality hold in a given society. This in turn requires some kind of welfare regime to ensure the material bases of equality. The people who are politically disadvantaged in the given society, those with fewer participatory resources and skills, will be the ones that the welfare regime is designed to benefit. Ideally the welfare regime would be formulated through the democratic participation of these people. They would need to participate alongside other citizens who also have a stake in such policies—taxpayers, for instance—to make claims about their needs and the policies that could best meet them. Moreover, they would need to make political claims about the *very fact* of their disadvantage and marginalization in the first place. By participating in such processes, previously marginalized citizens would be able to negotiate with others for policies that match their needs and values. This is precisely the problem, however. People needing participation-promoting policies are ipso facto unable to participate equally in their formation. Participation, therefore, cannot be both the problem and the solution. This is the nature of the circularity. The participatory ideal is circular because it presupposes equal agency at the same time it seeks to promote it.

This paradox—call it the *paradox of enablement*—is problematic for several reasons. First, it poses epistemological problems for politics. One of the most important functions of political participation is to register claims about one's needs, circumstances, opinions, and preferences. Participation, in other words, fulfills a vital *informational* function in politics. The paradox of enablement makes it impossible for a particular segment of the population to fulfill this function, however. Participatory inequality marginalizes people. It diminishes their voice in politics and culture, reduces the audibility of their claims, and decreases their impact on public affairs. Thus the opinions and preferences of this segment are less well registered in public decision making. Participatory inequality removes valuable information from public dialogue. As a result, attempts to promote people's participation will be prone to error and incompleteness.

Participatory inequality causes particularly serious epistemological problems when it mutes claims that people might make about their own exclusion from political processes themselves. When people are marginalized, by definition they have much less adequate means to demand inclusion. They are not only left out of the political system, but also deprived of the means to demand entry. This doubly paradoxical silence leaves the most marginalized people in a political black hole from which no information can escape. Their very existence becomes politically invisible.

A second problem is more pragmatic. The paradox systematically foils attempts to create public policy that both promotes equality and is democratically legitimate. It forces one to choose between equality and democracy because it seems that the two cannot be combined. Attempts to realize the participatory ideal will be sidetracked into one of two unsatisfactory compromises. The first compromise would choose democracy over equality. In this scenario, participation-promoting policies would be formulated through existing democratic processes. Ex hypothesi these processes would be characterized by unequal participation. The resulting policies would be democratic in a formal sense. They would not, however, be representative of the people they are designed to benefit. At best, such policies would be based on faulty information that would prevent them from meeting the needs of their intended beneficiaries. At worst, they could miss many who are marginalized by the political process while imposing illegitimate, paternalistic measures on others. Such a regime might be formally democratic, but it would violate the participatory ideal while trying to instantiate it.

The second compromise would choose equality over democracy. In this scenario democracy would temporarily be set aside in favor of an expert assessment of needs and means. Gaps in participatory equality would be assessed by social scientists. Such experts would estimate who is at a disadvantage in participation. Further, they would discern the ways in which such people are disadvantaged— unequal wealth, say, or unequal education. Finally, they would devise a policy apparatus to compensate for such problems. This process would not be democratic at the beginning, but it would be intended to start the process off on the right direction so that it could become democratic at some future date. This proposal is also subject to many problems. It runs the same risks of epistemological blindness and paternalism. The second scenario is based on operational assessments of what counts as participation. Social scientists would have to decide what skills and opportunities are important to democracy before they can determine the pattern of their distribution. This risks creating a gap between idealized experimental schemas and people's actual experiences of marginalization or exclusion. In addition, paternalism is a very large problem here. The history of social policy is rife with well-meaning attempts to help people help themselves. This has all too frequently resulted in the heavy-handed imposition of cultural norms, perverse incentives, and moral agendas on people ill-equipped to resist them. It is possible that a project of this kind could start an egalitarian boot-strapping operation leading to participatory equality. It is also possible, however, that such a process would miss its target over and over again, resulting in endless paternalism and no steady progress towards the participatory ideal.

Both of the compromise solutions I have examined run aground on problems of epistemology and paternalism. Each tries to resolve the circularity by setting one half of the circle aside: the half requiring policies to be formulated by their beneficiaries. In so doing, each also forfeits one of the chief advantages of participation: its tendency to foster civic skills. Thinkers from Tocqueville to Putnam have emphasized the extent to which participation teaches people participatory skills.[2] A valuable means of promoting equal participation is to provide participatory opportunities for those normally marginalized or excluded. Exactly this possibility is precluded by the two compromises I have examined. In addition to problems of epistemology and paternalism, then, each of these unsatisfactory approximations gives up one of the principal advantages of political participation.

The difficulties I have just traced are not simply the result of failed attempts to find a practical shortcut to participatory equality. They are inherent in the participatory ideal. As long as this ideal is construed as a purely abstract commitment to participatory equality, it is noncontradictory. As soon as one unfolds its two moments, however, internal paradoxes are quickly discovered. The participatory ideal requires institutional means for its own enactment, which must in turn be democratically formulated. In this case, however, such measures are legitimate and nonpaternalistic only if people already have equal opportunities for participation. Yet this is exactly the problem they are designed to remedy. If, in contrast, such measures are paternalistically formulated, they are directly self-defeating. They provide agency with one hand and take it away with the other. The moral is that participation cannot be the solution to problems of participation. Any attempt to make it so is inherently paradoxical.

## 5.2 The Problematic Connection between Autonomy and Social Rights

To see exactly how paradox sits at the heart of the participatory ideal, it is useful to examine it in finer detail. In chapter 4 I drew heavily on Jürgen Habermas's work to develop this view. It is worth turning to Habermas again as an object lesson in the nature of the problem. His work provides a more concrete example of the paradox I have just outlined, as well as resources for thinking constructively about a solution to it.

Autonomy, as we have seen, is the normative basis of Habermas's theory. It expresses the equal status that citizens must grant one another and provides grounds for explicating a conception of civil, political, and social rights. To investigate the paradox of enablement, I will focus on a smaller part of this picture: the connection between public autonomy and social rights. Because public and private autonomy are so thoroughly intertwined, it is somewhat artificial to separate them here. I am doing this only for ease of exposition: public autonomy is most closely connected with the idea of voice, which is my primary interest. This, of course, is an oversimplification that I undertake only reluctantly; a more complete picture would reveal complicated interdependencies between democracy, social rights, and both private and public autonomy.[3]

The most striking feature of Habermas's account of social rights is the fact that their justification is *empirically* and therefore *discursively* mediated. To explain what I mean by this, it is best to start by drawing a comparison with civil and political rights. In Habermas's account, civil and political rights are always justified ex ante, regardless of context. Any society attempting to guarantee public and private autonomy would need to enshrine some version of them in its constitution. At least a minimal approximation of civil and political rights must be put into the constitution from the beginning; these rights can later be modified to better fit the situation at hand, using the actual discourses that they help to protect and foster. Thus the general justification of civil and political rights does not depend on the actual use of political participation, which is required only to determine their specific, institutionalized content.

The justification of social rights is substantially different in Habermas's account. From a theorist's point of view, social rights are only *conditionally* justified.[4] This justification is hypothetical in character: if certain circumstances obtain, then some kind of social rights are justified as pragmatic presuppositions of democratic lawmaking. Specifically, social rights are called for when poverty, deprivation, or other forms of disadvantage decrease people's ability to be rational and autonomous citizens. They serve as corrective measures that are justified after the fact, against the background of a particular constitutional order that has failed to institutionalize the liberties it is designed to guarantee. The connection between autonomy and social rights is thus mediated through a complicated set of contingent, "external," empirical circumstances. It is not given implicitly as a necessary feature of democratic lawmaking.

The empirical contingency of social rights means that their justification is highly dependent on actual processes of public deliberation. Social rights can be justified only after a large set of empirical and interpretive issues has been settled, connecting the general requirements of autonomy with the specific characteristics of the situation at hand. To some extent the answers to these questions will rest on empirical claims about the facts of the matter or evaluative claims about shared principles and ideals. In important ways, however, such answers can also be determined by the requirements of deliberation itself. The very act of deciding such questions publicly imposes certain limitations on deliberation. These sorts of concerns are what I referred to in chapter 4 as "formal-pragmatic presuppositions" of the political process. They are implicit requirements that actual citizens would, with the passage of time, come to understand and implement. Formal-pragmatic presuppositions are small kernels of necessity mixed into the routine problem-solving functions of everyday deliberation. They are thus part of normal discourse about the empirical claims and value judgments that go into forming a democratic constitutional state.

We can see how formal-pragmatic elements are implicit in the deliberative process by considering some of the claims that would arise when social rights come under discussion. Such deliberations would range over several important and interconnected topics: (1) what it would mean to be autonomous in a particular social context; (2) how the empirical circumstances in question limit or constrain autonomy; and (3) what scheme of social rights can best remedy these problems.

(1) Most importantly, social rights cannot be justified until the citizens of a society have determined what it will mean to *be* a citizen in their society. They must develop a particular interpretation of autonomy and institutionalize it in a particular constitutional order. Their account must satisfy certain general properties that are pragmatically presupposed by deliberative democracy. Citizens, for instance, must have the basic discursive competencies to communicate effectively with others—to raise claims, engage others in reasoning about them, and so on.[5] They must also have more specialized abilities to engage in political deliberation—such things as access to the media and the ability to express a position clearly and persuasively. Without these capabilities, deliberative-democratic politics would be impossible.

Public autonomy does not, of course, consist solely of such pragmatically necessary features. It is first and foremost a culturally situated view of what it means to be a fully participating citizen in a given society. Public and private autonomy, like moral autonomy, are culturally and situationally specific achievements.[6] What it means to be autonomous is to an extent relative to the understandings of autonomy prevalent in one's culture and society. In a general sense, this includes notions of what capabilities a publicly autonomous person must possess, what kinds of opportunities and rights she must be provided, and what standards of equality ought to be used in public deliberation. This understanding is partly formal-pragmatic and partly context-dependent in nature. For instance, a given conception of public autonomy will require developing various *kinds* of participatory competence, though it is not clear from the start which ones will count as necessary. Further, it might be held to require achieving various levels or *thresholds* of these capabilities, or *equal* competence beyond a basic threshold. A notion of public autonomy thus requires many determinations of quantity and quality that are not spelled out from a formal-pragmatic point of view. It consists in a publicly developed interpretation of what it means to be a fully participating citizen, built around, but not completely specified by, the necessary, formal-pragmatic presuppositions of deliberative democracy.

(2) The need for social rights can be evaluated only against the background of a constitutional order built on understandings of this kind. Once a socially accepted notion of autonomy has been legally secured, then discrepancies and deviations from the ideal can be found. This requires citizens to contrast the idealized understanding of autonomous citizenship that they have developed with the way things really are. They must ask, for instance, whether some people are disadvantaged in the political process, how their autonomy is subverted, and what kinds of social rights would restore equality. Such practical, empirical discourses are oriented to achieving understanding about a complex social reality and the way it departs from various regulative ideals. It is particularly important at this stage that politically and economically marginalized people are able to make their needs public. In this view, the publicly held, legally institutionalized notion of autonomy is their strongest basis for demanding equality. It provides them with a solid basis for making claims to social rights and other kinds of assistance.

(3) Finally, discourses about autonomy and about social rights come together in discussions of the kind of social policy that a group of people wants. Deliberating citizens must determine what forms of social policy are most consistent

with their culture, history, and self-understanding.[7] They must decide what measures will produce the desired outcome in a manner consistent with their beliefs about the role of the state in social life and their overall economic preferences. In other words, they must come to agreement about the kind of policy that will most effectively integrate the functional needs of autonomy with given social and economic conditions and with partly conscious, partly taken-for-granted values.

Because social rights are actually formulated at this point, it is very important that all citizens affected by them have a substantive role in deliberation. History provides many examples in which the state was allowed the only voice in developing social policy. To avoid state paternalism, it is vital that those most affected by social rights be allowed to make claims about their needs and the measures that would best address them.[8]

This brief sampling of the discourses needed to justify social rights shows that contextually specific social rights cannot be justified or formulated solely on the basis of a *philosophical* conception of autonomy. Rather, the connection between autonomy and social rights must be drawn within particular circumstances through a fairly demanding process of public deliberation. Because of this empirical contingency and dependence on actual discourse, however, justification is a problem for social rights. According to Habermas's universalist standards of legitimacy, the discourses justifying and forming a system of social rights require the autonomous participation of all those affected by them.[9] We have seen several examples of this above. Full, autonomous participation is necessary to ensure that all are fairly represented in the consensus that is reached as a result of public deliberation, and further, that those most in need of social rights have been able to articulate their own needs and interests. If those most affected by social rights do not participate in their formulation, then such rights are not, strictly speaking, democratically legitimate. Even more importantly, they run the risk of being irrelevant or missing their mark, because the contextually specific input of people needing social rights has not been adequately taken into account. This kind of under representation does in fact seem inevitable because the people that social rights are designed to help are precisely those who are *not* autonomous, those who lack some of the means necessary to participate fully in public discourse. Thus by definition they cannot be full and equal participants in deliberation, and the scheme of social rights designed to promote their autonomy will necessarily be formulated by others.

This argument shows that Habermas's justification of social rights runs headlong into the paradox of enablement. An actual system of social rights is required to guarantee political equality, at least in all but the rarest and most felicitous cases. However, political processes are first necessary to justify and implement that system of rights. Habermas's conception normatively stipulates *both* that social rights are a precondition of legitimate political processes *and* that a politically autonomous public is necessary to interpret social rights. Each is a necessary precondition for the other. This is not a clean, "internal," formal-pragmatic relation of mutual *implication* or co-originality, however. It is rather a messy, empirical relation of co-*dependence*, an empirical paradox in which we must be able to determine which material preconditions need to be satisfied before we can satisfy them, and paradoxically, certain material preconditions must be satisfied before we can determine which material preconditions need to be satisfied.[10]

This analysis reveals an awkward fit between autonomy and social rights. In philosophical terms, we see that social rights cannot be conditionally justified using autonomy as a standard. Such a conditional justification depends additionally upon actual agreement about the details of interpretive issues surrounding the connection between autonomy and material inequality. However, this "external," discursively developed justification is circular: a substantive notion of autonomy must be developed before social rights can be justified, but a fair and well-functioning regime of public discourse awaits adequate social rights. This means that the justification of social rights is problematic because the input of those most needing such rights is by definition impaired. Social rights are expected to provide the basis for their own justification and legitimation, but they cannot.

In practical terms, the paradox takes the following form. Social rights are needed, according to Habermas, only when the autonomy of some citizens is not sufficient to enable their equal participation in political and legal processes. However, the people needing social rights must be able to articulate that need and must also be able to explain what kinds of measures would best address their problems. In the absence of this, the state's deliberative "information sensors" will not function properly, increasing the likelihood that people already marginalized from politics and law will remain so. Since the participation of these people is by definition impaired, this seems an almost inevitable outcome. Those who have the most to gain from social rights are excluded from full participation in discourse. When social inequalities are persistent and consistently target the same disadvantaged groups, the needs and interests of these people are systematically excluded from discourse. This prevents them from improving their political situation, thus reproducing social inequalities. The conditionality of justification for social rights thus translates into the perpetuation of political and economic disadvantage.

## 5.3 Practical Shortcuts: Constitutional Reform and Critical Social Science

Until now, this discussion has proceeded in more or less strictly philosophical terms. It could be argued, however, that such an approach is overly stylized—that the problems I have outlined are only problems on paper that can be fudged in various ways in practice. In particular, it seems that a practically oriented process of constitutional reform, assisted by a critically oriented social science, could alleviate them.

That solution would look something like this. We would conceive the realization of autonomy as an ongoing process of constitutional reform and development, rather than as a state of being, institutionalized in one stroke.[11] The formal-pragmatic presuppositions of autonomy would then serve as guidelines for realizing the true potential of popular sovereignty. Social rights supporting popular sovereignty would develop in a dialectical process in which political discourse becomes more substantively equal through ongoing processes of critique and correction. To get such a process off the ground, a minimal interpretation of autonomy would have to be enshrined in the constitution, providing guidelines for the development of civil, political, and later, social rights. In its most basic form, this set of rights would have to guarantee sufficient capabilities and freedoms to put marginalized people on the road to full autonomy. Once such a preliminary constitution had been established, better and more adequate interpretations of social rights could be developed in an ongoing process of public dialogue and constitutional reform.

This "bootstrapping" argument emphasizes the dialectical and temporal character of constitutional reform. Instead of seeing the constitution as a blueprint for constructing a democratic society *uno actu,* it views it as a normative standard for evaluating and promoting the development of democratic societies. Here systems of rights develop in tandem with the autonomy and rationality of the populace, each supporting the further development of the other. In this view, the relation between autonomy and social rights is no longer circular, but a spiral composed of mutually reinforcing processes of social development.

Although this proposal is appealing for its practicality and its more dynamic reading of the constitution-building process, it does not entirely escape the problems I have outlined. Because some people are *not* fully autonomous from the start, their voices are not heard as loudly and their needs are not articulated as effectively in public dialogue. In such conditions, it may be quite difficult to achieve the minimal conditions needed to get the bootstrapping process going. Specifically, it is not clear how close to full autonomy disadvantaged citizens would have to be before they could start developing their own autonomy-promoting policies within a competitive and unequal political environment. It may likewise be hard to sustain this process, given the constant inequality-generating pressures of the capitalist economy and the uncertainties of translating material progress into political success. The political path toward securing autonomy is an uncertain and difficult one at best. I do not mean to suggest that such a path is impossible, of course, only that its instabilities may disrupt any orderly progression towards greater equality.

To skirt these problems, it must be possible to assess the needs of the marginalized largely *without* their initiative or input. In the language of Habermas's double-standpoint social theory, deficits in autonomy would have to be identified primarily from an observer's perspective, because the participant's perspective cannot be clearly enunciated in public dialogue. An elementary system of social rights would have to be justified *without* balanced, equal public deliberation, but with the intent of moving toward this goal. This is an example of the strategy I referred to earlier as "choosing equality over democracy."

A process of constitutional reform aiming at inclusion needs assistance of a kind best provided from the more objective perspective of a reconstructive social science.[12] That is an investigation trying to discern the implicit, formal-pragmatic presuppositions of a set of practices. The critical capacities of such a science could provide a rough guide for reform, approximating the implicit presuppositions of democratic participation from a slightly distanced, theoretical perspective. This kind of science would try to determine what capabilities are needed for fair and equal democratic participation, identifying inequalities in their distribution. It would provide a kind of expert assistance in the development of legislation about social rights, picking up the slack for the democratic process's failure to represent all citizens' interests. This proposal asks those who *are* autonomous to discern the needs of those who are not. Individuals capable of viewing the world from another person's perspective would try to infer or approximate the kinds of social rights required by those less fortunate.

I am fairly sympathetic to this kind of practical solution. It forges a productive alliance between the deliberative-democratic paradigm and the social sciences, creating a bridge between practically oriented political theory and theoretically guided political praxis. This refined account does not fully avoid the difficulties I have identified, however. I foresee two groups of problems: (1) one with the implicit paternalism of such an approach, and (2) the other with its use of autonomy as a critical concept.

(1) The solution that I have described uses social-scientific research to replace the democratic deliberation of a certain sector of the public. This raises the specter of a welfare state nearly as focused on social engineering and nearly as paternalistic as the ones it is designed to replace. In this case, the old logic centered on well-being is replaced by one focused on autonomy, but with the same lack of participatory input already characteristic of many welfare bureaucracies.

It is not clear how much better than present welfare regimes such a policy would be. Recent advances in social science, particularly a new sensitivity to the pitfalls of interpretation and representation, would make it possible to avoid some of the paternalism inherent in this model. In addition, it is likely that the forms of public autonomy needed in a society would be fairly universal. The specific capabilities employed by people who are presently autonomous would likely benefit those who are not autonomous as well. On the other hand, this kind of universalism risks falsely assessing the needs of the people it is designed to help. Because disadvantage and political marginalization are usually distributed along the lines of group identity, there is considerable room for cross-cultural and cross-gender misinterpretation. There is also ample space for failing to recognize the particular needs of marginalized groups. It is quite possible, in other words, to overestimate the degree to which a given conception of autonomy is universal rather than particular. This is especially a danger when social inequalities are reproduced among the same groups of people through long periods of time. In this case, certain kinds of people will always be at a disadvantage in articulating their needs and interests because they are consistently marginalized in the political process.

In addition, it must be remembered that the social rights that would be put in place here differ considerably in character from civil or political ones. Civil and political rights are primarily insubstantial, procedural, negative protections that are formulated to be as general and universal as possible. Freedom of speech, for instance, is a principle that is not typically specified for particular contexts; it is instead enunciated in a general form that can be judicially applied when necessary. Social rights, in contrast, must always be formulated, funded, and administered to meet the needs of the people they are designed to serve. Poverty prevention programs are thus considerably more tangible and specific than laws safeguarding speech. The substantive and material character of social rights requires them to be carefully tailored to the situation in which they are applied. They are thus more prone to paternalism than are civil or political rights, especially in the absence of participation by those affected by them.

In theory, of course, this model's paternalism is only a transitional necessity since it is oriented toward the eventual enablement and autonomy of the whole public. The ends in this case justify the means: if this paternalism fulfills its function, people will be able use their newfound capabilities to design nonpaternalist policies. On the other hand, however, it is fairly clear that universal, full autonomy is only a regulative ideal, and that the state would be involved in a perpetual cat-and-mouse game with the capitalist economy and other autonomy-undermining forces. As autonomy is subverted in new and different ways among different groups of people, the state would always face new challenges, starting its bootstrapping and learning process over each time. In this case, paternalism would not be transitional but chronic.

On the whole, it is largely a matter of luck, circumstance, and social scientific insight whether the necessary beginnings of a bootstrapping process could be developed without adequate input from all concerned. The burden is largely placed on policy makers to ensure that policies promote autonomy without producing undesirable and perhaps undetectable side effects. To some extent, this places us roughly in the situation of today's welfare states: we must determine how to enact social policy without having sufficient participation from those it is designed to help.

(2) Even if such a process could be started off in the right direction, however, I am not sure that autonomy is a sufficient guide to sustain it. For a process of social development to bootstrap itself towards increasing autonomy and deliberative equality, it must be oriented towards a secure goal. But in that respect, I think, it is unclear how far the concept of autonomy can take us. The formal-pragmatic dimensions of communication have been well established. Habermas has developed a sophisticated conception of communicative interaction, outlining the kinds of claims and forms of argumentation necessary to develop an intersubjective understanding of the world.[13] A person lacking these capabilities would be seriously hindered in political communication, creating a strong presumption for help in developing them. Profound distortions in communicative competence are fortunately rather rare, however. And although more subtle distortions certainly do exist, they are macrolevel phenomena whose cost seems to be reckoned primarily in subtle forms of damaged social integration, rather than in lost

political autonomy.[14] In sum, communicative competence is crucial to political autonomy, but it is so basic that it does not provide us with a sensitive diagnosis of underdeveloped political capabilities.

The real weight of this argument properly rests, then, on capabilities and opportunities more specific to public political interaction. Problems in the equality and sufficiency of democratic deliberation can be measured, for instance, as deficits in one's ability to express opinions and have influence on political will formation.[15] This includes having the ability to be persuasive in public debate, having sufficient command of the language of discourse, gaining access to its media of dissemination, having time to devote to politics, and possessing sufficient social status to have one's arguments count as worthy of attention in dialogue.

A critical notion of autonomy like this can provide a good guide for formulating civil and political rights, but its implications for social rights are less clear. When we trace out the connections between autonomy and social rights, the ethical-political and formal-pragmatic aspects are hard to separate.[16] I believe that this is an inherent limitation of autonomy as a critical concept, chiefly because its material and structural dimensions are *in principle* indeterminate and inexact from a philosophical point of view. Thus a philosophical characterization of autonomy by itself cannot be rich enough to stipulate actual social rights.

It is no surprise, then, that many crucial aspects of a system of social rights cannot be determined outside of actual processes of public deliberation. For instance, formal-pragmatic considerations do not give a narrow-enough stipulation of the standard of "equality" that should be used with public autonomy.[17] Is equality here a matter of equal influence, equal opportunity to participate, or what? If we interpreted it as "equal capability for public discourse," which capabilities should count as important, and in what proportion? Would we literally balance the capacities of corporate actors with those of individuals? In what ways would the unequal capacities of for-profit corporations, government agencies, and voluntary associations be equalized? Which forms of "equivalence" will count in giving individual people roughly equal competencies and privacy, given that literal equality is impossible? In addition, the actual character of autonomy is unclear from a formal-pragmatic point of view. Does it mean equal access to deliberation, equal access plus equal capacity to deliberate, or equal effectiveness in deliberation? Is a certain social status an unavoidable precondition for the credibility of one's public arguments? If this is the case, is it a minimum status ("citizen"? "adult"? "deliberatively autonomous person"?), an equal status, or some combination of the two? And finally, the connections between deficiencies in autonomy and the social rights designed to correct them cannot be determined formal-pragmatically. Corrective social policies require the input of those affected to be accurately and nonpaternalistically applied. A formal-pragmatic study of autonomy itself does not specify exactly what corrective measures should be taken.

It seems to me that these questions can be sorted into at least two large groups. One concerns the material character of autonomy: what it takes to act as a citizen in a deliberative democracy, particularly in terms of the means and enablements that a citizen would require. Any group of citizens would need to determine how substantive and material this concept is. There is not any philosophical, context-independent way of establishing the connection between autonomy and specific material properties or distributive criteria, however. A second group of questions focuses on the extent of these material aspects. Is autonomy a threshold concept or a matter of equality? What kind of equality? How far does a society have to go in promoting the material and discursive equality of its members? How close an approximation of equality is enough? These quantitative questions show that autonomy does not set strict enough limitations on the system of social rights to function as a critical guide, outside of actual processes of deliberation.

Although these clusters of questions lie at the heart of the connection between autonomy and social rights, they do not seem to be cleanly resolvable in formal-pragmatic terms. Too many of their crucial aspects are evaluative in character, determinable only with reference to a particular culture and system of values. In these cases the question, "what does it mean for an individual to be publicly autonomous?" is closely bound up with the question, "what does it mean for each of us to be publicly autonomous in our society?" Similarly, the question "what kinds of social rights are necessary to promote autonomy?" is equivalent to "what kinds of social rights can best promote our autonomy consistently with our values, preferences, and circumstances?" Thus a purely formal-pragmatic investigation can't get us very far in this particular case. It can describe the connection between autonomy and social rights only in minimal terms, and the formal-pragmatic and ethical elements of this connection are extremely hard if not impossible to separate out. This implies that formal-pragmatic considerations alone will not allow us to decide whether social rights are justified in a particular context. Such questions are inherently empirical and interpretive, and therefore require resolution in public discourse.

The process of constitutional reform that we have been examining therefore exhibits many of the same problems as my more strictly philosophical rendering of the paradox, though not perhaps to the same degree. We see here that autonomy is not an entirely reliable guide for a practically oriented process of reform. This is largely a result of the fact that the formal-pragmatic core of this notion isn't available for use until it has been interpreted and applied in actual public deliberation. That is to say that the critical capacities of the theory don't work well unless assisted by balanced and fair processes of democratic deliberation. They provide ways of *approximating* an adequate system of social rights, but again, only subject to the limitations of unbalanced and unequal public discourse. And as we have seen, those who most need to be on hand in the discourses institutionalizing social rights are least represented in them. In this case, however, we are thrown solidly back into the paradox of enablement. This is not to say that a careful, social-scientific study of autonomy could not be an adequate guide for constitutional reform. It suggests instead that such a practical solution may not be as useful as we might hope because it is forced to deal with the same sociopolitical problems faced by current welfare states.

## 5.4   Toward a Broader Conception of Citizenship

A solution to the problems I have outlined should retain as many of the deliberative-democratic paradigm's valuable insights as possible, but find a surer path around the difficulties it encounters. In particular we should work hard to salvage insights about the connections between democracy and welfare. To conclude this discussion, I will attempt to reassemble these elements in a way that seems less likely to create problems. My solution furnishes the deliberative-democratic paradigm with a different approach to citizenship and social rights.

The problems I have outlined largely result from an overly narrow construal of what social rights are supposed to accomplish. Both Marshall and Habermas subordinate social rights to the functional requirements of democracy, providing them with a highly conditional justification. As I have shown, however, the relatively tenuous, discursively and empirically mediated nature of this justification leaves social rights vulnerable to the very problems they are designed to address. The problems I have surveyed arise precisely because social rights are seen as supporting players in the political process, rather than as more free-standing elements of citizenship.

Ultimately, the most effective strategy for resolving these problems is to expand the range of tasks allocated to social rights and make their justification more secure. Instead of giving social rights a handmaiden's role in ensuring the actual worth of other rights, they should be seen as having a direct role in realizing autonomy. In this case, three kinds of rights are necessary to realize public and private autonomy: not only civil protections and political rights, but also material aspects of equal citizenship. On this view, autonomy has an inherently material character. Citizens must guarantee one another the means to participate as equals in a broad range of social activities for the same reasons that they provide each other with political and civil rights. Various enablements, security guarantees, and freedom from exploitable vulnerabilities are thus necessary for being a full and functioning citizen. This change results in a broader and more substantive conception of autonomy and citizenship. It acknowledges that citizens *always* need material forms of freedom and security to realize autonomy, so it builds them into the very idea of equal citizenship from the start.

On this view, social rights are seen as necessary features of equal citizenship and are connected with it internally and unconditionally in the same way that civil and political rights are. As a general category, these rights are not justified with reference to empirical circumstances. They are not seen, in other words, as means to rectify occasional empirical problems encountered by a constitutional order built around civil and political rights. Instead, social rights have the same degree of universality and the same formal-pragmatic, unconditional justification as rights to civil protection and political participation.

The justification of social rights I have outlined is a formal-pragmatic one in a somewhat unusual sense. Social rights are not justified here by their use in avoiding deficits in political or legal agency per se. Rather, they are justified by the descent into paradox that would result if they were made conditional upon democratic deliberation. As I have just argued, such rights must be justified independently of actual democratic processes. The justification must, as it were, already be there when democratic citizens arrive on the scene. The very act of attempting to answer questions about autonomy and rights democratically thus presupposes background conditions of material equality. Again, the reason is a logical one: to suppose otherwise would be to descend into the paradox of enablement. This is an indirect argument. It shows that material guarantees must be an integral part of citizenship because to suppose otherwise would be inconsistent and paradoxical.

A stronger justification for social rights gets around many of the problems I have examined. This conception promotes the agency of citizens across a broad range of human activities. Its enlarged notion of agency is designed to promote equality in general, making it less likely that the state will need to do repair work in the wake of entrenched forms of social stratification or material inequality. By increasing people's capacities in a general sense, the material forms of disadvantage that undercut autonomy will be reduced and grave disparities among political capacities will be minimized. Autonomy is better promoted, then, by a more general conception of citizenship.

The difference between Habermas's view and my own is chiefly one of contingency. Although social rights have a formal-pragmatic justification in Habermas's view, it is one that obtains only in specific, empirical cases. He thus reduces the core functions of the welfare state to realizing formal guarantees of civil and political rights. Habermas argues that politically enfranchised citizens can develop more robust welfare policies through public deliberation if they so desire.[18] My proposal, in contrast, starts from the idea that it is too difficult to single out actually existing participatory deficits and connect them with social rights. Although formal-pragmatic analysis is a valuable tool, it reaches unfortunate limits when called on to justify social rights on a case-by-case basis. My proposal, therefore, is also formal-pragmatic, but it deploys this kind of argument in a much more general sense. To avoid paradox, I argue, we must see material equality as an integral part of democratic law-making. This proposal includes political capabilities among the favored forms of agency to be promoted by the state, but does not make the existence of social rights *contingent* upon them. This form of agency, like the freedoms guaranteed by civil and political rights, must be promoted regardless of fluctuating circumstance because of its noncontingent role in promoting autonomy.

The broader conception of citizenship and the more general notion of social rights that I have described preserve many of the advantages of the deliberative-democratic paradigm, but in a more substantive and less conditional form. Political equality is now promoted not in conditional terms but as an ongoing commitment of political procedure. This allows citizens to fine-tune welfare benefits in the same way that they can reconfigure the specific civil and political rights they grant one another. It also anchors social rights much more firmly in the notion of equal citizenship, providing them with a more solid public, political justification and narrowing the range of controversy about what counts as a justifiable social right. In this view the welfare state is seen above all as an institution designed to promote equal citizenship across a broad range of human activities. Like Habermas's model, it leaves much of the content of social rights open to political deliberation, diminishing the role of the theorist and opening up room for the actual decisions of real citizens. Above all, this model pays careful attention to the material preconditions of autonomy and establishes a conception of democratic citizenship that can realize them without paradox.

Although this revision of the deliberative-democratic paradigm meets the challenge of the paradox of enablement, it does so at a high level of abstraction. This proposal focuses on the justification of social rights, but says little beyond the idea that they must form a necessary component of citizenship. It claims that social rights should be justified independently of any particular circumstances, but it does not thereby say how we should determine the *content* or *purpose* of social rights. We know that such rights must be a necessary component of citizenship, but we do not know to what level of equality or sufficiency. Similarly, we do not know what specific kinds of measures would be called for. These issues show that the solution I have outlined solves only part of the problem. Many important questions remain to be addressed, ones that require a more complete elaboration of the relations between democracy and welfare lying at the heart of the deliberative-democratic paradigm.

# 6

# Reflexive Citizenship

A confrontation with the paradox of enablement has already prompted several important modifications in the deliberative-democratic paradigm. It calls above all for a different and more secure justification of social rights. In the revised version I have outlined, social rights must be a component of citizenship from the very start. They cannot be functional adjuncts of other commitments. Instead, such rights must be seen as pragmatic presuppositions of equal democratic citizenship. They are thus connected with it internally and unconditionally in the same way that civil and political rights are.

As I have articulated it so far, however, this is a rather thin view of citizenship. It contains only the idea that some kind of material equality must be a component of the broader view. There are no details about what this might be, however: what dimensions of equality or sufficiency it would involve, what kinds of rights are entailed, or what their purpose or content would be. More broadly, it is not clear what the consequences of this view are for democracy, the welfare state, or our understanding of the relation between the two. With an eye toward these questions, I will return to citizenship and the paradox of enablement to find some answers.

## 6.1 Circularity and Citizenship

In chapter 5 I identified a paradox at the heart of the deliberative-democratic paradigm—the paradox of enablement. I argued that we could resolve the paradox by providing a less contingent justification for social rights. When such measures are justified without reference to changing circumstances, their justification does not depend on unequal political processes. If they are instead attached directly to the idea of equal citizenship, then they are justified as necessary background conditions of deliberation itself.

A firmer justification for social rights inserts a guarantee of enablement into the circle from the start. Such a guarantee, I claimed, must be made whether or not it is called for by any particular, immediate circumstances. Only a standing guarantee would be adequate to break the circularity inherent in the participatory ideal, precisely because it is not contingent. As a free-standing guarantee, such a conception of rights is not dependent upon the materially circular political participation of the people.

This solution to the paradox of enablement functions at a fairly high level of abstraction. It focuses on issues of justification. It is important to note, though, that justification is not the only issue surrounding a system of social rights. Rights are not simply an empty functional category. Rather, they must take the form of concrete laws and policies. They must be formulated to do particular things for particular groups of people. There are actually two important problems with rights, then: one with their *justification* and one with their *content*. The deliberative-democratic paradigm as I have accounted for it so far tends to merge these questions. This is appropriate because they are in fact merged in daily life. For analytical purposes, however, it is useful to separate the two.

An analytical distinction between justification and content is very much alive in chapter 5. Many of the problems I outline there are claims about the difficulty of spelling out actual systems of rights—content—in a deliberative political system supported by the very same rights. Given the problems raised there, the solution I devised might seem to take us only halfway to resolving the paradox of enablement. One might wonder what difference it makes to solve issues of justification when actual democracy is still required to fill in the details. From this perspective the paradox of enablement seems not to be resolved so much as relocated. It is no longer primarily an issue of justification, but an issue of deliberation over the content of laws and policies.

To respond to this charge, it is useful to reexamine the nature of the paradox. Here Habermas's version of the deliberative-democratic paradigm again furnishes the best example. The principal problem that Habermas encounters is the simultaneous *open-endedness* of deliberation and its *inequality*. Autonomy is the standard of equality he puts forward, but it is an inherently vague one. Deliberative interpretation is needed to flesh out the meaning of autonomy and show how it connects with equality, but equal deliberation is of course the problem. The fact that issues of autonomy, equality, and sufficiency are underdetermined all the way down leaves citizens substantial leeway to interpret them as they see fit. At the same time, this open-endedness places great burdens on the populace. Their discourse bears the burdens of interpreting autonomy both to justify social rights and to determine their content. Such a heavy reliance on discourse in turn exacerbates the effects of deliberative inequalities. The more issues left for people to decide, the greater their freedom and the greater the negative effects of differences between them.

An unconditional justification for social rights removes one of two principal burdens on public discourse: the burden of justification. It stipulates from the start that such rights are needed, removing the issue of their importance from controversy. Such a justification thus narrows the scope of things that must be determined in public deliberation. If participatory equality is guaranteed in a general sense from the start, citizens do not have to demand it. They do not thereby fall into the trap of needing to make sophisticated arguments about the material nature of citizenship from a position of inequality. Rather, their focus is more restricted to claims about the form that such rights should take. Citizens are thus in a position to refine and customize the content of citizenship rather than struggling uphill for its universal extension.

This response does not eliminate the paradox of enablement, however, but merely narrows its scope. Removing the burden of justification from the deliberative docket leaves in place the burden of determining the content of systems of rights. Again, such a solution seems not to resolve the problem so much as relocate it. This is a misleading way to look at the situation, however. The expectation of solving the problem in one stroke is unnecessarily limiting. It is unrealistic to think that one *could* simply specify a state of affairs in which the paradox of enablement would not occur. Another approach would find a set of democratic procedures and guiding ideals that would allow a constitutional welfare state to resolve its own paradoxes democratically. This would harken back to the evolutionary model of constitutional reform I considered in section 5.3.

The constitutional reform proposal was promising. The idea, briefly, was to use a carefully crafted method of social-scientific investigation to detect and remedy inequalities. This would start deliberation off in the right direction, so that a temporary paternalism could evolve into a stable and egalitarian democracy. This is an example of "choosing equality over democracy" to prime the pump of egalitarian reform. In spite of its paternalistic overtones, this proposal has a great deal of potential. Ideally it would have a recursive structure, looping back on itself to create ever more equality. It thus takes advantage of the circularity inherent in the participatory ideal, converting self-limiting processes of democratic deliberation into self-reinforcing ones. Here circularity takes the form of an upward spiral rather than a downward one. For this to happen, though, the recursive reform process has to be oriented in the right direction. It needs some overall goal toward which it can progress. This need not be straight line, constant progress, just overall, incremental directionality. Teleology, in other words, is required to prevent endless looping or spiral descent.

Lack of teleology was in essence the problem I identified in chapter 5. The idea of autonomy was not sufficient to specify the kinds of rights needed to guarantee it. There were various questions about the kinds of capabilities an autonomous person must possess, what kinds of opportunities and rights she needs, and what standards of equality and sufficiency would hold for public deliberation. Further, it was not clear whether citizens' participatory capabilities would need to equal one another or whether autonomy was instead a threshold to be reached. Because these issues cannot be determined directly from the idea of autonomy, they were left to the deliberation of actual citizens. And here, of course, the open-endedness of deliberation led to the paradox of enablement.

To resolve the paradox, we need a clearer description of the goals that citizens must discursively implement. We need a telos for constitutional reform, one that adds direction to the process. To find such a goal, it is useful to change perspectives, imagining citizenship from a hypothetical, idealized point of view that describes the desired endstate. To execute this conceptual maneuver, it is instructive to look back at the participatory ideal. That ideal states that citizens should have sufficient and equal opportunities to participate in formulating the norms, laws, and policies under which they live. It is thus committed to maintaining participatory equality. Suppose for the moment that we could simply institute the dimensions of equality and sufficiency needed for the participatory ideal. What would that look like?

Given the discussion of chapter 5, the participatory ideal would need to ensure equality and sufficiency at a level such that the paradox of enablement would never arise. To prevent the paradox from occurring in the first place—hypothetically—all citizens would need the ability to make claims about the slightest tendency toward exclusion or marginalization. They would need the agency, in other words, to participate equally in forming the norms, laws, and policies that prevent exclusion. When all citizens have such capabilities, they would be able to head off the initial stages of a spiral descent into paradox.

The form of democracy I have just described is one in which citizens have the ability to revise the legal bases of democratic equality. Chief among these legal bases are the laws defining citizenship itelf. Such laws confer upon citizens the ability to revise the status that gives them the ability to revise it. More simply, this form of citizenship guarantees citizens the means to determine the conditions under which their participation is supported. That status is *reflexive*. It allows citizens to redefine and reformulate their own status *as* citizens. Such citizens, like Theseus, are able to refurbish the very vessel in which they sail. Reflexive citizenship provides a standard for this kind of practice by specifying core conditions of citizens' agency. Citizens can repair the ship in which they are sailing only when they are fully capable of specific kinds of participatory agency. The correct dimensions of equal and sufficient agency allow each citizen an equal chance to modify the status of citizenship itself.

Reflexive citizenship is a unique status. Strictly speaking, it cannot be imposed paternalistically. This conception uses welfare to create the conditions for self-determination. In so doing, it closes the gap between being subject to the law and being its author. Reflexivity creates the state that Rousseau characterizes as rendering people just as free as they would be on their own and obeying only themselves.[1] Like other conceptions of citizenship, the reflexive one constructs a legally encoded status and applies it to individuals. In so doing, it creates particular social relations, epistemologies, and kinds of person. This conception has a unique property not found in the others, however. Even if reflexivity were paternalistically applied to a person, the participatory character of that status allows one to leave or to modify it. This conception creates citizens who are capable of determining their own status and the rights and benefits attached to it. It thus foils the paternalism that could be present in other normative conceptions of citizenship.[2]

Continuing the thought experiment, consider how the idea of reflexive citizenship works within the context of constitutional reform. A nation of reflexive citizens would have the ability to define and redefine what citizenship means. Citizenship in such a regime would be a status legally open to change through democratic processes. Correspondingly, citizens would have the capabilities to reformulate the norms, laws, and policies governing citizenship itself. As long as these general conditions were met, citizenship would remain reflexive. Citizens would be able to modify the various parameters and nuances of citizenship by participating in such self-sustaining political practices. They would, in other words, be able to participate in choosing the circumstances of their own self-government and freedom. This political practice has the form of a happy circle, one that continually cycles back to maintain its own bases of equal and sufficient participation. In such circumstances, democracy itself becomes reflexive. Reflexive citizenship thus forms the conceptual and procedural core of reflexive democracy.

Such a practice of self-determination is, however, subject to one important limitation. That is the very reflexivity of citizenship itself. If citizens are like Theseus, repairing the ship in which they are sailing, the most obvious limitation on their conduct is that they keep the ship afloat. They may continually modify the *content* of reflexive citizenship, but they are not free to end its reflexivity. That would be a violation of other citizens' rights and a return to a society in which some participate while others live under a system of laws and norms not of their own creation. Such a political system would contradict the practices and intentions of citizens themselves. If citizens try to instantiate the participatory ideal *without* reflexive citizenship, they will fall headlong into the paradox of enablement. To avoid this paradox and make their own political practice consistent, they must ensure the right dimensions of equal and sufficient participatory agency for all among them. To draw out the metaphor to its fullest extent, citizens need to keep the ship afloat while they repair it. This metaphorical notion of an intact vessel represents the core content of reflexive citizenship that ensures equal and sufficient participatory agency itself.

We can see, then, that reflexivity provides a crucial standard for the deliberative-democratic paradigm. It is the test of an adequate regime of democratic citizenship. Regardless of the particular mix of laws and policies, regardless of the actual measure of equality or sufficiency, each of these components must be such that the overall regime allows its members reflexive agency. If it does not, citizenship becomes a source of inequality and paternalism rather than a status created by all to regulate their mutual interaction. Reflexivity thus provides a goal for processes of constitutional reform. It describes the state of affairs under which the paradox of enablement would not arise.

This ends our thought experiment. We can now leave the idealized perspective of a state in which the paradox of enablement does not occur. Back in the real world of political inequality, we can ask what is gained by having this kind of telos? From an actual citizen's perspective, the idea of reflexive citizenship allows people to assess whether a particular regime of rights increases each person's ability to act as an equal in determining the meaning of citizenship. Similarly, such a standard allows people to ask whether all who are considered citizens are able to participate equally in the definition of the status itself. Reflexive citizenship thus establishes a benchmark from which citizens can evaluate any proposed change.

The conjunction of reflexivity and citizenship provides unique conceptual tools for evaluating constitutional reform. Reflexive citizenship establishes a reference population—citizens—and requires one to investigate the success of each member in defining the status itself. By creating a reference population, reflexive citizenship takes on a force not found in other conceptions. Citizens—typically treated as subjects of the law—are recognized by the state. They are known and enumerated. In a regime of reflexive citizenship, any subject of the law should also have full abilities to be its author. The population of citizens subject to the law should coincide perfectly with the population reflexively able to be its authors. When the two groups do not coincide, there is reason to reexamine the rights and benefits of citizenship. This built-in standard overcomes the potential blindnesses and epistemological lacunae of other conceptions. People cannot fall into a political black hole of exclusion in such a regime because their role as subjects of the law always renders them visible. This visibility, in turn, carries with it the demand that anyone subject to the law must also be its reflexive author.

In sum, reflexive citizenship provides important resources for constitutional reform. It provides a standard both for the justification of social rights and for determining their content. This standard does not resolve the paradox of enablement in one stroke, but provides a direction for the democratic resolution of constitutional contradictions. It establishes a progressive standard for reform: any change must narrow the gap between the group of people subject to the law and the group fully capable of being its authors. Reflexive citizenship thus creates a directionality in the process of constitutional reform, providing an implicit telos for resolving the paradox of enablement. As such, it forms the core of a conception of reflexive democracy.

Interestingly, reflexive citizenship does not remove the circularity within the participatory ideal. Citizens must actually participate in real political processes to determine the conditions under which their participation will be sustained. The circularity of this relationship is, as I have said, inherent. This should not be surprising since the concept of reflexivity is at core circular. Its Latin root *reflexus* is a participle of the verb "to reflect," bearing all the connotations of things turned or bent back to their source. Reflexive citizens, by extension, are those who can circle back to maintain the sources of their own citizenship.

Rather than eliminate circularity, reflexive citizenship replaces the vicious circularity between participation and enablement with a *virtuous* one. Reflexivity is based on the idea that each citizen must be able to control the meaning of citizenship. If equal participatory agency is a citizen's right, and citizens are equally empowered to interpret and modify their rights, then reflexive citizenship requires that each citizen has means to protect, change, and modify the very rights that ensure her ability to participate in protecting, changing, and modifying them. Reflexive citizenship leaves the circularity in place, but provides a guiding ideal to orient reform in a positive direction.

## 6.2 Capabilities for Participation

The arguments I have used to introduce reflexive citizenship are fairly abstract. That is appropriate because this notion is designed to provide an idealized goal for actual processes of constitutional reform. Because the idea retains a large role for actual deliberation, however, it might seem too abstract to serve as such a goal. Reflexivity may give the impression of leaving any particular conception of citizenship just as undetermined as it would have been without this goal. In neither case is a concrete system of rights and procedures spelled out.

To allay these fears, it would be useful to spell out some of the pragmatic consequences of taking reflexivity as a goal. Although the participatory ideal stipulates that the content of actual systems of rights should be democratically determined, there are still important things one can say about this from a theorist's perspective. The requirement of reflexivity imposes specific limits on deliberation and the conceptions of rights, citizenship, and welfare that result from it.

The participatory ideal is built around particular conceptions of equality and sufficiency. Reflexivity sets limitations on these ideals, describing the level of agency at which citizens would be capable of participating as equals in defining the meaning of citizenship itself. Reflexive citizenship thus has a vital role in fleshing out a nonparadoxical conception of the participatory ideal. This would take the form of standards of equality and sufficiency for participatory agency.

To specify the kinds of equality and sufficiency needed in this context, it is useful to return to Amartya Sen's notion of capability egalitarianism. In chapter 3 I drew on Sen's work to resolve another version of the paradox of enablement—the problem of women's cultural agency. I claimed that capability egalitarianism provides a useful way to think about cultural agency as a component of citizenship. This notion is readily adaptable to reflexive citizenship in a broader sense as well.

According to Sen a capability is a "potential to achieve some functioning."[3] A functioning could be an activity—participating in a public debate, say—or a state of being—say being healthy or knowledgeable about current events. One has a capability when one's personal attributes and circumstances allow one to be or do something. For example, a capability to participate in a public debate would require personal attributes like the ability to speak the language in which the debate was held and cognitive abilities to structure arguments and understand others' points of view. Further, capabilities to participate would hinge on favorable circumstances of various kinds. One must be allowed into the room and permitted to speak, others must be prevented from monopolizing the conversation, and so on. One also requires basic, minimum resources to enable participation. Something as mundane as transportation, for instance, can often be a prerequisite for attendance.

Because capability egalitarianism promotes a person's *potential* to achieve some functioning rather than her functioning per se, it is a form of equal opportunity. This can easily be seen in the above example. In order to actually participate in a public debate, a person must first have the potential to do so. Potentiality, as Aristotle notes, precedes actuality.[4] In the idiom of distributive justice, we would say that opportunities necessarily precede actual achievements. For example, being able to speak the language of debate, being able to structure arguments and express them convincingly, having well-structured rules of discourse, all of these things enhance a person's *opportunity* to participate in public debates.

Sen is very careful to specify that capability equality requires *actual* as opposed to formal opportunity. Again, the above example illustrates this well. Suppose that a set of rules was in place ensuring fair and equal debate. Suppose further that all of the prospective participants spoke the language of debate, they were all well educated and all skilled in public persuasion. But suppose that the organizers located this debate on a snowy ice field somewhere in Antarctica, perhaps in a cynical bid to exclude public comment. They claim that this move is not objectionable because everyone who comes is welcome to participate. Everyone, they say, has an equal opportunity to participate because the debate is open to all. This kind of equality is purely formal, however. Formally equal opportunities provide a very thin sense of equality, as this example shows, because they still leave wide latitude for actual inequalities. Background inequalities are allowed to exercise a potent influence within a system of formally equal opportunities. Here, for instance, many people are excluded from the debate by the difficulty and expense of travel. Actually equal opportunities to participate would require the organizers to provide free transportation, or even better, move the debate closer to its participants. In Sen's terms, people would have equal capabilities only when all of the preconditions for participation were actually present.

Capability egalitarianism works particularly well as a guarantee of participatory agency. It can easily be focused on the kinds of opportunities required for participatory equality.[5] Speaking the official language of a government or debate is a kind of capability in this sense. It opens up opportunities that one would not otherwise have. Similarly, cognitive abilities and rhetorical skills are participatory capabilities because they provide a person with necessary means for participatory agency. In general, the kinds of capacities a person needs to be an active participant can all be compactly theorized as participatory capabilities. This approach has the advantage of requiring, by definition, actually equal opportunities for participation. It thus prevents marginalization and exclusion by establishing a standard for full and actual participatory equality. This conceptual device provides potent means to determine which voices are politically and culturally muted and ensure their amplification to an adequate level. Capabilities are a gauge for judging the dimensions of this amplification. By guaranteeing actually equal opportunities for voice, a conception of participation formulated in Sen's terms decouples participation from background inequalities and thus heads off the problems of political inequality that create the paradox of enablement.

To render citizenship reflexive, agency must be sufficient as well as equal. Capability egalitarianism provides the conceptual means to set such a level. Sufficient agency, like equal agency, can be seen as a kind of capability. According to the standard of reflexivity, citizens must minimally have the capability to ensure their own agency *as* citizens. They must be able, in other words, to ensure that they do not sink into political or cultural invisibility. No group can be at risk of falling into a downward spiral of political marginalization and increasing lack of participatory opportunities. To avoid such a downward spiral, citizens must be able to determine the *content* of citizenship. When all citizens can participate to an adequate level, they are able to claim the means to political equality. They can articulate rights and policy measures to ensure their ongoing agency. By extension, all citizens thus have the means to prevent their own marginalization.

Sufficiency and equality are deeply intertwined, even though they are separate criteria for participatory agency. It is quite normal for only some citizens to have the ability to redefine the meaning and content of citizenship. This is arguably the status quo in most democratic nations. In such cases sufficient agency is achieved by some but not others. Some citizens then control the meaning of citizenship for all, disenfranchising and marginalizing others. To foil this problem, sufficiency must be realized hand in hand with equality. Only when agency is both equal and sufficient can we claim that participation will enable citizens to sustain the means of their own agency.

The idea of reflexive citizenship does not, again, determine the precise content of citizenship or rights. That is, as I have said, both impossible and undesirable. Instead, this notion further narrows the scope of what actual citizens must decide. It lifts some of the burdens on actual discourse and eliminates some of the room for damaging inequalities to arise. The notion says specifically that citizenship must be reflexive, that actual citizens should attempt to make it so, that reflexivity will be a matter of devising standards of equal and sufficient agency, and that these standards can be thought of as capabilities. Reflexivity thus provides an orienting goal for constitutional reform, and it makes insightful comments about the *kinds* and *amounts* of agency necessary for a nonparadoxical conception of citizenship.

In chapter 3 I emphasized that capabilities provide an analytic perspective from which we can evaluate many different kinds of governmental, institutional, and personal relations. Equal capability is thus an abstract standard rather than a concrete set of institutions or practices. It is a particular kind of equal opportunity, applied to particular forms of agency as evaluated from political, cultural, and economic perspectives.

I have treated political and cultural capabilities separately in this discussion, largely because of their different functions. The separation is primarily analytical, however. Many of the same kinds of thing would count as increasing a person's political *and* cultural capabilities. Education, for example, improves the effectiveness of a person's voice in both political and cultural senses, improves her understanding of what she needs to say, and gives her greater self-confidence to say it. An achieved functioning in education is thus a capability for both political and cultural participation.

It should be no surprise that capabilities from the perspective of politics over-lap with capabilities from the perspective of culture, given what I have said about the intertwining of culture and politics. Political discourse always has cultural connotations, and political decisions institutionalize particular norms, values, and images of human life. Reciprocally, renegotiating cultural norms is an inher-ently political process. It requires people to thematize background norms, iden-tify the symbolic content of laws and policies, and argue for changes. Because politics and culture are so closely intertwined, what counts as a political capa-bility is likely quite similar to what will count as a cultural capability. The differ-ences between them are largely perspectival ones, derived from looking at the same underlying reality from two different angles.

A capability theory easily extends to economic agency as well. Like politics and culture, economic agency can be described as a matter of capabilities. Most obviously, one's economic agency is increased by possessing capital or highly desirable job skills—things classically associated with the economy. Economic agency can be promoted by many other factors, however. Sharing the interests, habits, manners, and tastes of the rich provides easier access to high-level employment, for instance.[6] These classically cultural attributes provide eco-nomic mobility by improving one's social "suitability" for occupying positions of privilege. To the extent that such attributes provide privileged access to income and occupations, they function as capabilities from the perspective of the econ-omy. To the extent that they enable one to act as an arbiter of social acceptabil-ity and status in defining systems of cultural value, they also count as capabilities from the perspective of culture.

In general, economic agency tends to promote a wide range of other capabil-ities. It gives a person better exit options from home and work. It thus enhances her position to renegotiate cultural norms and gives her better financial means to participate in public affairs. Economic agency therefore helps to promote cul-tural and political agency. Of course, economic agency is promoted by voice as well as exit. One's capability to articulate claims within the economic sphere improves one's economic situation. Arguing for higher pay or better work con-ditions is a form of economic agency. Voice, then, provides capabilities from the perspective of the economy. However, we have also seen that voice is necessary for renegotiating cultural norms and for articulating claims in the official politi-cal sphere. All of this shows that political, cultural, and economic agency over-lap in important ways. Their connections and disjunctions can be more precisely examined by making perspectival distinctions between the kinds of capabilities they provide. This set of distinctions allows us to observe how various traits and circumstances provide capabilities from the perspectives of the economy, culture, or politics.

## 6.3   Constitutional Reform and Actually Existing Inequalities

Warnings about abstraction notwithstanding, the conception of reflexive citizenship I have outlined is still quite abstract. This is potentially problematic because the success of this view ultimately hinges on how well it integrates with the actual discourse of real citizens to promote democratic equality. To demonstrate the utility of reflexive citizenship, it would be useful to show how it might accomplish this task. This would clarify the connection between reflexive citizenship in the abstract and actual rights and procedures. To do this, we need another thought experiment. This one is a simulation of the path that actual citizens might trace as they attempt to use the idea of reflexivity to guide their deliberations about the basics of a constitution. It is purely hypothetical, then, a heuristic illustration of the kinds of issues that actual citizens would have to consider.

Citizens bent on constitutional reform would have to take stock of the actually existing inequalities that characterize their political life. To simulate this kind of consideration, let us take the contemporary United States as a case study. The most detailed study of the factors promoting or hindering political participation there is Sidney Verba, Kay Schlozman, and Henry Brady's Citizen Participation Study. This work is a comprehensive investigation of the roots of participatory inequality. It is particularly useful for present purposes because it shows the importance of various capabilities for participation. Actual citizens would need something like this information to make their own decisions about citizenship and avoid the paradox of enablement.

Interest in politics, not surprisingly, turns out to be the strongest factor promoting a person's participation.[7] Tied for second place, however, are education, civic skills, and institutional recruitment. Educational level requires no explanation in this context. Civic skills are the everyday organizational and relational capacities that people need to conduct meetings, present ideas, and persuade others of their point of view. Recruitment gauges the extent to which one is encouraged by institutions—church groups, labor unions, civic groups—to participate in politics. Other so-called engagement factors like political knowl-edge and feelings of efficacy round out much of the list. Family income closely trails them as an important influence, however.

The range of participatory factors surveyed by Verba, Schlozman, and Brady fits snugly within a capability framework. The capability view works particularly well for theorizing the kinds of opportunities and skills that people need to be effective participants. Achieved functionings in each of these areas confer capa-bilities for participation. Verba, Schlozman, and Brady focus a great deal of attention, for instance, on civic skills, the mundane capacities of expression, thought, and persuasion that people use in participation. These skills are pre-conditions for successful participation, and they have a great impact on an indi-vidual's actual opportunity to participate. Education also has a similar impact because it cultivates the cognitive skills necessary to be an effective participant. Income is an important part of participatory capability as well, because insuffi-cient resources place strains on a person's life that crowd out politics. This is par-ticularly true of welfare recipients, who occupy the bottom rungs of the American income ladder and also exhibit the lowest levels of participatory capa-bilities and actual participation.[8]

A conception of reflexive citizenship drawn up in terms of capabilities pro-vides a dynamic approach to problems of equal opportunity. Civic skills, for example, are a pivotal category of opportunities for participation. Verba, Schlozman, and Brady show that civic skills are unequally distributed and that opportunities to develop them are also unequally distributed. In particular, the workplace is an important source of skill stratification. High-status, high-paying managerial jobs provide people with opportunities to practice and enhance par-ticular skills. Such people are more likely to spend time making presentations, chairing meetings, and persuading others. In contrast, jobs that involve more mechanical tasks, less self-direction, or less time interacting with others tend to leave civic skills correspondingly less developed. Churches and voluntary asso-ciations are also arenas for developing civic skills, however, and they help com-pensate to some extent for the dominance of the workplace in this domain.

This situation can be elegantly theorized using a capability framework. In order to acquire capabilities for political participation, people must actually achieve functionings in the various factors required for participation. On Sen's terms, however, before people can achieve such functionings, they must first have the *potential* to achieve them. A potential to achieve a functioning is a capa-bility. For example, people must have capabilities for civic skills, then achieve functionings in civic skills, in order to have capabilities for political participation. Workplaces, churches, and voluntary associations are important sites for cultivating such skills. This analysis shows linked chains of opportunities, one leading to the other. Certain kinds of opportunities need to be created in order to create further opportunities. Thus structural and institutional opportunities for acquiring civic skills are needed to make equal participation possible. Further, people must act on these opportunities to achieve the functionings they make possible. Finally, such opportunities must be actual ones, rather than formal ones impeded in various ways by other inequalities.

To better see how capability egalitarianism works as a theory of participatory agency, it is worth exploring some of the theory's fine-grained detail. When talking about capabilities, it is useful to distinguish between those that result from characteristics of a person versus those that are imposed by her structural and institutional environment. On one hand, one's capabilities are determined by personal abilities, talents, handicaps, and other attributes. These are what I will call the *agent-rooted aspects* of capability.[9] Equally important, however, are a person's circumstances. These *structural aspects* of capability describe the environment within which a person acts. They include all of the external factors that limit or promote a person's agency: laws, resources, physical facilities, and even the help or hindrance of others. This distinction enhances the concept's ability to deal with issues of political participation. Sometimes inequalities are simple, tangible differences between people. In other cases, however, they are best seen as asymmetries in the structural circumstances within which people act.

Some of Verba, Schlozman, and Brady's participatory factors are agent-rooted capabilities. Education and civic skills are agent-rooted, as are engagement factors like interest in politics or feelings of attachment to a political party. These kinds of competencies, attitudes, and preferences open up opportunities to participate. Other factors, in contrast, are structural. The extent to which political participation is solicited by organizations and associations is an example of this type. Because participatory capabilities are both agent-rooted and structural, promoting their equality requires several strategies. On one hand it requires developing the talents and capacities of individuals. On the other it requires leveling structures that amplify the voices of some and diminish the voices of others. Thus equality requires a dual focus on structure and individual characteristics.

Talk about equalizing capabilities raises an important problem. As I have noted, many of a person's capabilities are rooted in the person herself. They are aspects of who she is and what she can do. These personal traits—or as Sen would say, these achieved functionings—open up further opportunities for the person. In general opportunities are a good thing because they increase a person's freedom without constraining her options. Unlike other forms of opportunity, however, promoting agent-rooted capabilities could be viciously paternalistic. It would be problematic simply to *create* these kinds of capabilities because they are so directly associated with the agent herself. Civic skills, for example, open up many opportunities to their possessor and thus expand her capability set. Civic skills are learned through practice, however, so a program that simply created them would force a person to do particular kinds of things. Such a system would be highly illiberal to say the least. Because of the real danger of paternalism and coercion, agent-rooted capabilities should not be treated like ordinary opportunities. They must be enacted through more subtle means.

As a matter of definition, I will call capabilities like civic skills first-order opportunities: having them directly opens possibilities to participate. Similarly, knowing how to read gives one a first-order opportunity for further education; having a bicycle provides a first-order opportunity to ride a bicycle. In some cases, providing a person with a first-order opportunity is a good thing. Giving someone a bicycle, ceteris paribus, opens up possibilities she would not otherwise have. In other cases, however, giving someone a first-order opportunity is literally impossible. Inculcating civic skills in a person is beyond the current state of neurobiology and cybernetics. It would also, of course, be odiously invasive. In this case it is much better to provide a person with an opportunity to develop them, which she can take or leave as she chooses. An opportunity to develop civic skills can be defined as a second-order opportunity: it is an opportunity to develop opportunities. Actually *having* civic skills, in contrast, provides first-order opportunities for political participation.

Talk of first- and second-order opportunities is important in the context of welfare regimes. Capabilities are opportunities, and some of them are agent-rooted. They are opportunities made possible by personal characteristics. Creating such opportunities could be substantially invasive and paternalistic if it required directly modifying a person. In such cases we would not want to create first-order opportunities directly, but rather create opportunities to acquire these other opportunities. This nested structure avoids both the technical and moral difficulties with promoting capabilities that are rooted in the agent herself.

Civic skills follow this pattern. It would be invasive to make someone skilled in politics, but it would not be problematic to offer them an opportunity to develop such skills. An opportunity to develop civic skills would open further opportunities to political participation; it is thus second order. Again, a nested structure of opportunities avoids coercion when it consists of agent-rooted capabilities. This allows us to see that the issue is not one of equalizing people's civic skills per se. It is, rather, one of providing equal opportunities to develop such skills.

Happily enough, problems of invasiveness and paternalism do not arise in the case of structural capabilities. They are straightforward, garden-variety opportunities. Creating unwanted structural capabilities may be expensive and wasteful, but it is not dangerous. The Americans with Disabilities Act,[10] for instance, removed many structural barriers to mobility in public buildings. It thereby provided new capabilities to people whose access to public facilities was previously limited. The act opened up opportunities without coercion because it increased people's capabilities in a structural rather than an agent-rooted sense. The solution I have just outlined for improving civic skills functions in a similar way. It solves problems of paternalism by translating agent-rooted capabilities into structural ones. Rather than modifying people directly, this solution equalizes the structures of opportunity within which people act. When we talk about citizenship in the abstract, it is not a problem to view civic skills as capabilities without distinguishing their various types. When it comes to proposing concrete policy measures, however, those that promote agent-rooted capabilities can be dangerously paternalistic. To avoid the possibility of coercion, we must translate them into second-order opportunities instead. The measures needed to enact them will focus on promoting agent-rooted capabilities indirectly, by first promoting structural and institutional ones.

These considerations establish further parameters for a reflexive conception of citizenship. The notion of equal capabilities for participation describes the opportunity structure of a society. It calls for actual equality of opportunity in certain crucial dimensions—those providing citizens with equal and sufficient means to revise the meaning of citizenship itself. Citizens would need to create an opportunity structure promoting these kinds of capabilities. They would need to take special pains to ensure that their conception of citizenship is as universal and inclusive as possible. The notion of reflexivity establishes a standard for this because it stipulates that anyone who is considered a citizen should be reflexively able to modify that status. When there is a mismatch between those classified as citizens and those who are equally and sufficiently capable, measures will have to be taken to restore reflexivity to the population as a whole.

How citizens would deal with such lacunae is, of course, an open question. For purposes of illustration, though, we could imagine several strategies. One would focus on developing capabilities that are as universal as possible in their political utility. Education, for example, is already compulsory in the United States. Citizens could develop the universality of education further to make it equally *useful* to each citizen. This is in fact the function of the highly successful Headstart program, which focuses on promoting educational equality at an early age. Similarly, the character of one's job seems to matter greatly in developing political capabilities for adults. This may be a rationale for a reconfigured labor market paradigm, one focusing on the quality of self-direction allowed to people across the status hierarchy of the workplace. It may also give citizens pause to realize that unemployment is *politically* serious as well as economically debilitating. It undermines the acquisition of many capabilities by removing people from the sphere in which they are developed.

In this vein, it is interesting to wonder what kinds of innovations a regime of reflexive citizenship might spawn in the welfare state itself. Rather than thinking of welfare simply as a means of redistributing resources, citizens might think of it instead as a participatory venue in itself, one that can act as a "school of civic virtue." Here welfare regimes could directly establish opportunities for participation by allowing people to practice participatory skills. The much-maligned Community Action Program, a key element of the U.S. War on Poverty, was built on this very valuable insight.[11] It viewed welfare not simply as providing people with resources, but also as giving them direct opportunities to participate in implementing social policy. Its slogan "maximum feasible participation" established a norm of autonomy and skill development within social programs themselves. Although it encountered many political problems, this program provides a valuable example of how the *form* in which policy is implemented can have as much impact as the resources it allocates. A paradigm focusing on participatory capabilities provides many conceptual resources for expanding on this insight.

These further considerations about participatory capabilities help to give a fuller view of the kinds of things citizens would have to take account of in implementing a reflexive conception of citizenship. They show that on balance there is much that can be said about the details of reflexive citizenship from a theorist's perspective. Even though the concept itself is quite abstract, it lends itself well to concrete theorizing about rights, agency, and distributive inequality. Capability egalitarianism provides a fairly narrow description of what such a view should look like. Distinctions between agent-rooted and structural aspects of capability, between first- and second-order opportunities are technical issues that citizens will be forced to confront. As such, these concepts are unavoidable features of the constitutional reform process. We can therefore say, from a theorist's perspective, that such concerns are a necessary part of the actual system of rights implementing reflexive citizenship.

## 6.4　A Distinctive Vision of the Welfare State

Reflexive citizenship and the paradox of enablement are a dialectical pair that guide constitutional reform. The former is a standard for adequate participation, while the latter predicts lacunae in any attempt to realize it. Deliberating citizens will therefore need to compensate for the inherent limitations of their own knowledge by establishing a conception of citizenship that is as universal and comprehensive as possible. The considerations I have just surveyed outline the issues with which such citizens will have to deal. Reflexive citizenship should be guided by concerns about equal agency, but it cannot simply be read off of an analysis of participatory inequalities like a blueprint. Citizens will have to anticipate the paradoxes inherent in their own deliberations and attempt to deal with them.

The idea of reflexive citizenship provides a distinctive vision of the welfare state. Like the older social-democratic vision, this one builds state policy around a conception of citizens' rights. It departs from earlier paradigms, however, by focusing on a rich conception of participatory democracy. Citizenship is an inherently participatory status in this view, rather than one merely entitling people to a certain portion of goods. Correspondingly, the welfare state is viewed as an agency-promoting institution, one created by citizens to ensure that none of their number becomes politically or culturally invisible. This conception ensures that citizens have the participatory means to protect and maintain their own status as citizens.

More broadly, the view that I have outlined can be characterized as establishing a state of reflexivity in both senses of the term. In one sense, reflexive democracy depends upon the equal agency of its citizens. It thus requires the procedural means to promote such agency, creating, as it were, a state of reflexivity among its citizens. In a second sense, the actual, institutional state is charged with maintaining the bases of reflexive democracy. It must equalize opportunities and preserve a level playing field for political and cultural interaction. This conception is rooted in values of agency and participatory equality. In both of these senses, reflexive democracy takes a distinctively political direction for rethinking the welfare state.

Reflexive citizenship provides a concrete expression of the participatory ideal, showing how it could be realized against background conditions of social inequality. Further, this view shows that the participatory ideal must be maintained at a fairly high standard to avoid self-contradiction. It focuses specifically on political agency, providing a coherent expression of a political turn in the welfare state.

In this chapter I have interpreted reflexive citizenship as a standard for equal capabilities. In my interpretation these are more narrowly construed as participatory capabilities—as the circumstances, opportunities, and abilities citizens need to ensure the reflexivity of citizenship itself. The content of this vision must be left to citizens themselves, of course; a theorist can draw only the kinds of programmatic conclusions I have outlined here.

The idea of reflexive democracy specifies a minimal, core conception of citizenship. It focuses on a narrow set of human activities—the capabilities needed to participate in forming norms, laws, and policies. It further holds that *these* capabilities are vital in a way that others are not. They must be maintained at a level ensuring reflexivity. As long as citizens have the capacity to sustain the bases of their own agency, this view is relatively agnostic about what else they do. Reflexive citizens have full capabilities to articulate arguments about their own values and institutions. From this standpoint, they themselves become a source of normativity that is sustained and perpetuated by reflexive citizenship itself.

As such, reflexive citizenship produces both a minimal and fecund conception of the welfare state. It is minimal in the sense that it focuses on a relatively narrow range of concerns. It is fecund because it holds those concerns as basic. Once citizenship becomes reflexive, citizens can sustain their own political equality and deliberate over any other concerns they might find important. A conception of citizenship need not be complete or comprehensive if it addresses crucial concerns in a carefully targeted way. In this case, self-sustaining political equality turns out to be key to all other considerations. By addressing it, we unlock a rich source of normativity without having to fill in all of the details from a theoretical point of view.

Because of this conception's distinctively political character, it could seem both unnecessarily narrow and rather foreign to the welfare state's traditional concerns. One might claim, for instance, that this view narrowly fetishizes politics at the expense of class and economic equality. This is not the case, however. In chapter 2 I argued that our traditional understanding of economic justice could benefit from fresh normative insights. Reflexive democracy accomplishes this by allowing people to articulate mutually binding arrangements to govern their own society. An economic norm like protecting the vulnerable, for instance, would be a valuable topic of discussion for the people actually affected by it. They would be able to evaluate its merits in actual dialogue from a position of political equality. In the place of theoretical pronouncements about economic justice, this view substitutes democratically formed norms, laws, and policies. Many of these will undoubtedly focus on economic issues.

More importantly, ideas of economic justice are integral to the procedural framework of a political turn. The political processes I have described place many limits on the economy as well as culture and politics. Economic arrangements that undercut reflexive citizenship would be solidly off-limits in this view. It may well turn out, for instance, that certain kinds of vulnerability undermine reflexive democracy and produce the paradox of enablement. Such arrangements would not wait to be judged by the democratic deliberation of actual citizens because these arrangements undermine reflexive democracy's very grounds of possibility. Those economic conditions are directly ruled out of bounds by the view I have outlined. In the name of political equality, then, this view does specify particular norms of economic justice.

This argument makes clear that the political turn I have outlined is above all a *normative* one. It describes many social and material conditions that are necessary to promote reflexivity and avoid the paradox of enablement. In particular, it requires specific dimensions of economic, cultural, and political agency. Reflexive democracy thus draws economic, cultural, and political concerns under a single normative rubric, providing a unifying framework for thinking about all three at once. Each is significant to the extent that it promotes or hinders participatory equality. Economic, cultural, and political agency thus stand on equal footing as components of reflexive citizenship. The political turn does not leave the economy behind, then. It ultimately circles back to place limits upon the economy, and further, to provide a democratic basis for arriving at broader notions of what is economically fair and just. It does not sideline economic issues, but only provides a new and powerful basis for thinking about them.

Unfortunately my argument about reflexive democracy and citizenship so far remains at the level of theory. It claims that insofar as one wants to resolve the paradox of enablement, one must have something functionally equivalent to the conception of citizenship I have detailed. This argument ignores a crucial question, however: is the participatory ideal actually necessary, obligatory, or even desirable? Can we claim that such a view should be applied to particular welfare states? Does the participatory ideal have any normative traction in actual societies, or is it simply an idealized dream of democratic theorists? If participatory equality is not a compelling value, then it cannot provide a good basis for reflexive democracy or a new conception of the welfare state.

Working out the normative import of participation is significant for another reason. By stipulating particular standards for democratic interaction, I am displacing some decisions made by actual people. Conceptions of democratic procedure permitting unequal political or cultural agency would be ruled out of bounds in my conception, for instance. In this case the idea of reflexive democracy could be seen as a usurpation of actual democratic politics rather than something that promotes it. The view I have outlined would just be another chapter in the history of grand and well-intentioned schemes of social engineering. Despite its good intentions, such a view could be seen as just as paternalistic as any other attempt to "help people help themselves." In this case my argument would seriously backfire. Rather than promoting participation and resolving the paradox of enablement, it would simply transmute that paradox into a new form.

To answer these questions, I will continue to develop the internal logic of the deliberative-democratic paradigm. My focus will be on the normative basis of rights and their relation to actual political and cultural contexts. This paradigm provides a rich set of resources for coping with the problems I have outlined. Contrary to appearances, the potential rift between armchair speculation and on-the-ground democracy imposes important limits on what can be said from a theoretical perspective. These limits do not delegitimate political theory, however. Instead, they add further clarity to the tasks that a conception of reflexive democracy and welfare state citizenship must accomplish.

# 7

# The Normative Basis of Constitutional Rights

Normativity has been a constant preoccupation of this book. It is ironic, then, that my arguments for reflexive democracy have focused largely on its utility for solving paradoxes of participatory equality. This argument is strong on detail but weak on justification. It argues for reflexive democracy based on its promise for promoting equal opportunities for political and cultural participation. It is thus premised on the idea that participation, particularly the view I have called the participatory ideal, is worth pursuing. This simply pushes the need for justification back a step, however. It requires us to ask what justifies participatory equality in the first place.

It is particularly important to iron out this problem because the view I have outlined could be seen as a usurpation of democracy itself. Insofar as my claims about citizenship and rights are intended to have a prescriptive force, they could be seen as preempting laws made by actual citizens. My view, in this case, would come into conflict with our standard view of legal legitimacy. That is, loosely speaking, the idea that people ought to author the laws to which they are subjected. Citizens, in this view, should be free to make whatever laws they see fit. If this is the case, though, there should be no overall unity of purpose or design among various conceptions of citizenship or rights. They would simply conform to local problems and ideals. As a result, it seems that theorists should have little to say about how rights ought to be formed or how they should shape the actions of the administrative state. By extension, my conception of reflexive citizenship would be an imposition on the democratic legislation of actual citizens.

This widely accepted form of legal positivism does not exclude the project I am outlining, however. I believe it is possible to make theoretical claims about the form and content of the law. Moreover, some of these claims should be understood as limiting actual citizens' decisions about rights and citizenship. The idea of reflexive citizenship is such a claim. It is intended to rule out of bounds many other conceptions of citizenship, even many of those legislated by the sovereign lawmaking bodies of contemporary welfare states. Such a tendentious claim requires thorough justification, however. It not only contradicts our commonly accepted notions of popular sovereignty and legal legitimacy, it also seems to contradict the participatory ideal itself. That ideal claims that people should have sufficient and equal opportunities to participate in formulating the norms, laws, and policies under which they live. It is at least awkward, then, to claim that this participation must be limited by a theoretically developed ideal of citizenship specifying the status of citizens as well as many of their rights. In this chapter I will lay the basis for a defense of such a view. Only in chapter 8, however, will I be able to make good on the claim itself. There I will argue that reflexive citizenship is not a usurpation of democracy so much as a condition of its possibility.

Reflexive citizenship is rooted in the idea of constitutional rights. To begin my justification project, I will ask whether and how we can say anything from a theoretical perspective about such rights. How is it, against the background of worries about usurping the democratic sovereignty of actual citizens, that a theorist can make the kinds of claims I have about the form and content of rights? The idea of using rights to solve circularity problems originally arose in my discussion of Jürgen Habermas's work. As I noted in chapter 4, Habermas has developed a theory of rights designed to guide the formation of contemporary constitutional democracies. He lays out a general scheme of functionally defined categories that include various kinds of civil, political, and social rights. These rights are justified through what Habermas calls a formal-pragmatic argument. This allows him to claim that a constitution would need to institutionalize rights fulfilling each of the functions he specifies. Unfortunately the sense in which a constitution "needs" such rights is exactly the issue that is least well argued in this otherwise exemplary work.

In this chapter I will return to the deliberative-democratic paradigm with attention to issues of justification. In particular I will focus on Habermas's idea of formal pragmatics, which is designed to discover normativity implicit in our practices by "reconstructing" their inner logic. I will claim that the methodological innovations of Habermas's theory of rights are both under appreciated and under developed. To make use of these innovations, I will delineate their methodological structure more carefully, resituate the normativity of law in an unorthodox form of contractarianism, and outline an empirical research project connecting philosophical idealizations with actual political culture. This view finds a principled perspective for legal criticism *within* the positing of the law itself. It lays a basis for my claim that reflexive citizenship is not a usurpation of democracy so much as a precondition for making legitimate law in the first place.

## 7.1 The Normative Force of Reconstruction

Habermas draws his most important methodological inspiration from Immanuel Kant. Kant claims that morality is "internally binding" on the human will because individual acts are governed directly by commands of reason. In contrast, positive law is "externally binding" on human conduct. Individual laws do not command our actions through reason, but through our inclination to avoid penalties. Adherence to the law in general, however, is commanded by reason, and its content is rooted in morality.[1] The law, in other words, acquires its legitimacy from morality, and it is thus intertwined with morality in important ways. As a consequence, moral reasoning exerts a powerful regulatory influence on the law for Kant. It provides the basis, as we would now say, for a normative critique of the law.

This kind of legal reasoning was roundly rejected by legal positivists like Bentham and Austin at the turn of the nineteenth century. Setting aside the metaphysical background assumptions of natural law, legal positivists claimed that the law is legitimated not by its moral content but by its political genealogy: when law is posited by socially recognized authorities, it is legitimate. Legal positivists have largely won this argument. In so doing, however, they have also given up the normative high ground of critique. If recognized authority is all that is required to posit legitimate law, then there is little that anyone else can say by way of complaint.

In the past several decades, however, Kant's spirit has returned to haunt the Anglo-American legal tradition. Neo-Kantians have been particularly adept at capitalizing on one of the key insights of Kant's work, the notion that subjects *construct* their intersubjective world through their own faculties and actions.[2] If human action is crucial in some way to constituting the world, Kant reasoned, then an analysis of the subject and its practices can uncover normativity immanent within the practices themselves. The implicit limits that humans bring to their own actions provide binding guidelines for those actions themselves. John Rawls has referred to this kind of argument as "Kantian constructivism."[3]

Jürgen Habermas takes a similar approach to justification. Like Kant's constructivism, Habermas's arguments are based on an analysis of the world-constituting practices of the human subject. Like constructivism, they attempt to identify grains of normativity implicit in human practices. Like constructivism, they do this by tracing out implicit structures, rules, or preconditions within a practice. Unlike constructivism, however, Habermas's arguments form a partnership with interpretive social-scientific research in modeling human practices. Their conclusions and methods tend to be somewhat different from those of constructivism, then. Further observation is always possible, future observations could falsify present ones, and interpretations can always be revised or shown to be wrong. Habermas's arguments are not transcendental in the strict Kantian sense, then, but provisional, interpretive generalizations open at least indirectly to social-scientific testing.[4] To emphasize the empirical grounding of his analyses, Habermas calls his arguments "reconstructions" of human practices.

Habermas's reconstruction of communication, for example, derives its normativity from a philosophical-empirical analysis of speech. It tries to identify the "general and necessary conditions for the validity of symbolic expressions and achievements."[5] Habermas aims at a reconstruction of language that could explicate "concepts, criteria, rules, and schemata," the "generative structures underlying the production of symbolic formations."[6] He says that these can be found in "the intuitive knowledge of competent subjects,"[7] the "know-how of subjects who are capable of speech and action, who are credited with the capability to produce valid utterances, and who consider themselves capable of distinguishing, at least intuitively, between valid and invalid expressions."[8] "Reconstructive proposals," in other words, "are directed to domains of pre-theoretical *knowledge*, that is, not to any implicit opinion, but to a proven intuitive foreknowledge."[9]

Reconstruction, then, is a process of interpretation in which a practice's meaning to its participants must be grasped. It tries above all to discern a practice's internal structures, implicit or necessary presuppositions, and its practitioners' implicit knowledge of the proper way to conduct it. Thus reconstruction focuses particular attention on what must be presupposed in a pragmatic, action-oriented sense by participants in order to perform the practice in question.

Because of their provisional and fallibilistic character, one would think that reconstructions would have little claim to normativity. As a descriptive interpretation of some practice, reconstruction would seem to have little new to teach us about that practice. Further, its provisional character threatens to undermine any generalized conclusions that could be drawn. Habermas does not view the normative force of his arguments in this way, however. Like Kant, he sees reconstructions as making claims that overshoot the boundaries of their immediate context.[10] On Habermas's account, a reconstructive argument can generate context-transcending normativity by going beyond mere description to draw more general conclusions about a practice. In particular it analyzes the implicit formation rules of that practice, thereby acquiring the ability to pass judgment on any particular performance of it. A good reconstruction, according to this characterization, should be able to say whether or not a particular instance adequately fits the general rules that govern its formation. Habermas's analysis of language, for instance, gives a linguist the ability to challenge the well-formedness of an utterance and even to describe the conditions of sincerity and reciprocity necessary for language to perform its function. As such, the reconstruction takes on a normative force that mere description would not have. It can criticize some utterances for not following the implicit rules of their own language, and even criticize some social conditions for undermining communication as such.[11]

Habermas's "reconstructive approach to law" is advertised as a similar kind of argument. The conceptual core of this theory is the derivation of the system of rights—civil, political, and social—discussed in chapter 4. It is worth reviewing the details of this argument to highlight its conceptual architecture. Habermas calls this core argument "the logical genesis of rights."[12] He starts from the idea that contemporary, modernized societies share two important traits. They tend to be organized through some form of democratic political participation, and they tend to be structured through positive law. The conjunction of democracy and law has a number of important implications in Habermas's analysis. People organizing their lives together by means of democracy and law must see one another as equal citizens—or as he says, as "free and equal consociates under law." This fundamental idea, Habermas argues, can be viewed as a mutual granting of autonomy. Citizens implicitly agree, in other words, reciprocally to provide one another with equal freedom under the law. Such freedom takes two forms, each of which requires the other. One is the "public autonomy" of citizens as authors of the law, the other is the "private autonomy" of citizens as subjects of the law. The development of law governing citizens' common life is conducted through public discourse. Reflecting the conditions of democratic lawmaking, such discourses are ruled by the principle that statutes are legitimate only when they can meet with the assent of all citizens in a legally structured process of legislation.[13] Habermas refers to this principle of universalization as the "principle of democracy." Similarly, the form of law itself—legality as such, in other words—is constituted through the principle that people must have equal rights under the law, a principle that Kant calls the "universal principle of right."[14]

When the principle of democracy is interpreted within the framework of positive law, according to Habermas, it establishes the need for the broad categories of rights examined in chapter 4.[15] These rights are defined in terms of the functional requirements of a legal system legitimated by democratic political processes. They outline the kinds of legal guarantees people would need to act as citizens in formulating a fair and legitimate set of laws to govern their own conduct. The system of rights is not intended as a formal template that must be imposed on positive law, however.[16] Rather, it aims to explicate internal aspects of the democratic rule of law, laying out a set of empty categories that would have to be filled in by specific rights, formulated by actual citizens in actual democratic processes. Habermas's reconstruction, then, is not prescriptive in the sense of a free-standing moral principle applied from outside to the formation of law. According to him, rather, the normative and limiting force of his legal theory originates within the practices of legal "consociates" themselves. The system of rights is only formal in a characteristically Kantian sense—it is a form that we create out of our own actions.[17]

The resulting picture of rights shows them to be based above all on intersubjective forms of mutual recognition. A right, in this framework, is something that each citizen grants to the others, with the expectation that her own enfranchisement and protection will likewise be respected. Habermas compactly summarizes the point by noting that "as elements of the legal order [rights] presuppose collaboration among subjects who recognize one another, in their reciprocally related rights and duties, as free and equal citizens. This mutual recognition is constitutive for a legal order from which actionable rights are derived."[18] Rights in this picture are relational, democratically formed, and express the mutual recognition of the citizens articulating them.

In the end Habermas's legal theory remains faithful to the spirit of Kantian constructivism. His analysis focuses on human practices of world construction, specifically on citizens' creation of legal norms through discourse. This form of action carries normative significance. Constitutions and laws are posited against the background of presuppositions about the nature of the practice undertaken and the kind of result it must produce. Habermas's account of law thus sits somewhere between legal positivism and naturalism. Though the raw material of his analysis is positive law, he develops a normative framework capable of criticizing laws and political regimes from a more distanced perspective.

## 7.2 Reconstructing What?

To decide exactly what kinds of critical claims a reconstructive legal theory can make about the law, we will need to be clear about a number of its key methodological features. As a reconstruction, this argument gains normative traction to the extent that it accurately captures the inner logic of practices that we already engage in. We must be clear, then, about exactly which practices are being reconstructed. We also must be clear about the *kind* of argument that can be used to draw normative implications from these practices. We should ask, in other words, what kind of analysis is capable of locating an implicit meaning within practices we might otherwise take for granted. Further, we must be able to account for the move in this analysis from hermeneutic description to normative prescription. It must be clear how a reconstruction's normative force is able to transcend the limits of the individual observations on which it is based. We must then determine whether its normativity is strong enough to produce an insightful critique of law and the welfare state.

In what follows, I will try to answer these questions by working out a more carefully developed argument for something like Habermas's reconstruction of rights. I will start by sketching three ways of thinking about such a reconstruction. These are not intended as interpretations of Habermas's text itself. Rather, each extends and elaborates his line of thought in a particular direction. Each thus provides a methodologically distinct perspective on issues of justification and normativity in reconstructive argument, allowing me to compare their relative advantages and drawbacks.

The Rule-Pragmatic View

Given Habermas's emphasis on reconstructing the implicit presuppositions of a practice, one obvious way to think about the reconstruction of rights is by analogy to Wittgenstein's analysis of language use. Wittgenstein's later work focuses on actual language, which he views as a product of socialization in which people learn to follow the implicit rules of their community's linguistic practice.[19] By analogy, we could read Habermas's work as a reconstruction of the norms and rules structuring the actual practice of the democratic rule of law.

This proposal is radically contextualist about culture, conducting a hermeneutics of the cultural rule-consciousness within practices of democratic constitutionalism. For example, we could ask whether our shared democratic practice implies notions of equal participation that would require certain kinds of rights. Is there something in our actual political system or culture that might bind us to norms of public and private autonomy? This view asks what forms of equality and reciprocity are normatively presupposed within the political practices we now conduct.

Such a hermeneutic, reconstructive exploration might focus, for instance, on the actual practice of lawyers and judges applying the civil protections of the U.S. Constitution. The famous right to privacy discovered in the penumbrae of the Bill of Rights, for instance, is not literally in the text.[20] Rather, it is held to be an implicit background principle for other explicitly enunciated protections. In the reasoning of the Supreme Court, elements of the First, Third, Fourth, Fifth, and Ninth Amendments all imply a background commitment to privacy in a more general sense. One could make the claim, then, that the implicit rule structure of American democracy contains a principle of privacy. Other Supreme Court decisions have relied on this principle as an implicit rule as they groped to justify setting limits on the action of the press or on government intervention. Yet it was only Justice Douglas, in this reading, who saw explicitly what others had intuitively perceived: the existence of a functioning but unrecognized principle of privacy in the actual practice of American constitutional democracy. We could say that before Douglas, the principle had functioned as a rule without being recognized, just like the rules of language function as linguistic background knowledge. In this case, an unenunciated right to privacy is seen as an implicit part of the self-understanding of a political and legal tradition.

Similarly, we could say that norms of equality and autonomy are deeply embedded in American political and legal culture. The founding declaration of the republic, for example, declares the equal creation of all men to be self-evidently true. Various amendments to the U.S. Constitution guarantee rights based on equal citizenship. A rough form of equality is enunciated in voting rights, for example, removing exclusions based on "race, color, or previous condition of servitude," sex, age, or poll taxes. Even more tangibly, the founding moments of the republic—the declaration of independence and the Constitutional Congress—were arguably fairly pure examples of discursive reciprocity and autonomy among the representatives of the states. And these historical documents and events can be viewed against the background of a liberal, democratic, civic-republican political culture built on a long line of political theory from the Renaissance to the present. All of this taken as a whole establishes the institutional and cultural basis for saying that norms of equality, reciprocity, and autonomy have currency in this particular culture.

This view is normative in the sense of reminding someone of the bindingness of a rule that is already supposed to be governing their conduct. We could think of it analogously to the way people are socialized into the rules of a language. When a child says "I goed to the store," the typical adult response is "no, you *went* to the store." Here the child misunderstands the rule for constructing the past tense—some verbs have irregular conjugations that don't follow the normal pattern. The adult's correcting response in such cases is usually given without an explicit understanding of the particular grammatical rule in question. Most native speakers of English cannot recount the rules of its formation; they simply know what counts as valid in their particular language community. The adult's response, then, is the response of someone who knows how to use the language and who has an implicit but not necessarily explicit grasp of the rules governing its use.

Similarly, we could claim that a reconstructive theory of rights aims at correcting the behavior of someone who acts as though she does not understand the rules governing a given social practice. In this case a government failing to institutionalize the proper kinds of rights could be said to be internally confused about the implicit rules of our democratic legal practice. Although it claims to conduct a set of democratic practices, some of them are inconsistent with its own cultural conceptions of democracy. Criticism would thus have the function of pointing out internal ideological inconsistencies.

The rule-pragmatic view derives its normativity directly out of the cultural background of political and legal practices. It reconstructs the actual understanding of rights held by a particular culture or cultures. Thus it relies on the (ethical) self-understanding of democratic societies, which is to say, on their own implicit, largely taken-for-granted cultural commitments. To the extent that norms of reciprocity and autonomy are implicit within a political tradition, it can trace out their consequences for various kinds of rights. Such analysis is a matter of showing the dissonance between practices identified as deviant or inadequate and the broader, culturally deep set of principles and rules implicitly governing a society's practices.

The normative force of reconstruction on this view comes from charges of inconsistency or hypocrisy. It unmasks instances in which our political system makes a commitment but fails to follow through on it, or acts inconsistently by embracing a principle but not its concomitant preconditions. As such, this view is at best weakly normative. First, it is limited to the normative resources actually present within a particular political culture. Criticism is internal to the cultural horizon of a particular society and therefore, strictly speaking, cannot teach that society anything new. It can only identify points of inconsistency or hypocrisy within a given cultural horizon. Second, although it seems that hypocrisy and inconsistency ought to count as negative traits, their normative force likewise depends on social currency within a culture's system of rules, principles, and values. If a political culture does not value internal consistency, then pointing out inconsistencies within a set of constitutional principles has no normative foothold. Again, if the standard of normativity is social currency, then the theorist is always constrained within the horizon of such values. The normativity that can be derived on such a basis will always be limited to what Ronald Dworkin calls "articulate consistency,"[21] and sometimes even that will not be seen as normatively compelling. This is because the rule-pragmatic view gives us an account only of the social currency of principles and has nothing to say about their abstract validity.

The rule-pragmatic view is subject to a number of other problems as well. First, it relies upon an organic or actually existing consensus about political ideals that could provide a basis for interpretation. It presupposes that we *do* in fact have unified commitments to equality and reciprocity that are substantively robust enough to serve as a basis of normativity. Dependence on such a consensus in the case of politics is problematic, however. Reconstructing the implicit rule-consciousness of a political tradition is quite different from reconstructing that of speakers of a language. In the formal-pragmatic analysis of language, the theorist identifies an implicit rule-consciousness that agents actually possess and draw upon in constructing meaningful utterances.[22] Languages have important and omnipresent mechanisms for conserving meaning. People who use words in odd ways are challenged on the correctness of their usage. As such, language has an implicit, context-transcending though nontranscendental structure, one into which every competent speaker is socialized in learning the language. There is no equivalent process of socialization for conserving political traditions, however. Citizens may be challenged on their opinions, but each one can maintain idiomatic views on politics in ways that would be impossible in linguistic meaning. In actual practice, people frequently exhibit strange and contradictory understandings of the constitutional principles under which they live.[23] We might conclude, then, that political culture is a fiction not to be relied on.

Additionally, there is an important ambiguity in interpreting the rule structure governing people's actions. It is quite likely that most survey respondents would agree with statements like "it is not right for a person to exempt herself from laws that others must follow." Most people, in other words, would agree with something like the intuition that the law ought to be universal in scope—Kant's universal principle of right. People's actions reveal a different attitude, however. Traffic laws are routinely violated, tax returns are knowingly falsified, people use drugs with full knowledge of their illegality, and so on. People's actual practices, then, reveal a very different set of generative principles than those that they are prepared to embrace in the hypothetical setting of an opinion survey. This raises the important interpretive question of which set of rules ought to be the basis of a reconstruction of the law.

Noting these ambiguities, one may want to shift the focus of investigation. Both Habermas and Kant point out that law frees people from the burden of imposing principles on their own conduct—they are free to act instrumentally within the boundaries established by legality. In light of this, it could be methodologically wrongheaded to study the attitudes of people acting as *subjects*, rather than as *authors*, of the law. A compelling argument could thus be made for excluding the attitudes people reveal toward the law when they face it as subjects of legal restraint. We may instead want to focus on the background principles revealed in democratic legislative processes. We could note that there is a shared frame of reference within the practices of constitutionalism itself. In coming together to create an agreement governing their shared maximization of autonomy, citizens share certain presuppositions about what will be produced. Those are the facts that some document will be the result of their joint labor, that they have equal status as citizens under it, that the document will use mechanisms of law to enforce and stabilize the agreements it encodes, and so on. These background assumptions arise out of a shared political culture—the culture of democratic constitutionalism developed roughly from the Magna Carta and the English Civil War through the French and American revolutions to the liberation of Third World colonies and the Eastern Bloc. The constitutional and statutory codes that result from this tradition are materialized manifestations of its political culture.

The Anglo-American tradition of constitutionalism is certainly a long-established practice, but it is of course only part of our historical practice of politics and jurisprudence. In addition to the principled practices of legislation we have conducted over the years, the rule-pragmatic view must also take account of a great deal of instrumental behavior in the actual practice of American constitutional democracy. Political apathy, depoliticization in favor of consumption, procedural shortcuts by legislators to improve efficiency, deliberate marginalization of specific sectors of the populace, blatantly strategic behavior and rent seeking within the political sphere have all been parts of our actual political practice. One could say, then, that American political culture reveals a complex and contradictory set of implicit rules. On one hand, we have a tradition of principled commitment to liberty and equality; but on the other these principles are routinely set aside in favor of less noble goals. We are again left with the puzzle of deciding which rules the reconstructivist should see as decisive in governing our political and legal conduct.

Ultimately, the problems of the rule-pragmatic view are a result of its cultural contextualism. This view is normatively limited to the critical resources already present within a given culture. Ideality of any kind is problematic here. Because this view derives normativity from social currency, any attempt to go beyond an interpretation of actually existing culture exceeds the bounds of what is legitimate and normatively compelling. This view is thus subject to all of the fractures, contestation, contradiction, and compartmentalization found in any actual culture. Any critical standpoint derived on this basis would likely be both meager and highly contested.

The Functional-Pragmatic View

A second way of thinking about legal reconstruction relies more heavily on observational data than cultural hermeneutics. Like the rule-pragmatic view, it starts from the idea that our actual institutions and practices implicitly contain broader commitments. Like the above, it attempts to derive some kind of normativity from those commitments. This view starts by noting similarities between various constitutional traditions and postulating functional relations between their parts. From this, a kind of normative understanding can be developed of how constitutions are put together and how their parts ought to be related.

Such an account might start, for instance, from the observation that the "founders" and their descendants formed agreements about specific measures to be enshrined in the constitution. These are specific rights: rights to free speech, due process, equal protection, universal suffrage, legal representation, and so on. Each individual constitution has a unique constellation of such rights. However, we can observe contingent similarities among the modern, democratic societies. Among these are social integration through systems of positive law, the desire to institutionalize democracy, the desire to protect the private lives of citizens, and basic forms of reciprocity and equal status inherent in the initial acts of the constitution-forming process. We can also observe the subsequent elaboration of this system of rights—rights to property are altered under new conditions of taxation and technical development, rights to privacy are more specifically articulated, political participation is universalized, and so on.

From a social scientist's vantage point, we can classify such rights by their functions—as safeguarding one's private choice or promoting the public use of reason. From this point of view, we are able to generalize further by noting that some, if not all, of these rights have functional significance in protecting autonomy in some way or other. In reconstructive retrospect, then, we can infer that the existence of these rights must have been due to their functional significance in overcoming certain problems. Specifically, they meet the challenges posed by a process of political and legal sociation under modern conditions of democracy and rule of law. Such rights can take on a kind of universality in retrospect when we conclude that all societies of a given type (modern, rationalized, industrialized, integrated through law, etc.) will share common problems which require functionally similar solutions.

The functional-pragmatic view proceeds in an empirical, investigative fashion, making generalizations about actual practices of democratic constitutionalism. This view claims that rights are functionally presupposed by specific practices of democracy. It does not reconstruct pragmatic presuppositions in the sense of implicit rules, then, but pragmatic presuppositions in the sense of functional necessities inherent in projects on which people have already embarked. Its claims are social-scientific to the bottom because they are based on an understanding of the kinds of practical problems encountered by certain forms of social organization. It thus skirts all of the difficult interpretive issues that arise from using political culture as a normative foundation.

The functional-pragmatic view runs into difficulties of its own, however. First, it takes only an objectivating, third-person perspective on political and legal practices. It reconstructs these practices exclusively from an external, observational viewpoint. What it misses in so doing is an internal, participant's perspective on the meaning of the practices in question. Leaving this element out means that the reconstruction lacks a clear link to the lived experience of the citizens whose practices are under investigation. As such, the reconstruction remains outside of the citizens' sphere of norms and values.

Further, the functional-pragmatic view can give us no grounds for reconstructing democratic practice *in discourse-theoretic terms*. Habermas's system of rights is explicated in terms of the principle D that describes conditions of universality in discourse.[24] The discourse principle occupies a vital place in Habermas's reconstruction. It identifies conditions under which legitimate law can be developed—namely, those in which the law is formed through fair, procedurally regulated discourse. Habermas's picture of the democratic genesis of law is thus an explicitly discursive one. If we think of rights as functional problem-solving devices for democratic practice, however, it is not clear why the democratic practices we reconstruct should be seen as discursive or deliberative. Any form of democracy would require guarantees of public and private autonomy, even a nonlinguistic aggregation of subjectively held preferences like voting.[25] The analysis of functions, in this case, accords no special place to language. Thus Habermas's use of the discourse principle would be unwarranted in this context. If the functional-pragmatic view is seen as extending and clarifying Habermas's reconstruction, then, his use of discourse-theoretic concepts would be arbitrary and inconsistent.

Additionally, the functional-pragmatic view is normative only in the very weak sense of making predictions about the necessities acting on present practices. It could claim, for instance, that the commitments laid out in the U.S. Bill of Rights cannot be consistently met without a further right to privacy. This would be a functional argument: a right to privacy is necessary to protect speech and property and to prohibit unreasonable search and seizure and self-incrimination.[26] Such a move displaces the normative burden to a conception of *dysfunction*—to the idea that the difficulties encountered by democratic practice will undermine it if they are not resolved. The functional-pragmatic view reveals contradictions implicit in such practices and makes the claim, for example, that "if you're really serious about protecting free political speech, you must institutionalize something functionally equivalent to a right to privacy." In the case of free speech and the right to privacy, then, we would have to know when speech was not being properly protected and how a right to privacy could ameliorate the situation. A sound analysis of the particulars of the case would provide a functional argument for such a right. Absent some observable dysfunction, however, no such argument could be made.

The normative force of this view is quite weak. The theorist's only leverage lies in pointing to places where some functional need is not being met. Criticism here has the force of identifying empirical contradictions in social practices. It is an instrumental "should" ("you should hurry if you don't want to be late") rather than a moral or ethical one ("you shouldn't be late").[27] Like the rule-pragmatic view, it relies only on normative resources already present in the culture. Again, this form of criticism cannot teach a society anything new, but merely instructs it in the full unfolding of its present commitments.

## The Ideal-Pragmatic View

A third way of thinking about reconstruction emphasizes its philosophical aspects. This view focuses on the idealizations that give the logical genesis of rights its logical character. It traces the *conceptual preconditions* of the democratic genesis of law.

The theorist begins with an idealized set of concepts—in this case an ideal-typical view of democratic lawmaking. She abstracts from conditions of actual political interaction to an idealized state in which the political and legal system function as people think they ideally could. Thinking within this framework, she puts herself in the position of a participant and asks what sort of presuppositions participants would be forced to make in order to form and use such a system. In particular, she tries to discern what presuppositions would be *inescapable* for the proper conduct of the practice. In the case of democratic jurigenesis, reciprocity, equality, and autonomy are necessarily presupposed. Democratic citizens must view one another as equal authors of the law and as equally bound by its dictates. If they do not, then the practice they aim at is not the democratic rule of law. In an idealized sense, democratic rule of law therefore presupposes reciprocal and equal forms of autonomy.

To put this argument to use, we need some way of connecting actual cultures and practices with idealized schematizations of them. This can be found in the insight that participants actually *do* aim at an idealized form of practice in setting the goals of their own action. When I play the piano, I seek to recreate the tranquil expressive beauty of, say, Chopin. I do not aim at the erratic tempos, missed notes, and clumsy interpretation that usually results. Similarly, speakers of a language aim at an idealized mutual understanding, even though the result is frequently the fractured grammar, poorly structured utterances, and incomplete comprehension of daily communication.

According to the ideal-pragmatic view, participants in actual practices of democratic self-government would aim at similar idealizations. Citizenship in a democratic-constitutional state involves two functionally differentiated attitudes toward others. Citizens must view one another in an idealized sense as equal authors of the law *and* as equally bound by it. For participants to ignore either of these attitudes would be a performative contradiction. A person could not, as we have seen, both claim to engage in the democratic rule of law *and* deny others the functionally necessary forms of autonomy that he himself enjoys. Dual forms of autonomy are thus a necessary presupposition of law legitimated by democratic means. From this standpoint, the rest of the system of rights can be worked up in the way I have already outlined.

The ideal-pragmatic view has a substantial normative bite. Its force comes from the fact that it identifies idealized conceptual presuppositions of our own daily political and legal practice. On analogy with language, people participating in democratic government must (at least implicitly) view themselves as equal consociates in relation to their fellow citizens, they must decide to form laws in a discursively legitimate manner, and so on. Normativity thus comes directly out of daily practice, even though it is discovered only by means of a philosophical, ideal-typical argument. This argument claims that any society organized though law and democracy must recognize its own commitments to reciprocal protections of private life and reciprocal enablements of public discourse. The theorist thus identifies a productive tension between facts and norms, giving her strong leverage to criticize a society in terms that it must, in the end, embrace as its own.

Although the ideal-pragmatic view is appealing in many ways, there is an important sense in which it does not fit the mold of Habermas's other reconstructions. Methodologically, reconstruction relies on the implicit *teleology* of practices. In cases like language or piano playing, this telic structure is fairly obvious. They are practices explicitly aimed at bringing about a particular aim: shared understanding or a beautifully recreated piece of music. Similarly, Habermas's characterization of democracy has a telic structure. It is a communicatively structured political practice—a form of democracy, in other words, which is *deliberative* in nature. This practice aims at reaching understanding about shared goals and undertakings. It is thus subject to norms of universalization implicit in language. The logical genesis of rights, then, is based specifically on a vision of communicatively structured political practice that has a teleology similar to that of everyday communicative interaction.

In contrast, our actual practices of democratic lawmaking seem much more indeterminate. From one perspective they can be seen as communicatively mediated attempts to create a political system built on implicit principles of reciprocity and equality. From another perspective, however, they can also be viewed as attempts to create a workable modus vivendi that maintains social order and prevents violence. From the first perspective, we can view our current political processes as aimed at deliberation to an extent. There is at least nominal debate before voting in legislatures, and public opinion circulates through daily discussion and the media in a relatively free manner. From the second perspective, however, all of our actual political decisions are based on the aggregation of subjective preferences through voting. These preferences may be modified by discourse, but in the end the system itself is nondiscursive.

In these examples we can see that our actual practices of political decision making have an unclear teleology. From the first perspective, each participant is viewed as an equal author and subject of the laws. From the second, however, lawmaking has the much vaguer telos of maintaining order. Either of these is a plausible interpretation of our present political system. People act at times as engaged citizens in a project of mutual lawmaking, and at times as consumers of peace and prosperity. The difference between the two lies precisely in what is presupposed in the conduct of democratic legislation. In the first case, norms of equality, reciprocity, and autonomy apply. In the second, however, it would not particularly matter whether people were equally autonomous as long as disorder did not result. Our actual practices of democratic legislation have an indeterminate teleology, then, and are not strictly analogous to language in this regard. To say that the idealized presuppositions of Habermas's reconstruction are buried within our actual political practice thus requires further argument.

If idealized reconstructions do not fit squarely with actual practices, the normative claims of the ideal-pragmatic view are considerably undermined. A productive tension between facts and norms can emerge only when a reconstruction draws its source material out of the practices it plans to criticize. Thus Habermas intends that the system of rights as developed from the theorist's perspective will be recapitulated by actual citizens forming actual constitutions. Law is legitimate in his view only when it is formed by those whose action it binds.[28] The idea that the actual practice of citizens will recapitulate the theorist's normative argument is problematic, however.[29] It is not clear why a populace would decide to enact the norms described in the theorist's reconstruction as opposed to any others. We have no way of explaining how the constructive action of law-constituting citizens will match up with the theorist's more carefully considered reconstructive arguments. Even if citizens were shown by the theorist that such presuppositions were "inescapable" in a philosophical sense, we have no way of ensuring that they would act on them. The normative "ought" of the theorist's reconstruction is largely impotent in the face of the legitimate, sovereign political will of actual citizens. The reconstruction's normativity would have to rest on its use in actual public discourse, trying to convince citizens that there is a better way to manage their affairs. Citizens, in other words, would have to embrace the reconstruction as an insightful commentary on their own practices. The fit between an ideal-pragmatic reconstruction and actual practice would thus be left to the judgment of citizens themselves. In this case, however, it is not clear that a reconstruction is reconstructing actual practices; it seems more to be recommending different ways of doing things in the role of a friendly advocate. No particular normative grounding is needed for this kind of advice because its legitimacy rests solely on actual public acceptance.

Overall, the ideal-pragmatic view proceeds chiefly from a theorist's projection of a participant's point of view. It reaches deeply into the most abstract features of modern societies, identifying implicit characteristics of our present practices but at times overshooting the mark and carrying idealization beyond their bounds. This view postulates substantial constraints on our actual practices, using an idealized conception of validity to criticize and improve reality. Such an interpretation has the advantage of normative clarity and force. It provides a standard against which actually existing regimes can be measured. It has many of the problems, however, with which Kantian views are typically saddled. The level of idealization in this view distances it from particular lives, cultures, and political systems. As a result, the ideal-pragmatic view risks becoming too detached from the practices in which it claims to be based.

## 7.3 The Normative Background of Legal Practice

The different views of legal reconstruction that I have outlined suffer from differing and to an extent symmetrical problems. The rule-pragmatic and functional-pragmatic views are bound within the horizon of particular legal cultures and practices, without adequate tools to draw farther-reaching conclusions about them. Their very immanence within systems of positive law deprives them of the kind of strong normativity required to say anything interesting about this law. In contrast, the ideal-pragmatic view is normatively strong enough to place substantial limits on the correctness of actual constitutions. It does this, however, at the price of distance from particular political cultures and systems of positive law. To the extent that it idealizes these actually existing practices, it becomes foreign to them.

The question, then, is whether an adequate argument for constitutional rights can be developed somewhere in between. Immanence is needed to ensure the legitimacy of any reconstruction. Critical distance is also needed, however, to provide normative leverage against practices that do not measure up to the standards of a fair and free society. I believe that the ideal-pragmatic view alone has the potential to develop sufficient critical distance from actual practices while simultaneously discovering normativity *within* those practices themselves. This view holds out the promise of a normative force that cannot in principle be matched by either of its competitors. To build the ideal-pragmatic view into a more workable theory, however, I will suggest two modifications to it. The first of these is philosophical in character, building on the ideal or "logical" character of reconstruction. The second, outlined in section 7.4, is empirical, designed to knit together idealized reconstructions and actual practice.

My criticism of the ideal-pragmatic view has largely turned on the idea that Habermas assumes too much when he uses a robust notion of deliberative democracy to reconstruct the system of rights. By using a rich and rather idealized notion of democracy, Habermas brings a powerful normative point of view to bear on processes of democratic legislation. This is intended to identify the ways in which actual democratic practices do not—and indeed cannot—live up to the standards of an ideally conceived model of democratic deliberation.[30] In so doing, however, he widens the gap between the idealized notion of democracy employed in reconstruction and our actual practice. Messier, actually existing forms of democracy are much more resistant to idealization and much less interesting from a reconstructive point of view. And they are, I have argued, structurally dissimilar to idealized notions of deliberative democracy. This structural mismatch leads to a problematic gap between theory and practice that weakens the reconstruction's normative foothold in present-day political practice.

Although our actual democratic practice may lack the discursive character of Habermas's reconstructed model, it does share an important characteristic with it. Both deliberative democracy and its less ideal cousins are sophisticated, legally structured forms of *social cooperation*. Social cooperation is a form of practice dedicated to the collective pursuit of common goals. In order to enter into a cooperative venture, people must make basic presuppositions about the way they will relate to their fellow cooperators. Specifically, they must approach such an undertaking with the idea that their fellows are equal partners in a joint undertaking. These others are therefore entitled to reciprocal forms of recognition and equality within the practice in question. Reciprocity and equality, then, are basic, structural properties of cooperative agreement itself.

Social cooperation is a discursively mediated practice in a way that democracy per se is not. Cooperation occurs against a background of normative expectations about the need for the cooperating parties to agree on the goals they will pursue, how they will divide up tasks and labor, what means they should use to accomplish their shared undertakings, and so on. Reciprocity and equality are thus built into cooperation in a second way: as the structural characteristics of agreement and consensus in the *organization* of cooperation. Seeing one's fellows as partners in cooperation thus implies endowing them with the ability to negotiate about the task at hand. This characteristic of cooperation implies the need for language as a medium of decision making and action coordination. Even if the decision-making apparatus is eventually converted to some other medium (say money or votes), the basic relations of cooperators themselves must always leave open the possibility of dialogue about the character of their joint enterprise.[31]

I therefore propose to amend the ideal-pragmatic view in a slight but significant manner. To justify characterizing the democratic creation of law as a deliberative practice, we must first make a reconstructive detour through social cooperation per se. This allows us to see that, although our current democratic practice may or may not be discursive in character, it is founded on basic presuppositions of social interaction. The daily legal and political interactions of citizens are premised on the idea of cooperative practice. This presupposition makes democratic lawmaking subject to the kinds of normative constraints that would be placed on any cooperative enterprise. It additionally provides us with the conceptual grounds to see what unique forms these constraints take when they arise within the institutional context of a practice like democratic lawmaking, as opposed to some other form of cooperation. From this perspective we can derive a twofold conception of autonomy as a unique requirement of *political* cooperation. And again, a system of rights, likely somewhat different in content from those Habermas specifies, can be worked up in the way I have already rehearsed.

There is of course something very familiar about this idea. It has a strongly contractarian flavor. Free and equal individuals come together to found a society. Their natural freedom and equality carry over into the newly constituted political unit, being transmuted into protections and guarantees of citizenship. This classic conception is different in important ways from the view I am developing, however. It typically starts with the idea of freedom as a natural, inalienable right of presocial (atomized, liberal) individuals. Because individuals all enter the contractual situation in a condition of natural freedom, they start in a position of equal status as well. From this initial situation of freedom and equality, they can then contractually set aside certain aspects of the initial situation for their mutual advantage.

The version that we get by reconstructing practices of social cooperation would be quite different. It would not start from a fictionalized initial situation, and it would not characterize individuals as free and equal rights bearers *from the start* in a prepolitical sense. Rather, it would project backward from the fact of cooperative social interaction, claiming that freedom and equality are pragmatically presupposed regardless of the actual freedom and actual equality of individuals. In this picture, our performative will to cooperate implies the presumption that agreement can be reached about the goals and means of cooperative action. The teleology implicit in the cooperative selection and pursuit of goals requires treating others as equal partners in cooperation. This recognition of others as parties to a cooperative enterprise provides the foundation for mutual recognition of equal status. Equality and reciprocity would not come from a counterhistorically projected "natural" state, then, but from implicit presuppositions of actual, current practices. In particular, the voluntary, cooperative character of those practices endows them with a normativity that we can reconstruct as a basis for legal critique.

## 7.4  Connecting the Ideal and the Real

So far this argument has moved in a purely philosophical orbit. It has not touched earth solidly enough to make contact with actual political cultures or legal practices. I have argued, however, that a reconstructive theory of rights can work only if the reconstruction is firmly rooted in actual cultures and practices. Otherwise we run the risk of having reconstruction move so far beyond practice that it loses its normative footing. Avoiding this fate requires the kind of partnership between theory and empirical research that Habermas has championed in the past.[32] Toward this end, I would like to outline a research project that could connect productively with the normative project I have already described.

To begin, it is instructive to turn to some of the research that Habermas has used to support his other reconstructions. His analysis of language is dedicated above all to identifying the normative presuppositions implicit in everyday speech. Habermas approvingly cites Harold Garfinkel's work in this regard.[33] Garfinkel notes that the background context of speech can be teased out by disturbing it in a careful, deliberate manner. He has conducted a large array of experiments designed to breach the taken-for-granted consensus implicit in social interaction.[34] Of particular importance for current purposes is the fact that Garfinkel's work explicitly probes the implicit infrastructure of human *cooperation*. The discomfort resulting from a breach of everyday interaction is specifically perceived by participants as a collapse of the matrix of expectations that coordinates everyday cooperative endeavors.[35]

Garfinkel's experiments require the investigator to engage a research subject in some routine interaction, then to behave in a way suggesting that investigator and subject do not share the same understanding about the proper norms of behavior in the given situation. Some experiments, for instance, require the investigator to pretend that she does not understand the meaning of everyday small talk, or to act as a stranger among her own family, or to bargain with store cashiers over the price of a fixed-price item. In each of these cases, the visible and explicit discomfort of both subject and investigator provides ample data for interpreting the implicit, normative presuppositions of everyday social cooperation.

I believe that a similar strategy could be used for building the empirical bases of a reconstructive theory of law, and by extension, the welfare state. What is needed, in schematic terms, is a set of breaching experiments for legally structured behavioral contexts. These experiments would be designed to probe the implicit norms governing institutionalized forms of social cooperation, providing us with a map for reconstructing them. From this starting point, an ideal-pragmatic, reconstructive account could be worked up to identify the pragmatic and necessary presuppositions of each particular genre of cooperation. This, I believe, would provide us with empirical correlates for the philosophically driven reconstruction I have outlined.

Research on one-on-one economic interactions illustrates a part of this picture particularly germane to the welfare state. In the ultimatum game, for example, two subjects are separated from one another and told that they will be awarded a sum of money—usually $10 but sometimes as much as $100—if they can agree on a way of dividing the money between them. The procedure for arriving at this agreement is as follows. The first player makes an offer to the second; the second may then either accept or reject the offer. If player 2 accepts the offer, they divide the money as agreed. If player 2 rejects the offer, however, the entire sum is lost and neither player receives anything.[36]

Because of the structure of the game, the standard model of instrumental rationality predicts that player 2 should accept any positive offer—even the smallest increment. After all, the smallest possible amount of gain is better than nothing, which would be the result of declining player 1's offer. Similarly, player 1 should realize this and make only the smallest incremental offer to player 2. However, in actual plays of the game with real money, player 1 typically offers player 2 something on the order of 40 to 50 percent of the total. Similarly, any offer under roughly 30 percent of the total is typically rejected by player 2, even though he[37] realizes that he will get nothing instead of the offered amount.

These results reveal a normative context underlying and structuring everyday economic interactions. Player 1 violates norms of reciprocity and equality if his offer does not approach half of the total. These norms are implicit in the situation itself—implicit, in other words, in the idea that the players must cooperate and respect one another as roughly equal in status in order to succeed. If player 1 acts in strictly instrumental terms, he treats player 2 as a means to his own ends rather than as a partner in cooperation. Both players see such a lack of reciprocity as a violation of the normative background of their interaction. Thus player 1 tends to make an offer of roughly equal division, and player 2 tends to sanction any offer not approaching equality by terminating cooperation.

The ultimatum game illustrates a method of getting at the deep normative background of interaction. It reveals this background in action when people's expectations are violated. To my knowledge, no similar experiments have been conducted in the law. There are, however, studies that point the way toward such experiments. Empirical research on procedural justice reveals aspects of the normative background of the law. For example, people will accept governmental policy decisions that do not benefit them personally when they believe that decisions are arrived at through fair procedures.[38] They particularly value the ability to state their case before a decision is reached. Surprisingly, it does not seem to matter whether a person's statements are perceived to influence the outcome of the decision, as long as their side of the story is heard. Similarly, neutrality and impartiality are valued characteristics in legal decisions. Findings like these suggest that people do have normative expectations about legal and political practice, and these expectations are applied not only to individual actions but also to institutionalized procedures. Further, the norms in question are closely related to the bases of Habermas's reconstruction. They show that people expect to be treated with respect as discursive participants in law and politics.

Studies of procedural justice do an admirable job of connecting abstract work on law and politics with the concrete conditions of daily life. They do not, however, probe the structure of background norms in exactly the way needed for my purposes. Many of the situations examined in these studies are genuine breaches of the normative background of social interaction: arbitrary judicial decisions, personal insults at the hands of authorities, and so on. However, these studies rely primarily on people's reports of their own perception of the justice of daily situations. As such, they miss some of the narrative and interpretive richness of the other studies I have just surveyed, in which research subjects often reveal normative commitments they themselves were not aware of having. A key characteristic of normative background principles is their taken-for-granted nature: they are often so deeply embedded in social practice that they are not recognized as such.[39] The value of the breaching encounter between investigator and subject is precisely that it makes normative background principles viscerally present to participants while revealing them as commitments that participants may recognize as their own only in retrospect. This kind of investigation allows the investigator to probe beyond the range of what I have called "social currency," revealing additional commitments that are entailed by people's practices but not consciously embraced by them. This highly abstract level of commitment to principles like reciprocity and autonomy is the necessary starting point, as we have seen, of an ideal-pragmatic reconstruction. Such commitments require special experimental methods, however, to be elucidated.

With these methodological considerations in mind, we could imagine a slightly different investigative strategy. In many of the U.S. states, citizens can place initiatives on the ballot by gathering signatures from a specified number of registered voters. As an election nears, it is common to be approached in public places by people carrying clipboards who are gathering signatures for some initiative or other. We could imagine a situation, then, in which unsuspecting voters are approached by an investigator with various ballot initiatives—say, proposals to disenfranchise women from the vote because of "their weaker nature and irrationality," or to arrest and imprison suspected drug dealers without due process. The point behind such an exercise would not, of course, be to gather data on the acceptability of such proposals. Rather, it would be to elicit the kind of strong sanctioning behavior that Garfinkel observed in the microstructure of human interaction. The responses elicited in each case would likely show the character and depth of people's commitments to principles like political equality or equal treatment before the law. The examples I have given here purposely push the boundaries of good taste, of course, and perhaps go beyond the limits of what would be necessary to elicit the expected responses. A more carefully planned program of interpretive research, however, could provide us with a promising path to follow in reconstructing the normative basis of the law.

## 7.5   The Fecund Normativity of Social Cooperation

We can now outline some of the methodological innovations that reconstruction makes possible in legal theory. Reconstruction is above all a strategy for tracing out the implicit presuppositions of actual practices. It does not impose foreign moral viewpoints on the law, but develops a normative perspective *from within* the boundaries of actually existing practice. Reconstruction starts with the normative kernel of an already given practice and builds it into something that circles back to modify this practice. It can be seen, then, as a form of criticism rooted firmly in positive rather than natural law. In this sense reconstruction makes minimal theoretical claims and commits none of the sins of natural law. It should be seen as consistent with the everyday legal practice of actual people, not as an externally imposed corrective to it.

To develop a workable reconstruction of the law, I have attempted to knit theory and practice together into an empirically rooted yet idealized normative model. The philosophical and empirical aspects of this project are designed to dovetail into one productive research program. If this is done correctly from both sides, the result will be one cohesive account of the bases of constitutional rights. This account would provide us with a basis for criticizing particular laws from within their own normative horizon. At the same time, this view would exceed the bounds of what is immediately given in current legal practices, providing a principled perspective for criticizing them.

A reconstructive theory of rights provides a basis for a fecund project of justification and legal reform. It gives us means to justify not only forms of civil and political rights but also substantial social welfare rights and procedural limits on economic interaction. It allows the possibility that theory can harmoniously combine with actual democracy, illuminating some of its implicit commitments and self-contradictions. My remarks on reflexive democracy and citizenship are intended in this spirit. They are designed to illuminate commitments made within social cooperation itself—commitments made, in other words, by actual democratic citizens. If this theory fulfills its task, a welfare state built around reflexive citizenship would not impose rights and policies on actual people. It would simply render consistent some of the practices they have already undertaken. In the chapter that follows, I will try to make good on this claim, showing that the participatory ideal and reflexive citizenship are implicit presuppositions of social cooperation. This argument will allow me to develop a full-blown version of the view I have only sketched so far: a normative conception of reflexive democracy, articulated in terms of political equality, legal legitimacy, and welfare.

# 8

# Political Equality, Legal Legitimacy, and Welfare

Near the beginning of this volume I claimed that an adequate normative approach to the welfare state would require going beyond the limitations of tit-for-tat quarrels between opposing moral intuitions. As I said, this means stepping outside of debates about *meum* and *tuum*, about property rights versus redistribution, or economic individualism versus social solidarity. With a nod to Max Weber, I argued that the critical standpoints most vulnerable to rejection are those imposed on a welfare regime from outside. Those are vulnerable because it is difficult to claim that any one perspective is more applicable than another. Given these limitations, a more promising standpoint would be one rooted *within* our social and political practices. What we need, I claimed, is a conception of welfare taking its start within our own horizon of values and commitments. Our understanding of politics, law, and welfare is much more solid when we see normative commitments as rooted in cooperative practices that we have already undertaken. Such a viewpoint provides a sharp contrast to points of view lacking a strong normative foothold in actual societies and cultures.

In this chapter I draw together the various stands of that argument as a basis for reflexive democracy. I will return to the ideas of participatory equality and reflexive citizenship that I developed in the first six chapters, but now with a focus on justification. To connect ideality and reality in a productive way, I will work within a contemporary social, political, and cultural context—the recent United States welfare reforms. My goal in using this example is to show that the participatory ideal actually has normative traction in our society, providing a more solid basis for a political turn in welfare. I will focus on political components of agency and return again to the circularities inherent in attempts to promote it. Now, however, we have more robust means to talk about the legal and conceptual bases of citizenship. This discussion returns to the topic of reflexivity with a focus on the crucial connections between political equality, legal legitimacy, and welfare. This line of argument connects the ideal and the real in the way I outlined more schematically above. It also provides an occasion to show how this position makes incisive judgments about actual institutions, laws, and practices.

## 8.1  Reflexive Legitimacy

Jean-Jacques Rousseau famously addressed the political effects of material inequality when he wrote that "no citizen should be so rich as to be capable of buying another citizen, and none so poor that he is forced to sell himself."[1] He goes on to say that extremes of wealth and poverty make liberty a commodity to be bought and sold, generating social grounds for both tyrants and those who would support them. This colorful statement is, needless to say, a rather coarse measure of the political impact of material inequality. Serious distortions in the political process can occur well before people are sold or tyrants rise up. More subtle, everyday inequalities in resources and capabilities produce large-scale distortions in who speaks and who is heard. Subtle differences in material fortune create important political inequalities well short of Rousseau's threshold. We must not wait for the buying and selling of people to start worrying about political equality. Rather, less dramatic inequalities should also be an object of concern.

The idea of reflexive citizenship that I developed in chapter 6 provides a finer standard for participatory equality. It states that each citizen must have an equal opportunity to participate in formulating the status and privileges of citizenship itself. This conception is at once about citizenship, agency, participation, and the material underpinnings of all of these. The question that remains to be answered, though, is what normative force could such a demanding notion of equality have? How do we know that something like the participatory ideal I have described should actually bind our political choices, our government, and our system of laws and policies?

The approach outlined in chapter 7 suggests that normativity should come out of a society's own practices. When we actually examine our current behavior as a source of norms and principles, however, our political practices yield contradictory answers. On one hand, political equality seems to be one of the most deeply entrenched values in the developed democracies. Our own political past includes a long history of expanding enfranchisement. Property qualifications were dropped, poll taxes were struck down, sex limitations were removed. Public education is free through high school, promoting equalization of the bases of citizenship. In addition, we seem firmly committed to exporting democracy to the rest of the world, first to the post-communist East and then to the Islamic Mideast. Other nations are told that their citizens are entitled to have a say in the government and laws under which they live. These actions imply basic commitments to the idea of political equality itself.

On the other hand, our political tradition is also a story of exclusion, marginalization, and restricted participation. Early democrats supposed that the franchise should be limited to those with "permanent fixed interests" in their nation of residence—property, in other words.[2] This idea has a long history of support in our political tradition by thinkers as illustrious as Kant, Hegel, and Mill.[3] Voter registration was notoriously used to disenfranchise African-Americans until very recently. Women only received the vote in the United States in 1920. More insidiously, campaign contributions function as a largely unchallenged basis for political inequality in our present system. It is problematic, then, to claim that political equality is an uncontested value in American political culture. The majority of our actual practices undercut any claims we make about more principled commitments.

These conflicting tendencies ably demonstrate a point I made in chapter 7, that culture is an unstable and unreliable basis for a normative conception of law. Each of these tendecies is observed, in different ways, in American political and legal culture. This shows the normative complexity of our culture, and by extension, its unsuitability to serve as a fast and ready basis for something like the participatory ideal. We cannot assume that political equality is an uncontested value. If we try to read normative claims directly out of our political culture, we will become mired in all of the contradictory principles and commitments that mark any actual culture. A different strategy is required, one that can establish the normative force of political equality without depending on our own changeable and conflicting testimony.

To accomplish this task, I will outline a view that takes its inspiration from concrete political contexts without being completely embedded in them. This argument interprets the implicit commitments within our present practices. Specifically, it shows that we are implicitly committed to political equality, even in cases where our practices seem to show the opposite. To do this, I will take up the line of argument that ended chapter 7. Social cooperation, I believe, is a productive starting point for showing that we already have a normative commitment to political equality.

As Emile Durkheim famously points out, law structures complex systems of social cooperation.[4] Modern societies are highly differentiated. Their degree of differentiation allows for a division of labor that increases the overall productivity of society while reducing the number of specialized tasks that any one person needs to master. As such, law makes possible complex, mutually beneficial interactions, allowing a richness of material and cultural life that is not attainable by isolated individuals. Social cooperation is not simply an abstract feature of society as a whole, however. It is a common motivation for practices repeated over and over again in daily life. We work for wages, observe customary manners and forms of politeness, use money, and obey the law most of the time. These practices all contain presuppositions about the nature of cooperative interaction, presuppositions that are sometimes shared in an implicit sense and sometimes spelled out in law.

In order to participate in cooperative endeavors, people must adopt specific behavioral norms and attitudes and assume that others have done the same. Most importantly, they must be willing to treat others as reciprocal partners in formulating the *terms* of their cooperation. This is a constitutive presupposition of cooperation itself. It would be unreasonable to expect people to participate in a cooperative venture without agreeing to the conditions under which their participation would be reciprocated by the cooperation of others. To establish a cooperative enterprise without such agreement is coercive rather than cooperative. It would indicate that, although a person may derive some benefit from the arrangement in question, her participation is forced rather than voluntary.

Because participation is consensual and revocable on all sides, each person has the same basic status within a cooperative practice. The fact of voluntary participation implies equality in a basic sense. Even though the actual practice in question may later be conducted in an asymmetrical or hierarchical manner, this can be done only on a more fundamental presupposition of participatory equality and freedom. Each person expects to be treated as an equal in cooperation, and she must see others in the same way. She must, in other words, recognize that others participate under the same conditions and presuppositions that she does. This confers on each of them a reciprocal, equal status.

As the structure of many sophisticated, modern forms of cooperation, law is informed by the norms and expectations characterizing cooperative practice in general. Principal among these is the presupposition that law encodes the terms under which people cooperate, and it is therefore subject to the cooperators' agreement. Law is, in other words, a consensual structure within which people agree to act. This insight defines a conception of legal legitimacy. Here the law is legitimate to the extent that it is *legitimatable* through political agreement. The French Declaration of the Rights of Man and of the Citizen puts this point well. Article 6 asserts that "All citizens have a right to concur, either personally or by their representatives, in [the law's] formation."[5] Reciprocally, Jeremy Bentham notes that a law with which citizens were *prevented* from concurring would clearly be illegitimate.[6] Citizens' ability to consent to the laws is a deep and fundamental presupposition of our particular form of social cooperation, arising from the fact that the laws structure our cooperative interactions.

Presuppositions of voluntary and reciprocal cooperation are typically given legal form in a conception of *citizenship*. In modern, institutionally differentiated societies, citizenship takes many forms depending on the particular meaning that people give it. It must, however, contain certain essential elements. One of these is a guarantee of political participation, so that people can negotiate the terms of their cooperation. Citizenship must, in other words, encode some idea of political rights.[7]

As we have seen in chapter 4, Jürgen Habermas conducts an insightful analysis of the presuppositions that people must make in order to develop a legitimate body of laws within a democratic political system. He characterizes the reciprocity of citizens as a matter of simultaneously being subject to the laws and being their author.[8] Subjection to the laws is legitimate only when one has a meaningful role in creating or at least authorizing them. A meaningful role means being able to discuss the content of the laws until an agreement is formed about what they should contain. Some kind of open-ended dialogue leading to an agreement, then, is one of the constitutive presuppositions of authoring the laws. In order to be subject to the laws, a person must first have the opportunity to participate in their formation. She must also be satisfied with the extent and quality of this participation. Habermas sums up these presuppositions in what he calls the principle of democracy. That principle states that "Only those statutes may claim legitimacy that can meet with the assent of all citizens in a discursive process of legislation that in turn has been legally constituted."[9] Habermas emphasizes the discursive character of assent as a crucial part of being an author of the laws.

The features of cooperation and legitimacy that we have just surveyed impose limitations on the political process. In order to view each other as equal authors of the law, people must be committed to some idea of *democratic equality*. Everyone ought to have equal capabilities in the deliberations that formulate the laws. People must function as equals in drawing up the laws in spite of any social, cultural, or material differences that may exist between them. This gives rise to a number of procedural considerations structuring public dialogue.[10] Anyone must be allowed to take part in discourse. People must be able to introduce any concern they have into discussion, and they must be allowed to question other's assertions and ask for justification. Reciprocally, people must be able to give reasons for what they claim in public discussion, even if their reasons are a justification for not giving adequate reasons. These features of public discourse spell out the meaning of social cooperation under the law. They identify the presuppositions that we make when we claim that law is legitimate. They are not heuristic rules or moral principles, then, but constitutive assumptions of legal legitimacy as such. They are, in other words, conditions that people must attempt to meet in order to formulate legitimate laws. Any law-forming process must have these formal properties in order to count as valid under our current cooperative practices. Specifically, these properties must ensure some minimal form of democratic equality.

The form of democratic equality needed to legitimate law is a version of the view that I have called the participatory ideal. The idea that people should have sufficient and equal opportunities to participate in formulating the norms, laws, and policies under which they live is a basic presupposition of cooperation. The various considerations about participatory equality that we have just examined are exactly those coded into the participatory ideal's talk of sufficient and equal opportunities to participate. The ideal, in this sense, is part of the conception of legal legitimacy I am developing. It is a conception of participatory equality presupposed in social cooperation.

In sum, practices of social cooperation require us to make specific presuppositions about the equal status of fellow cooperators, about each person's right to consent to the terms of cooperation, and about each person's participatory equality in arriving at these terms. This conception is based on the idea that people make certain presuppositions about the practices they engage in and these presuppositions determine important aspects of their conduct towards others. Participants in social cooperation must therefore *presuppose* that others are equal and reciprocal partners in cooperation, actively intending to treat others in this way.

To see why participatory equality is presupposed in cooperation, it is important to emphasize the intentional dimensions of our practices. Equality is a counterfactual presupposition that is, as Kurt Vonnegut, Jr. hyperbolically reminds us, an ideal impossible to realize in the strictest sense.[11] Nonetheless, we could not claim to cooperate with others as equals if equality were not an active intention and an ongoing project. In order to cooperate, participants must honestly attempt to make good on an ideal that is in practice elusive. From this perspective, failure to treat others as equals is not a failure of cooperation but a mistake to be corrected. It is, more generally, part of a continual process of making actual practices live up to more idealized intentions.

When participants in social cooperation presuppose equal abilities to consent to the terms of cooperation, they are focusing on characteristics of the *procedures* through which laws are created. Those procedures must allow each participant equal say in establishing the ground rules for further cooperation, regardless of what the ground rules actually turn out to be. The legitimacy of laws, then, is conferred and derived from the fairness of the procedures creating them.

A similar attitude toward legitimacy has been observed in some of the experimental studies I discussed in section 7.4. Judgments of the fairness of both political and legal procedures are largely independent of outcome. Procedures are judged on their own merits, not on whether they produce a desired result. Political and legal procedures are more often seen as fair when people have adequate time to express their views, when they believe that those views have been heard and carefully considered, and when people are included in determining what procedures should be followed in reaching a decision. In general, government policy is more often seen as legitimate when it is openly discussed. It is important to note that these studies largely probe people's experiences as subjects of the law rather than as its authors. Nonetheless, they confirm the general importance of procedure over outcome in people's perceptions of legitimacy, and highlight the extent to which procedural fairness is a background presupposition of political and legal cooperation.

It is important to emphasize that the procedural fairness of lawmaking is a *presupposition* of social cooperation, not a *precondition*. The distinction is an important one which turns, again, on the importance of people's intentions in cooperating with one another. Legal legitimacy, in the account I have given, is based on a set of counterfactual presuppositions about practices that are already under way. When people deliberate about the set of laws that govern their conduct, they must have some vision of the kinds of procedures that would ensure fair and balanced discussion. They must have a notion of what it would mean to ensure that all participants have equal opportunity to express their opinions, and what it would mean to agree on a system of laws. This is not to say that these conditions must actually be *met;* only that procedures are designed to accomplish the task of meeting them. In terms of democratic political participation, this means adopting procedures that embody the intention of promoting equal participation. In formulating such procedures, citizens demonstrate the sincerity of their desire to cooperate. They show that they understand the shortcomings of their own deliberative processes and will actively attempt to correct these processes in order to make good on their commitment to treating each other as equals.

The fact that legitimacy is based on the intentions animating a system of laws has important consequences. It implies that a law is not automatically illegitimate if the idealized presuppositions of lawmaking have not been met. If this were the case, all law would be illegitimate because such demanding conditions of reciprocity and equality can only be approximated but never completely realized. What is important is not that the conditions be met in actuality, however, but that they function as guiding ideals of the process itself. In other words, the system of laws must incorporate mechanisms to compensate for contingent, shifting inequalities that would undermine its legitimacy. It must be a self-correcting process, such that inequities in its formation are systematically detected and corrected. The law, in other words, must be *reflexive:* it must encode measures to support the conditions of its own legitimacy.

The reflexive legitimacy of the law is inextricably tied to reflexive democracy. This merely reflects the already intimate connection between democracy and legitimate law. In a general sense, democracy is a political practice that legitimates law. Law, in turn, provides a procedural framework structuring democracy. This intimate connection holds in the same way between reflexive legitimacy and reflexive democracy. When a set of laws must provide its own bases of legitimacy, it is required to maintain the equality and sufficiency of the democratic procedures that legitimate it. In this sense, law creates structural circumstances within which actual citizens can in turn create new law. New laws, in turn, proceduralize further democratic lawmaking, which in turn creates new laws. In sum, when citizens establish the procedural conditions for reflexive democracy, they are simultaneously establishing the democratic conditions for reflexive legitimacy. Reflexive legitimacy and reflexive democracy are thus flip sides of the same coin.

The intentional, reflexive character of legitimacy has a second important consequence. It implies that legitimacy is a property of *systems* of law rather than individual laws. The conditions of legitimacy are determined by presuppositions that actors must make in order to structure their own cooperation by means of law. As such, legitimacy is a criterion describing the system's ability to ensure that it is formed through the cooperative participation of all citizens. It is a property of the legal system itself, rather than any of its parts.

We can draw these observations together into a reflexive conception of legal legitimacy. My argument claims that a legal system must attempt to ensure the conditions necessary for its own legitimacy. These are conditions that provide all citizens with equal opportunities to author the laws. A system of laws is legitimate when it is structured so that such conditions could in principle be met. The system need not be perfect; it need only contain procedural mechanisms for its own correction. Rather than expecting a perfect system, we only expect one that contains institutionalized and incremental means for its own improvement. Legitimacy here is rooted in processes and procedures rather than states of affairs or fixed conditions.

It is important to note the differences between this notion of legitimacy and the classic, contractarian one. Contractarianism bases legitimacy on implied consent to a quasi-legal contract. Consent to the laws is implied by one's ongoing residence in a given nation-state. The social contract is implicitly signed, in this view, when one does not actively opt out of it. In contrast, practices of social cooperation give rise to legal legitimacy in a very different way. When people undertake such practices, they simultaneously adopt certain aims, goals, and beliefs about the practices they are engaging in. One could not consistently claim to cooperate with others and simultaneously deny these general features of cooperative practice. When we engage in legally structured practices of cooperation, we simultaneously engage the machinery of legitimacy that I have outlined. This conception is created within and by our own practices; it is *internal to* the practices in question. Its standards are not negatively implied by our failure to leave a given geographical area, but positively created by practices we purposely engage in.

## 8.2   Constitutional Rights and the Paradox of Enablement

So far I have established that the law must be structured to secure the democratic bases of its own legitimacy. This form of democracy is described by the participatory ideal. In order to justify this principle, I have emphasized the extent to which the participatory ideal serves as the background for legal legitimacy. Equal and sufficient participation is a necessary presupposition of social cooperation. It is presupposed whenever we enter into cooperative practices. This shows that participatory equality is in fact an important value in our political system. Even when it is not valued consistently or directly, it is presupposed by other things that we do value. Now I will extend this argument to show how the participatory ideal's circularity problems jeopardize legitimacy. To avoid such problems, a system of laws must include some conception of reflexive citizenship. In short, I will argue that legitimate laws can be made only under very particular conditions of democratic reflexivity.

Following thinkers like Jürgen Habermas and Robert Alexy, I have noted that legal legitimacy requires procedural guarantees to ensure participatory inclusion. It is important to recognize, however, that formal equality of participation is not enough. Formal equality does not meet the presuppositions of social cooperation. People must have actually equal opportunities to participate if they are to claim that each has had an equal opportunity to consent to the terms of cooperation.

Presuppositions of participatory equality are in tension with the current state of affairs in American society. Americans participate in politics at substantially different rates, depending on their income, education, and employment status.[12] A person in the least affluent segment of the population, for example, is half as likely to vote as a person in the richest. She is also half as likely to participate in political protests and half as likely to contact a political representative. The same pattern holds true of education: people with college degrees participate almost twice as often as those with no high school degree. Similarly, professional and managerial workers participate almost twice as frequently as service and unskilled workers.[13]

In the language I introduced in chapters 3 and 6, socially patterned differences in participation are capability deficits. They are to some extent inequalities in people's participatory skills; to another extent they are inequalities in structural and institutional opportunities to participate. Such inequalities, I have argued, can best be ameliorated through a welfare regime focusing on participatory capabilities. Such a regime would need to equalize the resource base of participation to some extent. More directly, though, it could also change the way welfare is implemented, encouraging direct participation in policy itself. In this way policy could directly promote participatory skills while eliminating the material bases of inequality.

Welfare regimes of any kind are created through politics and legislation. Most of the significant turning points in welfare policy, for instance, have been the result of organized attempts by the beneficiaries of such policies to have their needs and claims recognized. Political activism has been a crucial element in the formation of government welfare programs and distributive policies. Protest, electoral activism, and the political organization of the unemployed were instrumental in many American New Deal programs.[14] Similarly, the Scandinavian welfare states were largely built through the political mobilization of workers and farmers, especially when the two groups formed coalitions.[15] The provision of goods and services by the state is rarely a spontaneous gift.[16] It is, instead, the result of political participation itself. In a general sense, then, the policies needed to ensure equality are formulated through political means.

Welfare is part of the legal system. All of the measures I have described in this book—democratic procedures, capability-supporting policies, conceptions of citizenship, and so on—would be institutionalized through law. Welfare states are organized by means of statutes and constitutional provisions. Like other aspects of the law, welfare policies must be formulated through democratic political procedures in order to be legitimate. Only in this way can the people affected by them consent to their enactment. Legally institutionalized welfare programs are legitimate only when they are part of a legitimate legal system, one based on the consent of the people living under it.

The preceding argument provides new insight into the paradox of enablement. Laws are formulated in political processes. At the same time, the political realm is legally structured and institutionalized. Political participation both creates the law and is sustained by it.[17] The law becomes self-referential and internally circular, then, as a result of its reliance on participation. Similarly, the law's self-referentiality creates problems when material inequalities are present. The circularity inherent in this paradox is thus mediated through the law, and the paradox of enablement becomes inscribed within the law.

The law's circularity and self-referentiality place welfare at the center of legal legitimacy. The welfare-providing functions of the law are crucial for maintaining the material basis of participation. Welfare is a vital mechanism for ensuring that all citizens have the means to participate as equals. Participation, however, is vital for articulating needs and interests in forming welfare law. On one hand, welfare is necessary to ensure equal and sufficient participation in forming the laws. On the other hand, equal and sufficient participation is necessary to legitimate the system of laws that includes welfare. So although the law in general is deeply intertwined with participation, the circularity problems it inherits from participation are most crucially felt in its welfare-providing functions.

When welfare policies are formulated to promote sufficient and equal participation, this relationship will be a happy one and its circularity will be unproblematic. In this scenario, citizens participate as equals to air their differences and form agreements. Fair decisions are reached about the structure of the political process, the nature of the laws, and the distribution of material goods. If these decisions are made carefully, the system that results will support sufficient and equal participation on an ongoing basis.

However the opposite scenario is also possible. If welfare policies fail to ensure sufficient and equal participation, then the voice of some will be amplified over the voice of others. In this case not all people will be authors of the law; some will merely be subject to it without taking part in its formation. In this sense, the essential presuppositions of social cooperation are violated. Some people are forced to cooperate on terms that they do not have the ability to authorize or modify. More tangibly, those people will also be less able to articulate their own needs and interests. Lacking the material means to participate as equals, they will be less effective in participation. Therefore such people will be trapped in the position of lacking the means to participate while also lacking the participation to acquire such means. This situation creates a downward spiral of declining political effectiveness, increasing political marginalization, decreasing access to opportunities, and increasing exclusion from the material resources necessary for political participation. Here the circularity becomes vicious rather than benign.

This kind of vicious circularity imposes particularly stringent limits on the usefulness of means-tested welfare benefits. Means testing confers benefits based on financial need rather than the citizenship criteria I have outlined. Like income, means testing is correlated with low political participation. In the United States, for instance, recipients of means-tested benefits show half the political participation of the general population and half the participation of those receiving non-means-tested benefits like Social Security, veteran's benefits, or Medicare.[18] Ironically, those most dependent upon the government are also the least well equipped to communicate with it.

The parallel lack of participation between low-income people and recipients of means-tested benefits is undoubtedly no coincidence. Means-tested programs are by definition limited to people with low incomes. However, the association of means testing with low participation presents a paradox that is not shared with low income per se. This correlation implies that constituents of means-tested programs have significantly less political voice than those outside these programs. As such, they have correspondingly less ability to make claims on the system, to articulate public arguments about their needs, or to affect the form and amount of benefits they receive. Ironically, recipients of means-tested programs report stronger than average motivation to participate on issues specifically concerned with welfare. This motivation is not strong enough, however, to overcome their much smaller resource base.[19] As a result, the recipients of the most minimal and stigmatized social programs are also least able to defend or modify those programs, much less to use them as a device for improving their own political agency.

Means testing, of course, is designed to target benefits to the needy and thus eliminate such problems. To the extent that it is successful, however, it improves people's means and removes them from the program in question. Paradoxically, at the time that such people acquire better means to participate in politics and legitimate the programs that benefit them, they are no longer directly impacted by those programs. From the perspective of participatory equality, then, means testing is paradoxical. Those who qualify as clients of the program are substantially less able to provide political feedback on its acceptability, while those who possess the capabilities to provide political feedback are disqualified from the program. We can draw only one conclusion from this paradox. A mean-tested welfare system is a political black box. Its recipients are by definition those with low incomes. As long as participatory capabilities vary with income, these people will be least able to comment on the system's acceptability. Means testing does not resolve the paradox of enablement, then, so it cannot provide the welfare basis needed to legitimate a system of laws.

Means-tested welfare is fully entangled in the paradox of enablement, but welfare based on reflexive citizenship has no such problems. Whereas means-tested welfare recipients receive no help in building the political voice needed to become full participants in the legislative process, reflexive citizens by definition have equal and sufficient capabilities to participate. Rather than a descending spiral of political marginality, reflexive citizens are guaranteed the means to full political membership. Reflexive citizenship renders circularity problems harmless, and even better, it converts them into virtuous circularities.

Means testing is paradoxical because it mirrors the pattern of participatory inequalities. It conditions benefits on the same circumstances that lead to participatory deficits. Conditioning benefits on immediate, demonstrated need leads to epistemological problems and paternalism, as we have seen in chapter 5. We do not know when inequalities will pop up, and by definition those affected cannot tell us. Reflexive citizenship avoids such problems by avoiding this kind of conditionality. As a conception of universal citizens' rights, it is not conditioned on claimants' capabilities to articulate their own needs. Agency is guaranteed for all.

Means-tested benefits differ from those awarded on the basis of reflexive citizenship in justification as well as effect. Because means testing is paradoxical, it is also inconsistent with the presuppositions people make when entering into social cooperation. People could not claim to view one another as political equals, yet institute a conditional, viciously circular system of welfare. This holds true of any other welfare regime that fails to guarantee equal opportunities for participation. Such a regime fails to uphold the intention citizens share, that each of them should be equally able to consent to the system of laws. Reflexive citizenship, in contrast, consistently embodies and supports the assumptions such people make about their own cooperation. As a result, reflexive citizenship is justified by practices we already engage in. Other formulations of welfare policy are inconsistent with these practices. Consistency between the goal of cooperation and the means of realizing it is the characteristic that separates these two.

I have justified reflexive citizenship by showing its utility for ensuring that some of our most idealized intentions are achieved in real life. It is worth pointing out that this justification relies on empirical circumstances only in a very particular and elliptical way. Reflexive citizenship is needed to prevent participatory inequalities. It is not *contingent* on them, however. We have strong conceptual and logical reasons to promote participatory equality, even when inequalities are not observed at any particular point in time. Ongoing, stable guarantees of agency are needed to counteract the empirical *possibility* of participatory inequalities, not any particular instance of them. They are needed precisely because of the epistemic uncertainty of knowing when and how people's agency will be compromised.

Because the paradox of enablement shows up as a problem within the law, it is not surprising that the means for resolving it would also be legal. Specifically, the law needs to encode a status for citizens ensuring equal and sufficient agency. Guarantees of material equality have to be made unconditionally to ensure political equality. They must be legally encoded in a way free from contingencies—as constitutional rights. This is why a conception of citizenship must sit at the heart of reflexive democracy. It provides the legal basis for guarantees of equal agency. When such guarantees take the form of citizens' rights, they hold whether or not participatory inequalities can be seen to be present at any particular moment. Adequate guarantees are necessary from the start because conditioning them on circumstance is self-contradictory. It involves a vicious circularity in which those disadvantaged by inequality are least able to articulate claims for redress. Thus political equality must be an ongoing project of welfare states, not simply an occasional task. For all of these reasons reflexive citizenship constitutes a particularly good solution for participatory problems.

## 8.3 Participatory Realities and the Contemporary Impasse

In the past several sections I have argued that a solid conception of constitutional democracy must be firmly rooted in the practices of real citizens. Paradoxically, it must also have the normative force to correct these practices and suggest ways in which they are limited or wrong. Reflexive democracy is such a view. It shows that common, everyday practices of social cooperation presuppose basic commitments to participatory agency. In principle, then, equal opportunity for participation ought to take precedence over other kinds of claims. In particular, it ought to trump the kinds of claims that have motivated welfare cutbacks in recent years.

To make good on this argument, I will now return to the example with which I opened this book. The American welfare system richly illustrates the internal tensions to which actual political cultures are prone. American public opinion seems largely in accord with the system's current state, particularly its reforms during the past decade. Nonetheless, the social background of the American welfare system is both normatively confused and self-contradictory. It amply demonstrates why political culture is an unreliable basis for a system of rights. It also shows how my own view can take its basis from the practices of real citizens while retaining the normative force to correct these practices.

Welfare has fared poorly in American politics over the past several decades. American politicians have adeptly capitalized on the electorate's suspicion and dislike of welfare programs as a reason for dismantling them. Jennifer Hochschild's study of attitudes towards distributive justice reveals some of the cultural background for these attacks.[20] Hochschild documents the complexity and confusion of people's intuitions about equality. Her study is based on intensive one-on-one interviews and thus reveals the fine grain of her subjects' normative intuitions.

Hochschild finds surprising consistency in distributive norms across income groups. Her subjects' attitudes towards political and civil rights are strongly and unambiguously egalitarian. They believe that all citizens should share the same political and civil rights, a commitment often stemming from their reported belief in inherent human equality. Similarly, these subjects strongly support national health insurance, guaranteed jobs, and more-progressive taxation. When asked about their vision of utopia, subjects consistently describe a society more egalitarian than the status quo. Rather surprisingly, this egalitarianism holds regardless of the respondent's income or occupation. Attitudes shift, however, when the topic is more purely monetary. Here the study subjects hold strongly differentiating views, affirming the sanctity of private property and opposing any post-hoc egalitarianism in its redistribution. They hold similarly individualist and differentiating attitudes toward the economy in general, believing that labor markets distribute goods in a correct though unequal fashion.

The dominant pattern among respondents is therefore a bifurcated belief in political equality and economic difference. By dividing the social world into separate spheres, most respondents feel comfortable upholding radically different norms. When the lines between spheres blur, therefore, these subjects display considerable discomfort and lack of confidence. Questions about economic redistribution seem to provoke this reaction in particular because they are seen as partly economic and partly political issues. Here distributive norms come into conflict, provoking variously uncomfortable attempts to reconcile them. Subjects seem to experience these normative conflicts with visceral unease and a felt need to reconcile opposing norms.

Hochschild's interviews amply demonstrate my claims about the normative confusion of actual cultures. Although most subjects fall into a dominant pattern of economic differentiation and political equality, others are consistently egalitarian or consistently differentiating. There is, not surprisingly, no absolute consensus about equality in either the political or economic realm. Further, Hochschild shows that there are substantial tensions within the dominant pattern of belief. She reveals the complex and often contradictory texture of individual conceptions of equality and differentiation.

Martin Gilens finds a similarly ambivalent attitude towards egalitarianism and redistribution in American culture.[21] Like Hochschild, Gilens discovers a reservoir of support for most social programs. Like Hochschild, he also finds that Americans hold strongly to market norms in their evaluation of welfare. People tend to evaluate social programs based on moral criteria of desert. If recipients are perceived as hard working or as victims of larger socioeconomic forces, the public tends to support programs aimed at helping them. If, on the other hand, recipients are perceived as lazy and lacking initiative, the public opposes such programs.

According to Gilens, the American welfare system has encountered substantial opposition because it is perceived as facilitating laziness and undermining the work ethic. The programs making up the bottom of the American safety net, programs like Aid to Families with Dependent Children (AFDC), Temporary Assistance for Needy Families (TANF), and food stamps, are subject to a number of unfortunate misconceptions. Most Americans believe that blacks are the primary recipients of these programs. Further, they believe that blacks are lazy and that welfare undermines the work ethic and allows people to shirk individual responsibility. As a result, public opinion draws a racial line between the deserving and undeserving poor, believing that welfare encourages laziness and gives a free ride to people who could be working. According to Gilens, most Americans support the functions and expenses of a modern welfare state. They object, however, to programs that counteract the logic of the labor market and undermine responsibility. American welfare programs have run afoul of these values in recent years, largely due to misconceptions about the racial characteristics and work ethic of welfare recipients.

Both of these studies reveal substantial normative confusion within American political culture. In Gilens's case, Americans are relatively clear about their values: they reward effort and punish laziness. Their perceptions of how welfare embodies these values are highly confused, however. Welfare is connected via race with ideas of moral hazard and dependency. Welfare recipients are perceived as lazy and dependent because they are perceived as black. This chain of associations is based on factual misperception. It is an unwarranted belief system that results in unfairly demonizing certain parts of the American policy regime. Gilens shows that our normative attitudes toward work and moral desert are inaccurately applied to the welfare state.

Hochschild parallels this analysis, but identifies deeper inconsistencies in American political culture. She shows that Americans reconcile conflicting distributive norms by locating them in different domains of social life. This allows people to be political egalitarians at the same time that they are economic differentiators. What Hochschild's subjects largely fail to grasp, however, is the interconnection between the norms they hold separate. Political equality is often inconsistent with systematic and persistent economic inequality. Even though Hochschild's subjects support political equality, they seem largely unaware of the empirical difficulties of separating the economic and political spheres. They thus seem unaware that their conceptualization of equality is untenable: under current American social conditions it is not possible to obtain a clean separation between politics and economics. The psychological tactic of maintaining separate distributive norms for separate spheres is therefore unsustainable.

The inseparability of the political and the economic is carefully demonstrated in the 1990 American Citizen Participation Study, already discussed in chapter 6. It reveals the subtle texture of actually existing inequalities in turn-of-the-century America, finding significant inverse relationships between people's income and political participation. The most affluent people are nine times more likely to give money to a political campaign, four times more likely to volunteer for one and 40 percent more likely to vote than are the poorest people.[22] They are also twice as likely to participate in political protests than the poor and twice as likely to contact a political representative.

Differences in income are not only correlated with participation itself, but more particularly with the kinds of skills people need to participate in political life. The richest people are three times as likely as the poorest to participate in a meeting in which decisions are made, organize a meeting, give a presentation, or write a letter in an average work day. They are also twice as likely to use such skills in nonpolitical organizations like clubs or service groups and one and a half times as likely to use them in church.[23] These differences show that skill use is stratified across a range of social activities. In the workplace, stratification seems to result from the kinds of jobs people have rather than their income per se. Professionals, for instance, practice such skills on the job one and a half times as often as clerical or sales people, and almost three times as often as laborers or service employees. In sum, a person's wealth and occupation seem to make a large difference in her political activities across the board. It seems to make a particular difference in the activities most pivotal in expressing her needs and interests in the political process.

This research implies that political participation has important material preconditions. Unequal resources amplify the voices of some and diminish the voices of others. Political agency seems to be connected in important ways with people's material fortunes. Of particular import is the effect of wealth and income on the less tangible forms of political participation. Differences in voice between rich and poor seem not solely based on the ability of money to amplify what one says, nor on the ability of money to furnish one with the freedom to say it. Rather, wealth is correlated with people's discursive capacities in a more specific, agent-rooted sense. Occupying a position of authority and prestige gives a person greater opportunities to develop civic and political skills, skills as mundane as speaking before a group, formulating ideas clearly, planning meetings, and motivating others.[24] It gives him, in short, more effective cognitive and verbal means to express his interests and needs in public dialogue.

The American Citizen Participation Study identifies contradictions within the dominant pattern of belief described by Hochschild. People attempt to relieve the tensions between differing distributive norms by distinguishing separate political and economic spheres. Research on participation shows the actual interconnectedness of the economic and the political, however. Because participatory agency is heavily influenced by wealth and employment, economic differentiation undermines political egalitarianism. Separating economic and political spheres may provide psychological solace to people seeking to reconcile contradictory norms, but it does not reflect the realities of contemporary American society. Both Gilens and Hochschild show, then, that Americans' attitudes towards welfare are complex and confused. Many of the core functions of the welfare state are widely supported. Americans also seem deeply egalitarian in their opinions about politics and the basic worth of others. At the same time, however, they try to reconcile contradictory norms by embracing factually untenable beliefs. As a result, any welfare system justified on this basis would rest on very shaky grounds.

Unfortunately, recent changes in the American welfare system seem to track this unstable mix of contradictory beliefs quite closely. American welfare rhetoric has focused increasingly on notions of individual responsibility in recent years. It hews closely to the kind of market logic described by Hochschild and Gilens, in which effort is rewarded and laziness stigmatized. Because welfare recipients are seen as lazy and dependent upon public assistance, they are classed as undeserving poor who have failed to exercise the kind of initiative and responsibility expected of other citizens. Congress clearly endorsed such a view when it terminated AFDC in 1996 with the Personal Responsibility and Work Opportunity Reconciliation Act (PRA). In this law Congress makes individuals responsible through a combination of less-eligibility measures, time limits, reporting mandates, and work requirements. As such, it institutes a program that seems to follow closely the logic of public opinion outlined by Gilens and Hochschild. Individual responsibility is a strongly differentiating norm; it enforces a great deal of economic independence. Further, it draws a sharp line between "deserving" and "undeserving," giving anyone not choosing to work a strong push off the welfare roles.

These features of the American welfare system clash with more basic presuppositions of the American system of law and politics. Like any other modernized society, the United States has a highly differentiated economy, a sophisticated political apparatus, and a complex system of laws for organizing social cooperation. Participatory equality has primary importance in legitimating these kinds of cooperation-stabilizing structures. It is presupposed in cooperation itself and is therefore prior to any specific institutional details that people might cooperatively devise. Normatively speaking, Americans must find some way to ensure participatory equality before embracing, say, norms of individualism and differentiation in the economy. On my view, then, the American public not only deceives itself in a factual sense when it embraces conflicting distributive norms. It also avoids primary responsibilities that citizens have toward one another. Only a welfare system capable of supporting reflexive democracy would be able to meet these requirements. When the American public opts for a more minimal, means-tested system not focused on the capabilities of its citizens, it fails to meet this standard.

It is no surprise, then, that the ideal of self-responsibility enunciated in the PRA directly contradicts the responsibilities that citizens have toward one another as a result of their mutual cooperation. The PRA's overriding goal is to remove people from the welfare rolls. It emphasizes personal responsibility for economic risks and enforces it through a stringent residualism. As such, it contains no direct provisions to equalize or support political citizenship. It fails to institutionalize the guarantees necessary to ensure the mutual autonomy of citizens. It is, then, in principle blind to the democratic presuppositions of social cooperation. This is seen in a number of the PRA's specific provisions.

(1) Like food stamps and subsidized housing, TANF is a means-tested program. It requires states to establish criteria of need for awarding benefits, in keeping with the PRA's stated goal of targeting benefits to needy families.[25] It is thus subject to the political circularity inherent in any means-tested program. As long as participation continues to be less among the recipients of means-tested benefits, the constituents of programs like TANF will on average participate less. This implies less political voice and less input into the shape and size of the programs designed to benefit them. To the extent that TANF participants leave the program and increase their income, they should be expected to become more politically capable. At the same time, however, they are no longer governed by the paternalistic measures of the program itself. Thus TANF recipients are much less likely to act as citizens in the political processes that shape

the program; they are much less likely to protest or, for that matter, to legitimate its various tests and requirements. TANF, then, becomes a black box from the perspective of democratic politics. This is a result of the circularity inherent in the connection between political participation and means testing.

(2) The PRA conditions benefits in other ways that undermine political participation. Benefits are time limited in the PRA,[26] subject to cooperation in paternity reporting,[27] and they apply only to people with dependent children.[28] These limits preclude any systematic attempt to equalize political capabilities. They ignore the possibility that people without children may fall short of political equality, or that some people may need more education, more resources, or greater protection than the two- and five-year caps on benefits allow.

(3) Through a combination of time limits and incentives, the PRA mandates states to move people into the job market as quickly as possible. These measures tend to push people into low-wage jobs.[29] By sacrificing quality for speed, the PRA traps workers in the bottom tiers of the economy. This is not only a wage trap, but a participation trap as well. Although the workplace is the most important site for acquiring political capabilities, it functions as such only for the upper levels of employment status.[30] Managers and professionals have jobs that encourage the same organizational and verbal skills that are useful in politics. Rank-and-file jobs, on the other hand, do not. The PRA's work requirements have been supported by both conservative and liberal commentators who claim many social and individual benefits for work. Work in itself is no panacea for participatory problems, however. To be effective in this realm, the PRA would need to create capability-enhancing jobs for its subjects. Currently it tends to move them into the sector of the job market that does the least to promote political capabilities.

(4) Education has been shown many times to be vital for equal political participation. Its effect seems to be an indirect one—it gives people the motivation to become engaged in politics.[31] The PRA includes certain types of educational activity in its list of work requirements, enabling people to improve their skills and job marketability while receiving benefits.[32] These include vocational training (capped after a year), skills training related directly to particular jobs, and high school attendance for those who have not graduated. These provisions make a valuable contribution to equalizing political participation. Education is much more likely to lead to the development of important deliberative skills than is a low-status job. Whereas only the upper echelons of employment promote deliberative skills, education is more universal in its reach. It is thus fitting

that a welfare program should allow individuals to substitute education for work mandates.

However, the PRA's education benefits are narrowly targeted at work skills training, which limits their effectiveness in promoting labor market mobility or political capabilities. They are also subject to the same time limits and narrow criteria of need as other benefits. In addition, authority is largely left to the states to determine whether or not an individual is allowed to participate in education as opposed to work,[33] and TANF requires states to choose the combination of education and work that will move a given individual "into whatever private sector employment the individual is capable of handling as quickly as possible. . . ."[34] Education benefits are thus conditioned in ways that seriously limit their beneficial effects.

As I have noted, the best strategy for avoiding the paradoxes of political circularity and illegitimate law is to universalize benefits on the basis of citizenship. A conception of reflexive citizenship, for instance, would guarantee equal participatory agency across income groups.[35] The PRA explicitly excludes any conception of citizenship or entitlement, however. The first section of title 1 states very explicitly that the act confers no federal or state entitlement on its recipients.[36] The act's funding mechanisms further preclude any guarantees of status or capability enhancement. Unlike the earlier AFDC, federal funds are now provided as a block grant rather than as an open-ended, per capita guarantee of matching funds.[37] These funds can be increased or decreased depending on a state's performance in enforcing work requirements, decreasing out-of-marriage births, and meeting various other targets. As a result, the federal government does not guarantee states the funds to raise individuals up to a meaningful level of living. It makes no standing commitment to equality of any kind, much less to equal political citizenship. Instead, the PRA's commitment to federalism and fiscal minimalism will most likely reproduce existing inequalities.

These policy details allow us to see the social logic of "responsibility" in the PRA from a different angle. Unlike Unemployment Insurance, TANF is not conditioned on previous employment history. Unlike the Earned Income Tax Credit, it does not presuppose that one is currently employed. TANF thus occupies a crucial niche in the American legal system. Along with programs like Headstart, public housing, and food stamps, it makes up the very bottom of the American safety net, providing benefits for people left behind by the labor market. It has a vital role, then, in ensuring the material basis of legitimacy for the entire system. Along with the other components of the American welfare system, its proper function should be first and foremost to ensure that inequalities in political agency are adequately corrected. The PRA chooses a different direction, however. It does not ensure smooth transitions into work for all of its recipients, nor does it hand them off smoothly to employment-conditioned programs like the Earned Income Tax Credit. Further, it does not provide jobs that enhance citizenship skills. Instead, the PRA emphasizes the social and financial self-sufficiency—"personal responsibility"—of needy people. It does this without and instead of ensuring political equality, at a time when the democratic processes that ought to legitimate American law are in fact significantly unequal. Unfortunately, our commitments to legitimate law cannot be upheld solely through self-sufficient economic agency in the labor market. As a result, the PRA's conception of responsibility is inconsistent with the forms of mutual obligation implicit in our legal and political system. We must conclude, then, that the PRA is internally inconsistent. By failing to ensure the material bases of political participation, it undermines the legitimacy of American law in general.

In the perspective I have outlined, responsibility cannot simply be a matter of drawing a line between the affairs proper to the state and those proper to the individual. The market economy in which individuals are to be responsible is legally constituted and structured. If the laws constituting the market are to be legitimate, they must be formed through the equal and sufficient participation of all citizens. The need for equal political participation imposes limits on the system of laws, which in turn imposes limits on the market. Effective guarantees of political agency are required to ensure the legitimacy of the law and the market. Before individuals can be required to act responsibly in the marketplace, then, the basic conditions of legal legitimacy must first be secured. An effective welfare system is necessary to secure such conditions. This system must operate with a fairly robust conception of citizenship, one that acknowledges the inherent connection between participation and material inequality. It seems, then, that personal responsibility *presupposes* some conception of welfare rights. Welfare is not, as neo-liberals have claimed, the opposite of responsibility.

The problem with the current American welfare regime is a procedural inattention to political equality within the legal system itself. The fundamental criterion that enables citizens to take responsibility in the American legal and political system is not met. This is the responsibility that citizens must take for each other in order to ensure the bases of a system of equal and reciprocal cooperation. Instead the American system treats welfare as a moral and motivational failure on the part of individuals. It limits the responsibilities of the state by redefining those of individuals and seeks to resolve social problems by ending "dependency" and returning people to the labor market. The conception of reflexive democracy I have outlined shows, however, that society, law, politics, and economics cannot be so easily disentangled. The social and political bases of the law prevent a quick retreat from state responsibility. Before the state can claim to have discharged its duties, it must establish a framework in which the law—including welfare law—can be legitimately created.

## 8.4 A Distinctive Justification of the Welfare State

At the beginning of this volume, I set out a standard—a wish list, really—for what a solid normative conception of the welfare state would look like. Looking back to Max Weber's critique of early welfare states, I said that a good conception would meet Weber's cautions against "emotionally colored ethical postulates" without conceding the project as a whole. It would, in other words, develop an immanent critique of our current institutions and practices, using values and commitments already present in those institutions and practices. Such a justification would thus avoid imposing critical perspectives or moral points of view from outside. And yet, I said, this project must avoid a kind of straightforward embeddedness in its current cultural milieu. That would risk simply reproducing the status quo without teaching us anything new.

The view I have outlined in this book meets these requirements. It is embedded within a particular context—the institutions and practices of modernized, democratic, constitutional nation-states. It holds up a mirror to those societies without simply reflecting back the image they are used to seeing. The mirror in this case reveals widespread distortions in our internalized self-image. We see ourselves as democratic, egalitarian societies created for the mutual benefit of all members. Yet we systematically ignore inconsistencies in this view, particularly the extent to which some voices are allowed to dominate political and cultural discussions while others remain quiet.

A more consistent view, I have argued, is one in which our preferred self-image is backed up by legal measures that ensure actual equality as a necessary component of actual cooperation. Our conception of democracy and welfare, I believe, ought to be consistent with the core practices and beliefs of our society. This view avoids the romanticism that Weber found in early social democracy. It is not based on "emotionally colored ethical postulates" of justice or human dignity. It is not rooted in any particular conception of a good society or a fully developed human being. Rather, the ultimate justification of this view is based on formal properties of the law, a project dear to Weber's heart. Our legally institutionalized practices of social cooperation are inconsistent without particular commitments to the agency of the law's authors. At its core, this view is based on a kind of logical minimalism Weber would have to embrace: the idea that a system of laws should be internally consistent.

I have claimed that welfare is a necessary component of democratic legitimacy. It guarantees that procedural mechanisms exist to secure the material preconditions of fair participation. Welfare is important here not as an *outcome*—not as generating the kind of substantive equality to which Weber objected. Rather, it is important as a *process*, as a formal component of the democratic creation of law. Without this component, a system of laws lacks the means to ensure its own legitimacy, just as surely as if it failed to provide people with rights to participation.

This perspective on welfare arises out of the law itself. It is not an external viewpoint imposed on the law, but a limitation that the legal framework imposes on itself. It is a criterion that comes out of the basic, formal requirements of political legitimacy that inhere within law as a structure of social cooperation. As such, this criterion provides us with a way to evaluate systems of law. It is formal in Weber's sense because it evaluates basic structural properties of the system of laws. However, this criterion is also substantive in Weber's sense because it lays down particular goals and end states for welfare policy to pursue. A system of laws must include a guarantee of agency sufficient to ensure that people will be able to function as equal participants in authoring the laws. This is a substantive outcome of the kind that so dismayed Weber. In this case, however, substantive goals are specified by formal properties of the law. They are not "emotionally colored ethical postulates" generated out of a free-standing conception of social justice external to the law. The notion of legal legitimacy that I have outlined here takes its shape solely from internal properties of democratic lawmaking.

The advantages of this approach can be highlighted by contrasting it with a view of welfare that has had a large impact on American public policy in recent years. Lawrence Mead's "new paternalism" also draws connections between citizenship, welfare, and cooperation.[38] He observes that the conception of citizenship operative in American social policy emphasizes benefits and entitlements without corresponding obligations. Opposing this conception, Mead draws on a countertradition in American politics that he calls civic conservatism. In this conception of citizenship, benefits and obligations go hand in hand. Citizens can expect to benefit from social membership only if they contribute to the polity. These obligations are conceived specifically in terms of labor. To receive welfare benefits, citizens should be expected to work. This, Mead claims, is an attitude toward social obligation that is common in contemporary American culture, and it is crucial to defining what it means to be a full participant in American society.

At first blush the civic conservative notion of citizenship might seem parallel to my own. Mead's idea of the reciprocal character of contribution and benefit corresponds in certain ways with my own delineation of the presuppositions of social cooperation. Further, Mead's analysis of expectations actually implicit in American culture is similar to my own attempt to locate normativity within our actual practices. Our positions are quite different, however. Mead is certainly right about the symbolic and moral importance of work in American culture and its de facto link to social status.[39] However, such homegrown moral ideals cannot be translated directly into a conception of citizenship.[40] They represent only one particular norm of human behavior among the multitude found in our culture. Taken as a group, these ideals are disparate, often contradictory, and typically lack unanimity. Most importantly, they are *nonconsensual*. Such norms circulate through society as prescriptive images of human life; they are not the product of equal participatory processes establishing mutually acceptable guidelines for cooperation. Informal, nonconsensual moral ideals are not a sound basis for a conception of citizenship. They are, as Mead himself notes, expectations paternalistically applied by some citizens on others, rather than expectations citizens set for themselves.

Lacking a sound notion of citizenship, the civic conception does not provide an adequate explanation of why work is something citizens owe to society. It cannot provide a rationale for this idea because it does not articulate sufficient grounds to explain mutual obligations of any kind. The inchoate moral intuitions on which the civic conception is based are important features of public opinion, but they have no normative force beyond their status as recommendations. They do not collectively make up a conception of citizenship, but only suggest measures that could be enacted after more solid grounds for citizenship were collectively agreed on.

This is the kind of lapse that reflexive democracy is designed to address. In my conception, participation is not concerned first and foremost with work but with coming to an understanding about the nature and conditions of cooperation itself. It is above all a political practice through which other aspects of cooperation can be decided. If a particular society agrees, on the basis of equal and sufficient participation, to condition welfare benefits on work, it may do so. Such a decision would be legitimate only when measures were in place to ensure equal and sufficient participation, however. Thus welfare could be limited or conditioned only to the extent that guarantees of participatory equality were not undermined.

Paternalistic policy measures could be legitimate only if they were *self-imposed*. Such measures could be self-imposed, however, only through legitimate processes of lawmaking. The problem of participatory inequality needs to be solved, then, before government can legitimately become an agent of coercion. Reflexive democracy necessarily precedes paternalism. Interestingly, the conception I have outlined is not a direct argument against work requirements or other paternalistic welfare measures. It is, rather, an argument against paternalism that is not the result of citizens freely imposing limits on their own actions through legitimate legislation. Legitimate paternalism can only be an example of what Kant might call freely binding one's own will, or what Jon Elster's more colorful, Homeric imagery would portray as "binding oneself to the mast."[41]

## 8.5 A New Conception of Democracy and the Welfare State

Bill Clinton campaigned for the U.S. presidency in 1992 on the promise to "end welfare as we know it." Putting aside his eschatological rhetoric, reflexive democracy would have much the same effect. It would require fairly profound changes in our views of government, social policy, and welfare. Earlier I conjectured that the problem of the welfare state is not one of institutional design, but rather a failure of the imagination. The true crisis, in other words, is conceptual rather than institutional. I have tried to redeem this claim in words if not deeds. The past chapters outline a new set of concepts for the welfare state, ones focusing on key areas of our political, cultural, and economic life. These concepts give us a different way of thinking about the functions of welfare and provide new justifications for it. At the same time, they also have much to say about democracy itself and its intertwinement with welfare.

The conception of reflexive democracy that I have described opens substantial areas of public life to democratic participation. It is committed to the participatory ideal, the notion that people should have sufficient and equal opportunities to participate in formulating the norms, laws, and policies under which they live. Through this commitment, however, the new paradigm also acquires corresponding burdens to ensure that the demos is up to the task. In particular, the background conditions of public deliberation must be such that a turn to politics does not simply increase the dominance of already privileged interests. Because social inequalities frequently translate into political inequalities, some mechanism must exist to ensure participatory equality in the face of forces that would destabilize it.

The idea of reflexive democracy is designed to meet this challenge. It resolves the paradox of enablement, ensuring the internal consistency of the democratic-constitutional state. Reflexive democracy not only ensures that citizens have equal means to participate in creating the laws, but also that they have equal means to ensure their own ongoing equality. Such a notion of reflexivity is the only way to guarantee that equal participation is a stable feature of the constitutional state. Reflexivity in this sense is a self-maintaining structure for democratic deliberation.

Reflexive democracy has, at its core, a notion of citizenship that is also reflexive. Citizenship is reflexive here because it is the most important procedural condition of reflexive democracy. For democracy to be reflexive, citizens must be able to control the legal status that sustains their own agency as citizens. To make sense of this abstract structural principle, I have theorized citizens' participation as a matter of capabilities. One's capability to participate is a matter of personal abilities and characteristics combined with environmental strictures and enablements. The welfare state is charged, in this view, with promoting and equalizing people's participatory skills and opportunities. It fosters agency and active participation. From the start, then, this vision is substantially different from a client-oriented, dependency-creating welfare state that redistributes goods to passive recipients. A reflexive conception promotes the activity of citizens rather than replacing it.

A capability-based model also provides powerful means for theorizing actual equality of opportunity in participation. It goes beyond merely formal equality—one person, one vote, for instance—to address persistent inequalities in the use people can make of resources at their disposal. By equalizing capabilities, it acknowledges the need for equal background conditions and establishes a level playing field for participation.

The capability model also makes possible a qualitative shift in the way we think about welfare. Rather than thinking of welfare simply as a package of goods, the *form* in which it is provided becomes very important. A capability-promoting state could directly provide citizens with opportunities to develop participatory skills. It could thus promote their participatory capabilities in a more general sense while simultaneously encouraging the very participation that legitimates welfare in the first place. In one stroke, welfare regimes could become sites for practicing participation *and* institutions legitimated by it. This double-edged benefit is made possible only when the form of welfare—the involvement of its beneficiaries—becomes a focus as important as the actual package of goods and services a regime provides.

Reflexive citizenship differs from traditional models of citizenship. It is the status that people would have to attribute to each other in social cooperation. It describes the political, cultural, and economic bases of participatory agency. Reflexive citizenship contrasts, then, with universalist conceptions based on *membership* rather than participation. In the classic conception, national membership entitles one to a particular packet of rights and benefits. The bureaucratic classification of being a member creates the status of passive recipient. Reflexive citizenship, in contrast, endows people with the means to continue in the active status of participant, which entails being able to participate in the processes guaranteeing participation in the first place. It is, then, a different kind of universalism.

Reflexive citizenship contrasts even more sharply with many actually practiced notions of citizenship in today's developed nations. These are highly particularistic and place a large emphasis on an individual's economic status. Such regimes informally differentiate citizenship according to a person's success or failure in the marketplace. Economic success enhances the effectiveness of political rights and cultural participation, creating de facto higher levels of citizenship for the successful. The conception I have outlined is explicitly designed to prevent this kind of differentiation. It is universalistic not only in the way it awards benefits, but more radically in the forms of equal status and agency that these benefits are designed to guarantee.

Reflexive democracy thus provides a cluster of interconnected concepts that form a unique vision of the welfare state. These include the participatory ideal, reflexive citizenship, reflexive legitimacy, and the idea that agency should be seen as a matter of capabilities evaluated from political, cultural, and economic perspectives. In addition, reflexive democracy provides a unique *justification* for the welfare state. It locates a basis for participatory norms in practices in which we are already engaged. Our cooperative practices presuppose ongoing commitments to participatory equality. We might call these "revealed commitments" as opposed to ones that are openly declared or consciously held.[42]

Such commitments are no less real, however. If we intend our interactions to be cooperative, something like reflexive democracy is necessary to fulfill those intentions. This is simply the result of structuring a legal system so that participatory inequalities are systematically avoided.

Justification through revealed commitments resolves many of the difficulties that I have traced in other conceptions of the welfare state. I argued in chapter 2 that economically oriented conceptions of welfare could benefit from the additional normative resources of a theory of voice. Justifications based on deeply structured class interests provide an ambitious critique of the capitalist economy but thereby distance themselves from actual contexts and actual people. Justifications based on moral norms, in contrast, are appropriately contextual and firmly rooted in the normative context of specific cultures. They are thereby limited by the extent of the de facto acceptance of the norms in question, however. The line of justification I have outlined walks a middle path between these contrasting problems. It avoids dependence on particular norms and values, but remains rooted in particular societies by focusing on society-wide practices of social cooperation.

Although reflexive democracy focuses primarily on equal participation, it does have important implications for distributive equality in a broader sense. Rather than devising an abstract metric of distributive justice, this view establishes a political benchmark of equality that allows actual citizens to work out distributive norms for themselves. It thus avoids the philosophical burden of deciding on just patterns or processes for distributing goods. It solves these problems instead by specifying the minimal conditions that would allow such issues to be decided through the political dialogue of actual citizens.

This conception of democracy and the welfare state would require a substantial deviation from our current path, but it is rooted in practices we already engage in and commitments we already hold. The idea of a capability-promoting state parallels the kinds of policy preferences that pollsters currently observe, including broad support for policies that promote independence and agency.[43] It is based on widely accepted values of democratic sovereignty, equal opportunity, and participatory politics. As such, this conception draws on core elements of liberalism and civic republicanism. It does not reject our current political culture, but describes the means for its full and consistent realization.

The ideas I have outlined trace a political turn in the welfare state. This turn supplements existing justifications for welfare with new, political ones. It is built on the observation that democracy is a fragile achievement that must be carefully maintained. A democratic state must itself be democratically legitimate, providing its citizens with equal opportunities to formulate the norms, laws, and policies under which they live. To do this, it must have procedural means to promote political, cultural, and economic equality. These observations reveal deep interconnections between democracy and the welfare state. They show that any state taking democracy seriously must be *reflexive*. Reflexive democracy makes political equality a procedural concern. In this view, welfare is a vital mechanism for ensuring the material bases of democracy itself. Only by tilling the soil of democracy can the state reflexively maintain the bases of its own legitimacy.

Reflexive democracy puts issues of equal agency first and foremost on the state's agenda. It draws connections between various forms of agency as seen from the perspectives of economy, culture, and politics. These forms must be balanced and promoted to ensure that all citizens can participate on an equal footing. Because political agency is key to maintaining the reflexivity of democracy, however, it takes normative center stage in this vision. It is vital to synthesizing the norms, laws, and policies that undergird citizenship itself.

The political turn I have described unifies political, cultural, and economic concerns under a normative conception of democracy. This is not a turn away from the venerable project of economic egalitarianism and social democracy, however, so much as a thoroughgoing rethinking of that project. It reminds us that politics, culture, and the economy are not cleanly separable, but complexly interconnected. Reflexive democracy brings these domains into a dynamic equilibrium by taking simultaneous account of the material character of democracy and the political significance of welfare.

# Notes

## Chapter One

1. Personal Responsibility and Work Opportunity Reconciliation Act of 1996, Public Law 104–193, 22 August 1996, section 101 (8)–(9). Hereafter "PL 104–193."

2. Cf. Nikolas Rose, *Powers of Freedom: Reframing Political Thought* (New York: Cambridge University Press, 1999), esp. chap. 4; Wendy Larner, "Post-Welfare State Governance: Towards a Code of Social and Family Responsibility," *Social Politics* 7 (2000): 244–265.

3. Lawrence Mead, ed., *The New Paternalism: Supervisory Approaches to Poverty* (Washington, D.C.: Brookings Institution, 1997); and Lawrence Mead, *Beyond Entitlement: The Social Obligations of Citizenship* (New York: Free Press, 1986).

4. Richard Titmuss, *Social Policy* (London: Allen and Unwin, 1974), 30–31.

5. Frances Fox Piven and Richard Cloward, *Regulating the Poor: The Functions of Public Welfare* (New York: Vintage, 1971).

6. Gøsta Esping-Andersen, *The Three Worlds of Welfare Capitalism* (Princeton: Princeton University Press, 1990).

7. C. B. Macpherson, *The Political Theory of Possessive Individualism* (New York: Oxford University Press, 1962).

8. "An Act for the Relief of the Poor," 5 Elizabeth I, c. 3, 1563; "An Act for the Punishment of Vagabonds, and for Relief of the Poor and Impotent," 14 Elizabeth I, c. 5, 1572; "An Act for the Setting of the Poor on Work, and for the Avoiding of Idleness," 18 Elizabeth I, c. 3, 1576; "An Act for the Relief of the Poor," 39 and 40 Elizabeth I, c. 3, 1598; "An Act for the Punishment of Rogues, Vagabonds, and Sturdy Beggars," 39 and 40 Elizabeth I, c. 4, 1598; "An Act for Erecting of Hospitals or Abiding and Working Houses for the Poor," 39 and 40 Elizabeth I, c. 5, 1598; "An Act for the Relief of the Poor," 43 and 44 Elizabeth I, c. 2, 1601.

9. John Locke, "An Essay on the Poor Law" (1697), in *Political Essays,* ed. Mark Goldie (New York: Cambridge University Press, 1997), 189.

10. *Sic.* Jeremy Bentham, "Pauper Management Improved" (c. 1797), in *The Works of Jeremy Bentham,* vol. 8, ed. John Bowring (New York: Russell and Russell, 1962), 369–439.

11. Sidney Checkland and Olive Checkland, eds., *The Poor Law Report of 1834* (New York: Penguin, 1974); Sidney Webb and Beatrice Webb, *English Poor Law History,* 3 vols. (Hamden, Conn.: Archon Books, 1963).

12. Gwendolyn Mink, *Welfare's End* (Ithaca, N.Y.: Cornell University Press, 1998), chap. 2; Lawrence Mead, *Beyond Entitlement,* chap. 6.

13. G. A. Cohen, "The Structure of Proletarian Unfreedom," in *Analytical Marxism,* ed. John Roemer (Cambridge: Cambridge University Press, 1986).

14. Robert Goodin, "Social Welfare as a Collective Social Responsibility," in Robert Goodin and David Schmidtz, *Social Welfare and Individual Responsibility* (New York: Cambridge University Press, 1998); Robert Goodin, *Reasons for Welfare: The Political Theory of the Welfare State* (Princeton: Princeton University Press, 1988).

15. Max Weber, *Economy and Society,* 2 vols. (Berkeley: University of California Press, 1978), 886.

16. See also Kevin Olson, "Participatory Parity and Democratic Justice," in Nancy Fraser, *Adding Insult to Injury: Social Justice and the Politics of Recognition,* ed. Kevin Olson (London: Verso, forthcoming).

## Chapter Two

1. Asa Briggs, "The Welfare State in Historical Perspective," *Archives Européennes de Sociologie* 2 (1961): 228.

2. Emile Durkheim, *The Division of Labor in Society,* trans. W. D. Hall (New York: The Free Press, 1984 [1893]), 28.

3. Gøsta Esping-Andersen, *The Three Worlds of Welfare Capitalism* (Princeton: Princeton University Press, 1990), ch. 1; *Social Foundations of Postindustrial Economies* (New York: Oxford University Press, 1999), ch. 4.

4. Esping-Andersen, *Three Worlds,* ch. 2; *Social Foundations,* ch. 5.

5. Leo XIII, "Rerum Novarum" (1891), in *The Papal Encyclicals,* vol. 2, ed. Claudia Carlen (Ann Arbor: Pierian Press, 1990). Pius XI, "Quadragesimo Anno" (1931), in *The Papal Encyclicals,* vol. 3, ed. Claudia Carlen (Ann Arbor: Pierian Press, 1990).

6. Iris Marion Young, *Justice and the Politics of Difference* (Princeton: Princeton University Press, 1990).

7. Peter Baldwin, *Politics of Social Solidarity: Class Bases of the European Welfare State 1875–1975* (New York: Cambridge University Press, 1990); Jerald Wallulis, *The New Insecurity: The End of the Standard Job and Family* (Albany, N.Y.: SUNY Press, 1998).

8. G. A. Cohen, "The Labor Theory of Value and the Concept of Exploitation," *Philosophy and Public Affairs* 8 (1979): 338–360; Jon Elster, *Making Sense of Marx* (New York: Cambridge University Press, 1985), 127–141; and Ian Steedman, ed., *The Value Controversy* (London: Verso, 1981).

9. John Roemer, *Egalitarian Perspectives: Essays in Philosophical Economics* (Cambridge, UK: Cambridge University Press, 1994), 104–111; modifying his *A General Theory of Exploitation and Class* (Cambridge, Mass.: Harvard University Press, 1982), 202–211.

10. Roemer, *General Theory*, 194–237. A nontechnical summary can be found in John Roemer, *Free to Lose* (Cambridge, Mass.: Harvard University Press, 1988); and in his "New Directions in the Marxian Theory of Exploitation and Class," in *Analytical Marxism,* ed. John Roemer (New York: Cambridge University Press, 1986).

11. Axel Honneth, *The Struggle for Recognition: The Moral Grammar of Social Conflicts,* trans. Joel Anderson (Cambridge, Mass.: MIT Press, 1995); Charles Taylor, *Multiculturalism: Examining the Politics of Recognition,* ed. Amy Gutmann (Princeton: Princeton University Press, 1994).

12. Arlie Hochschild, *The Second Shift: Working Parents and the Revolution at Home* (New York: Viking, 1989).

13. Friedrich Engels, *Origins of the Family, Private Property, and the State* (New York: Penguin, 1985).

14. Robert Goodin, *Protecting the Vulnerable: A Reanalysis of Our Social Responsibilities* (Chicago: University of Chicago Press, 1985), 149.

15. Robert Goodin, *Reasons for Welfare: The Political Theory of the Welfare State* (Princeton: Princeton University Press, 1988), 175–176; Goodin, *Protecting the Vulnerable,* 195–196.

16. Goodin, *Reasons for Welfare,* 160–173.

17. Ibid., chap. 7.

18. Ibid., 180.

19. Cited in Goodin, *Reasons for Welfare,* 165.

20. Albert Hirschman, *Exit, Voice, and Loyalty* (Cambridge, Mass: Harvard University Press, 1970).

21. Carole Pateman, *Participation and Democratic Theory* (New York: Cambridge University Press, 1970).

## Chapter Three

1. William Beveridge, *Social Insurance and Allied Services* (London: Her Majesty's Stationery Office, 1942), sec. 107.

2. Jane Jenson, "Who Cares? Gender and Welfare Regimes," *Social Politics* 4.2 (1997): 182–187.

3. Jane Lewis, "Gender and Welfare Regimes: Further Thoughts," *Social Politics* 4.2 (1997): 160–177; Ann Shola Orloff, "Gender and the Social Rights of Citizenship: The Comparative Analysis of Gender Relations and Welfare States," *American Sociological Review* 58 (1993): 303–328.

4. Barbara Hobson, "No Exit, No Voice: Women's Economic Dependency and the Welfare State," *Acta Sociologica* 33.3 (1990): 235–250.

5. Helga Maria Hernes, *Welfare State and Woman Power: Essays in State Feminism* (Oslo: Universitetsforlaget, 1987); Julia O'Connor, "Gender, Class and Citizenship in the Comparative Analysis of Welfare State Regimes: Theoretical and Methodological Issues," *British Journal of Sociology* 44.3 (1993): 514; Ruth Lister, "'She Has Other Duties'—Women, Citizenship, and Social Security," in *Social Security and Social Change: New Challenges to the Beveridge Model*, ed. Sally Baldwin and Jane Falkingham (New York: Harvester Wheatsheaf, 1994), 37.

6. Lisa D. Brush, *Gender and Governance* (Walnut Creek, Calif.: Altamira Press, 2003); S. Laurel Weldon, *Protest, Policy, and the Problem of Violence against Women: A Cross-National Comparison* (Pittsburgh: University of Pittsburgh Press, 2002); R. Amy Elman, *Sexual Subordination and State Intervention: Comparing Sweden and the United States* (Oxford: Berghahn Books, 1996).

7. Nancy Fraser, "After the Family Wage: A Post-Industrial Thought Experiment," in *Justice Interruptus* (New York: Routledge, 1997).

8. Peter Taylor-Gooby, *Social Change, Social Welfare, and Social Science* (New York: Harvester Wheatsheaf, 1991), 190–213.

9. Nancy Fraser, *Adding Insult to Injury: Social Justice and the Politics of Recognition*, ed. Kevin Olson (London: Verso, forthcoming); "Recognition without Ethics?" *Theory, Culture, and Society* 18.2–3 (2001): 21–42; "Rethinking Recognition," *New Left Review*, 2nd ser., 3 (2000): 107–120; "Social Justice in the Age of Identity Politics: Redistribution, Recognition, and Participation," in *The Tanner Lectures on Human Values*, ed. Grethe Peterson (Salt Lake City: University of Utah Press, 1998); and "From Redistribution to Recognition? Dilemmas of Justice in a 'Post-Socialist' Age," in Fraser, *Justice Interruptus*.

10. Fraser, "From Redistribution to Recognition?" 13–16.

11. Barbara Cruikshank, *The Will to Empower: Democratic Citizens and Other Subjects* (Ithaca, N.Y.: Cornell University Press, 1999); Mitchell Dean, *The Constitution of Poverty: Toward a Genealogy of Liberal Governance* (New York: Routledge, 1991).

12. More technically, this model would be institutionalized in a *liberal-democratic* state. I do not use that term here, however, to avoid potential confusions with the "liberal" welfare regime type. All contemporary welfare regimes—liberal, social-democratic, and conservative—are politically liberal-democratic in the sense of institutionalizing basic freedoms of popular sovereignty and civil protection.

13. John Stuart Mill, *On Liberty* (1859), ed. Stefan Collini (New York, Cambridge University Press, 1989), chaps. 3–4.

14. Cf. Julia O'Connor, Ann Shola Orloff, and Sheila Shaver, *States, Markets, Families: Gender, Liberalism, and Social Policy in Australia, Canada, Great Britain, and the United States* (New York: Cambridge University Press, 1999).

15. Carole Pateman, *The Sexual Contract* (Stanford, Calif.: Stanford University Press, 1988).

16. Rickie Solinger, *Beggars and Choosers: How the Politics of Choice Shapes Adoption, Abortion, and Welfare in the United States* (New York: Hill and Wang, 2001), chap. 5.

17. Pierre Bourdieu, *Distinction: A Social Critique of the Judgement of Taste*, trans. Richard Nice (Cambridge, Mass: Harvard University Press, 1984).

18. Diane Sainsbury, *Gender, Equality, and Welfare States* (New York: Cambridge University Press, 1996), 191; Linda Haas, *Equal Parenthood and Social Policy: A Study of Parental Leave in Sweden* (Albany, N.Y.: SUNY Press, 1992), 59–60; Karin Sandqvist, "Swedish Family Policy and the Attempt to Change Paternal Roles," in *Reassessing Fatherhood*, ed. Charlie Lewis and Margaret O'Brien (Newbury Park, Calif.: Sage Publications, 1987); Annika Baude, "Public Policy and Changing Family Patterns in Sweden: 1930–1977," in *Sex Roles and Social Policy*, ed. Jean Lipman-Blumen and Jessie Bernard (Newbury Park, Calif.: Sage, 1979), 145–176; Helena Bergman and Barbara Hobson, "Compulsory Fatherhood: The Coding of Fatherhood in the Swedish Welfare State," in *Making Men into Fathers: Men, Masculinities, and the Social Politics of Fatherhood*, ed. Barbara Hobson (New York: Cambridge University Press, 2002); Christina Bergqvist, "Childcare and Parental Leave Models," in *Equal Democracies? Gender and Politics in the Nordic Countries*, ed. Christina Bergqvist et al. (Oslo: Scandinavian University Press, 1999); Christina Bergqvist, Jaana Kuusipalo, and Audur Styrkarsdóttir, "The Debate on Childcare Policies," in *Equal Democracies?*

19. Ulla Björnberg, "Equity and Backlash: Family, Gender, and Social Policy in Sweden," in *Organizational Change and Gender Equity*, ed. Linda Haas, Philip Hwang, and Graeme Russell (Thousand Oaks, Calif.: Sage Publications, 2000), 61.

20. Sainsbury, *Gender, Equality*, 191; Haas, *Equal Parenthood*, 69.

21. Haas, *Equal Parenthood*.

22. Linda Haas and Philip Hwang, "Programs and Policies Promoting Women's Economic Equality and Men's Sharing of Child Care in Sweden," in *Organizational Change*, 145–146.

23. Haas, *Equal Parenthood*, 64.

24. Haas, *Equal Parenthood*; Ariane Sains, "Charting the Papa Index," *Europe* (2001): 44.

25. Yvonne Hirdman, "The Gender System," in *Moving On: New Perspectives on the Women's Movement*, ed. Tayo Andreasen, et al. (Aarhus: Aarhus University Press, 1991); "State Policy and Gender Contracts: The Swedish Experience," in *Women, Work, and the Family in Europe*, ed. Eileen Drew, Ruth Emerek, and Evelyn Mahon (New York: Routledge, 1998); "Women—From Possibility to Problem? Gender Conflict in the Welfare State—The Swedish Model" (working paper, National Institute for Working Life, Stockholm, Sweden, 1994): 5–45.

26. Linda Haas and Philip Hwang, "Company Culture and Men's Usage of Family Leave Benefits in Sweden," *Family Relations* 44 (1995): 28–36. Women's propensity to take leave seems not to be affected by public versus private employment. See Haas, *Equal Parenthood*, 109–110.

27. Haas, *Equal Parenthood*.

28. Ibid., 91.

29. Ulla Björnberg, "Equity and Backlash: Family, Gender, and Social Policy in Sweden," in *Organizational Change*, 61.

30. Hirdman, "Women—From Possibility to Problem?"

31. Haas, "Programs and Policies," 139–141.

32. Fraser, "From Redistribution to Recognition?"

33. Michel Foucault, *Discipline and Punish: The Birth of the Prison* (New York: Vintage Books, 1979).

34. Cf. Kevin Olson, "Distributive Justice and the Politics of Difference," *Critical Horizons* 2.1 (2001): 5–32.

35. Amartya Sen, "Capability and Well-Being," in *The Quality of Life*, ed. Martha Nussbaum and Amartya Sen (New York: Oxford University Press, 1993); *Inequality Reexamined* (Cambridge, Mass.: Harvard University Press, 1992); *Commodities and Capabilities* (Amsterdam: North-Holland, 1985); "Well-Being, Agency, and Freedom: The Dewey Lectures 1984," *Journal of Philosophy* 82.4 (1985): 169–221; "Equality of What?" *The Tanner Lectures on Human Values*, vol. 1, ed. Sterling McMurrin (Salt Lake City: University of Utah Press, 1980).

36. Olson, "Distributive Justice and the Politics of Difference," 25–29.

37. Cf. Seyla Benhabib, *The Claims of Culture: Equality and Diversity in the Global Era* (Princeton: Princeton University Press, 2002), especially chaps. 3–5.

38. Marlo Thomas, *Free to Be . . . You and Me*, ed. Carole Hart (New York: McGraw-Hill, 1974).

39. Christine Horne, "Sociological Perspectives on the Emergence of Social Norms," in *Social Norms*, ed. Michael Hechter and Karl-Dieter Opp (New York: Russell Sage Foundation, 2001), 6–8; Russell Hardin, *One for All: The Logic of Group Conflict* (Princeton: Princeton University Press, 1995), 60–65.

40. Harold Garfinkel, *Studies in Ethnomethodology* (Englewood Cliffs, N.J.: Prentice-Hall, 1967).

41. William Blackstone, *Commentaries on the Laws of England* (1765–1769) (Chicago: University of Chicago Press, 1979), vol. 1, bk. 1, chap. 15.

42. Haas, "Programs and Policies."

43. Clarissa Kugelberg, "Swedish Parents at a Multinational Conglomerate," in *Organizational Change*.

44. Elman, *Sexual Subordination;* R. Amy Elman and Maud Eduards, "Unprotected by the Swedish Welfare State: A Survey of Battered Women and the Assistance They Received," *Women's Studies International Forum* 14.5 (1991): 413–421; R. Amy Elman, "Unprotected by the Swedish Welfare State Revisited: Assessing a Decade of Reforms for Battered Women," *Women's Studies International Forum* 24.1 (2001): 39–52.

45. Haas, *Equal Parenthood*, 13; Helga Maria Hernes, *Welfare State and Woman Power: Essays in State Feminism* (Oslo: Universitetsforlaget, 1987), 19.

46. Baude, "Public Policy," 153.

47. Albert Hirschman, *Exit, Voice, and Loyalty* (Cambridge, Mass.: Harvard University Press, 1970); Barbara Hobson, "No Exit, No Voice."

48. Similarly, Haas (*Equal Parenthood*) finds a correlation between men's choice to take leave time and their spouse's job status and income. Men partnered with upper-income, upper-status women were much likelier to take parental leave and to share it equally. Presumably this reflects the woman's improved bargaining position in the form of both exit options and voice, as well as the higher education level of such couples and the likelihood that the woman is the higher wage earner.

49. Walter Korpi, "Faces of Inequality: Gender, Class, and Patterns of Inequalities in Different Types of Welfare States," *Social Politics* 7 (2000): 141.

50. Weldon, *Protest, Policy.*

51. Hernes, *Welfare State and Woman Power.*

52. Anne Phillips, *The Politics of Presence: The Political Representation of Gender, Ethnicity, and Race* (New York: Oxford University Press, 1995).

53. Kurt Vonnegut, Jr., "Harrison Bergeron," in *Welcome to the Monkey House* (New York: Delacorte Press, 1968).

54. Noting, as Judith Butler does, that "sex" is itself a construct and that normalized heterosexuality enforces the binary gender distinction between male and female. Judith Butler, *Gender Trouble: Feminism and the Subversion of Identity* (New York: Routledge, 1990).

## Chapter Four

1. Judith Butler, "Merely Cultural," *Social Text* 15.3–4 (1997): 265–277.

2. Jack Knight and James Johnson, "What Sort of Equality Does Deliberative Democracy Require?" in *Deliberative Democracy: Essays on Reason and Politics,* ed. James Bohman and William Rehg (Cambridge, Mass.: MIT Press, 1997).

3. Jean-Jacques Rousseau, *On the Social Contract* (1762), in *Basic Political Writings,* trans. Donald Cress (Indianapolis: Hackett, 1987), bk. 3, chap. 17. See also Bernard Manin, "On Legitimacy and Deliberation," *Political Theory* 15:3 (1987): 338–368.

4. James Bohman, *Public Deliberation: Pluralism, Complexity, and Democracy* (Cambridge, Mass: MIT Press, 1996), chap. 3; and "Deliberative Democracy and Effective Social Freedom: Capabilities, Resources, and Opportunities," in *Deliberative Democracy.*

5. Cf. Robert Dahl, *Democracy and Its Critics* (New Haven: Yale University Press, 1989), 109.

6. Among recent authors, two exemplary works are Carole Pateman, *Participation and Democratic Theory* (New York: Cambridge University Press, 1970); and C. B. Macpherson, *The Life and Times of Liberal Democracy* (New York: Oxford University Press, 1977). Also note the similarity with John Rawls's principle of (equal) participation: "all citizens are to have an equal right to take part in, and to determine the outcome of, the constitutional process that establishes the laws with which they are to comply." Rawls, *A Theory of Justice,* rev. ed. (Cambridge, Mass.: Harvard University Press, 1999), 194.

7. T. H. Marshall, "Citizenship and Social Class," in *Sociology at the Crossroads* (London: Heinemann, 1963).

8. Marshall, "Citizenship," 107.

9. Ibid., 74.

10. Jürgen Habermas, *Between Facts and Norms: Contributions to a Discourse Theory of Law and Democracy* (Cambridge, Mass.: MIT Press, 1996); *Inclusion of the Other,* trans. Ciaran Cronin and Pablo De Greiff (Cambridge, Mass.: MIT Press, 1998); "Constitutional Democracy: A Paradoxical Union

of Contradictory Principles?" *Political Theory* 29.6 (2001): 766–781; and "On Law and Disagreement: Some Comments on 'Interpretive Pluralism,'" *Ratio Juris* 16 (2003): 187–194.

11. Habermas, *Between Facts and Norms*, 118–122.

12. Ibid., 118–131.

13. Ibid., 123. Translation amended to avoid terminological confusion.

14. G. W. F. Hegel, *Elements of the Philosophy of Right*, trans. H. B. Nisbet (New York: Cambridge University Press, 1991 [1821]), secs. 300–314, especially sec. 306; John Stuart Mill, *Thoughts on Parliamentary Reform* (1859), in *Collected Works*, vol. 19 (Toronto: University of Toronto Press, 1977), 311–339; and "Considerations on Representative Government" (1861), in *On Liberty and Other Essays* (New York: Oxford University Press, 1998), especially chap. 4; Karl Marx, "On the Jewish Question" (1843), in *Karl Marx: Selected Writings*, ed. David McLellan (New York: Oxford University Press, 1977); Rawls, *Theory of Justice*, rev. ed., 179–180; Frank Michelman, "Welfare Rights in a Constitutional Democracy," *Washington University Law Quarterly* 1979.3 (1979): 659–693; and "Possession vs. Distribution in the Constitutional Idea of Property," *Iowa Law Review* 72 (1987): 1319–1350.

15. A clear and insightful explanation of formal pragmatics can be found in Thomas McCarthy, *The Critical Theory of Jürgen Habermas* (Cambridge, Mass.: MIT Press, 1978), chap. 4. I will also discuss this genre of justification in detail in chapter 7.

16. Habermas, *Between Facts and Norms*, chap. 4. Also 126.

17. Ibid., 307–308, following Nancy Fraser, "Rethinking the Public Sphere: A Contribution to the Critique of Actually Existing Democracy," in *Habermas and the Public Sphere*, ed. Craig Calhoun (Cambridge, Mass.: MIT Press, 1992).

18. Habermas, *Between Facts and Norms*, 354–359, 379–384.

19. Ibid., 151–157; and "Struggles for Recognition in Constitutional States," *European Journal of Philosophy* 1.2 (1993): 128–155.

20. In this last phrase I implicitly modify Habermas's assertion that the rationality of deliberation is founded *purely* on the rationality of its procedures (*Between Facts and Norms*, 296–297, 408–409, 442). Surely a more adequate view combines the rationality of the populace with the rationality of the framework in which they deliberate. After all, the two condition one another: the people must (rationally) devise specific interpretations of procedural rules; but these rules promote rational deliberation only if they correctly capture the pragmatic presuppositions of democracy. We would have to say, then, that democratic deliberation is "subject centered" in some senses and "subjectless" in others.

21. Benjamin Constant, "The Liberty of the Ancients Compared with That of the Moderns" (1819), in *Political Writings* (New York: Cambridge University Press, 1988).

## Chapter Five

1. T. H. Marshall, "Citizenship and Social Class," in *Sociology at the Crossroads* (London: Heinemann, 1963), 127.

2. Alexis de Tocqueville, *Democracy in America,* trans. Harvey Mansfield and Delba Winthrop (Chicago: University of Chicago Press, 2000); Robert Putnam, *Bowling Alone: The Collapse and Revival of American Community* (New York: Simon and Schuster, 2000).

3. Günther Frankenberg provides a good illustration of such a picture in "Why Care?—The Trouble with Social Rights," *Cardozo Law Review* 17 (1996): 1384.

4. Jürgen Habermas, *Between Facts and Norms: Contributions to a Discourse Theory of Law and Democracy* (Cambridge, Mass.: MIT Press, 1996), 123, 417–418. It is interesting to note that John Rawls makes a similar move. He refers to civil rights, political rights, and some "social minimum" as "constitutional essentials" and separates them off from more general questions of "social and economic justice." The "social minimum" is similar in justification and role to Habermas's social rights. Thus material redistribution has a double character for both thinkers. Redistribution is required in a minimal sense for civil and political equality; but it can be instituted on a broader scale only as a result of political consensus. For Rawls this separation is partly based on the idea that consensus is much harder to discover on distributive questions than on basic questions of civil and political equality. John Rawls, *Political Liberalism* (New York: Columbia University Press, 1993), 227–230.

5. Jürgen Habermas, *The Theory of Communicative Action,* vol. 1, trans. Thomas McCarthy (Boston: Beacon Press, 1984), chaps. 1 and 3; and Thomas McCarthy, *The Critical Theory of Jürgen Habermas* (Cambridge, Mass.: MIT Press, 1978), chap. 4.

6. Joel Anderson, "A Social Conception of Autonomy: Volitional Identity, Strong Evaluation, and Intersubjective Accountability" (doctoral dissertation, Northwestern University, 1996), chap. 7.

7. Gøsta Esping-Andersen insightfully traces the influence of such factors on a nation's choice of policy options. *The Three Worlds of Welfare Capitalism* (Princeton: Princeton University Press, 1990).

8. Habermas, *Between Facts and Norms,* 365, 426.

9. Ibid., 107–111, elaborating upon his *Moral Consciousness and Communicative Action* (Cambridge, Mass.: MIT Press, 1990), 62–68.

10. Frank Michelman insightfully identifies a similar, though structurally different circularity between deliberative democracy and the procedures that institutionalize it. Michelman, "Law's Republic," *Yale Law Journal* 97.8 (1988): 1499–1501, 1505; "How Can the People Ever Make the Laws? A Critique of Deliberative Democracy," in *Deliberative Democracy: Essays on Reason and Politics,* ed. James Bohman and William Rehg (Cambridge, Mass.: MIT Press, 1997); "Constitutional Authorship," in *Constitutionalism: Philosophical Foundations,* ed. Larry Alexander (New York: Cambridge University Press, 1998); and "Morality, Identity and 'Constitutional Patriotism,'" *Ratio Juris* 14:3 (2001): 253–271.

11. Habermas, *Between Facts and Norms,* 39, 384; "Constitutional Democracy: A Paradoxical Union of Contradictory Principles?" *Political Theory* 29.6 (2001): 766–781; "On Law and Disagreement: Some Comments on 'Interpretive Pluralism,'" *Ratio Juris* 16 (2003): 187–194.

12. See chapter 7 for more detail about the idea of reconstructive arguments in political theory, legal theory, and the social sciences.

13. Habermas, *Theory of Communicative Action,* vol. 1, chaps. 1 and 3.

14. Habermas, *Theory of Communicative Action,* vol. 2, trans. Thomas McCarthy (Boston: Beacon Press, 1987), esp. 140–152.

15. See James Bohman's insightful discussion of capabilities for public reason, which draws on Amartya Sen's work to conceptualize problems in the distribution of competencies for democratic participation. Bohman, *Public Deliberation: Pluralism, Complexity, and Democracy* (Cambridge, Mass.: MIT Press, 1996), chap. 3; "Deliberative Democracy and Effective Social Freedom: Capabilities, Resources, and Opportunities," in *Deliberative Democracy.*

16. On the idea of aspects of practical reason and the dangers of not separating them, see Thomas McCarthy, "Legitimacy and Diversity: Dialectical Reflections on Analytical Distinctions," *Cardozo Law Review* 17 (1996): 1083–1125; and Jürgen Habermas, "Reply to Symposium Participants," *Cardozo Law Review* 17 (1996): 1487–1503.

17. Cf. Ronald Dworkin, "What Is Equality? Part 4: Political Equality," *University of San Francisco Law Review* 22 (1987): 1–30; Bohman, *Public Deliberation*, chap. 3; and Bohman, "Deliberative Democracy."

18. See note 4 above.

## Chapter Six

1. Jean-Jacques Rousseau, *On the Social Contract* (1762), in *Basic Political Writings*, trans. Donald Cress (Indianapolis: Hackett, 1987), bk. 1, chap. 6.

2. Cf. Barbara Cruikshank, *The Will to Empower: Democratic Citizens and Other Subjects* (Ithaca, N.Y.: Cornell University Press, 1999).

3. Amartya Sen, "Capability and Well-Being," in *The Quality of Life*, ed. Martha Nussbaum and Amartya Sen (New York: Oxford University Press, 1993); *Inequality Reexamined* (Cambridge, Mass.: Harvard University Press, 1992); *Commodities and Capabilities* (Amsterdam: North-Holland, 1985); "Well-Being, Agency, and Freedom: The Dewey Lectures 1984," *Journal of Philosophy* 82.4 (1985): 169–221; "Equality of What?" *The Tanner Lectures on Human Values*, vol. 1, ed. Sterling McMurrin (Salt Lake City: University of Utah Press, 1980).

4. Aristotle, *On Interpretation*, in *The Basic Works of Aristotle*, ed. Richard McKeon, trans. E. M. Edghill (New York: Random House, 1941), chaps. 12–13.

5. James Bohman, *Public Deliberation: Pluralism, Complexity, and Democracy* (Cambridge, Mass.: MIT Press, 1996), chap. 3; and "Deliberative Democracy and Effective Social Freedom: Capabilities, Resources, and Opportunities," in *Deliberative Democracy: Essays on Reason and Politics*, ed. James Bohman and William Rehg (Cambridge, Mass.: MIT Press, 1997).

6. Pierre Bourdieu, *Distinction: A Social Critique of the Judgement of Taste*, trans. Richard Nice (Cambridge, Mass.: Harvard University Press, 1984).

7. Sidney Verba, Kay Schlozman, and Henry Brady, *Voice and Equality: Civic Voluntarism in American Politics* (Cambridge, Mass.: Harvard University Press, 1995), table 13.6, p. 389.

8. Verba, Schlozman, and Brady, *Voice and Equality*, 206–219.

9. Kevin Olson, "Distributive Justice and the Politics of Difference," *Critical Horizons* 2.1 (2001): 25–29.

10. Americans with Disabilities Act, Public Law 101–336 (1990).

11. Daniel Patrick Moynihan, *Maximum Feasible Misunderstanding: Community Action in the War on Poverty* (New York: Free Press, 1969); Peter Marris and Martin Rein, *Dilemmas of Social Reform: Poverty and Community Action in the United States,* 2nd ed. (Chicago: University of Chicago Press, 1982).

## Chapter Seven

1. Immanuel Kant, *The Metaphysics of Morals* (1797), trans. Mary Gregor (New York: Cambridge University Press, 1996), esp. AA 6:218–221.

2. Immanuel Kant, "Transcendental Analytic," *Critique of Pure Reason* (1781/1787), trans. Norman Kemp Smith (New York: St. Martin's, 1965).

3. John Rawls, "Kantian Constructivism in Moral Theory," *Journal of Philosophy* 77 (1980): 515–572; and "Themes in Kant's Moral Philosophy," in *Kant's Transcendental Deductions,* ed. Eckart Förster (Stanford: Stanford University Press, 1989). Also see Brian Barry's insightful discussion in *Theories of Justice* (Berkeley: University of California Press, 1989), 264–271.

4. Joseph Heath, *Communicative Action and Rational Choice* (Cambridge, Mass.: MIT Press, 2001), chap. 8; Michael Power, "Habermas and the Counterfactual Imagination," *Cardozo Law Review* 17 (1996): 1005–1025; and Roderick Chisholm, "What Is a Transcendental Argument?" *Neue Hefte für Philosophie* 14 (1978): 19–22.

5. Jürgen Habermas, "Reconstruction and Interpretation in the Social Sciences," in *Moral Consciousness and Communicative Action* (Cambridge, Mass.: MIT Press, 1990), 31. See also Kenneth Baynes, "Rational Reconstruction and Social Criticism: Habermas's Model of Interpretive Social Science," in *Hermeneutics and Critical Theory in Ethics and Politics,* ed. Michael Kelly (Cambridge, Mass.: MIT Press, 1990); and Thomas McCarthy, *The Critical Theory of Jürgen Habermas* (Cambridge, Mass.: MIT Press, 1978), 276–279.

6. Jürgen Habermas, "What Is Universal Pragmatics?" in *Communication and the Evolution of Society,* trans. Thomas McCarthy (Boston: Beacon Press, 1979), 8, 13.

7. Habermas, "What Is Universal Pragmatics?" 9.

8. Habermas, "Reconstruction and Interpretation," 31.

9. Habermas, "What Is Universal Pragmatics?" 14. Emphasis in the original.

10. Habermas, "Reconstruction and Interpretation," 31–32.

11. Jürgen Habermas, *The Theory of Communicative Action,* 2 vols., trans. Thomas McCarthy (Boston: Beacon Press, 1984 and 1987).

12. Jürgen Habermas, *Between Facts and Norms: Contributions to a Discourse Theory of Law and Democracy* (Cambridge, Mass.: MIT Press, 1996), 121ff.

13. Ibid., 110.

14. Kant, *Metaphysics of Morals,* AA 6:230–231.

15. Habermas, *Between Facts and Norms,* 122–123.

16. Ibid., 445.

17. Ibid., 445–446.

18. Ibid., 88.

19. Ludwig Wittgenstein, *Philosophical Investigations*, trans. G. E. M. Anscombe (Oxford: Blackwell, 1997 [1953]).

20. *Griswold v Connecticut*, 381 U.S. 479 (1965).

21. Ronald Dworkin, *Taking Rights Seriously* (Cambridge, Mass.: Harvard University Press, 1977), 87–88.

22. Jürgen Habermas, "What Is Universal Pragmatics?" 26.

23. Mary Ann Glendon, *Rights Talk: The Impoverishment of Political Discourse* (Glencoe, Ill.: Free Press, 1991), chap. 1–2.

24. Habermas, *Between Facts and Norms,* 107.

25. T. H. Marshall, "Citizenship and Social Class," in *Sociology at the Crossroads* (London: Heinemann, 1963).

26. Again, *Griswold v Connecticut*, 381 U.S. 479 (1965).

27. Jürgen Habermas, "On the Pragmatic, the Ethical, and the Moral Employments of Practical Reason," in *Justification and Application: Remarks on Discourse Ethics*, trans. Ciaran Cronin (Cambridge, Mass.: MIT Press, 1993).

28. Habermas, *Between Facts and Norms,* 110, 127.

29. Cf. Robert Alexy, "Basic Rights and Democracy in Jürgen Habermas's Procedural Paradigm of the Law," *Ratio Juris* 7.2 (1994): 227–238; James Bohman, "Complexity, Pluralism, and the Constitutional State: On Habermas's *Faktizität und Geltung*," *Law and Society Review* 28.4 (1994): 905.

30. Habermas, *Between Facts and Norms*, 326.

31. Cf. Rousseau's insightful reconstruction of the institution of government out of a form of pure collective will. Rousseau, *On the Social Contract* (1762), in *Basic Political Writings*, trans. Donald Cress (Indianapolis: Hackett, 1987), bk. 3, chap. 17.

32. Jürgen Habermas, "Philosophy as Stand-In and Interpreter," in *Moral Consciousness*.

33. Habermas, *Theory of Communicative Action*, vol. 1, 124–141.

34. Harold Garfinkel, *Studies in Ethnomethodology* (Englewood Cliffs, N.J.: Prentice-Hall, 1967).

35. Thomas McCarthy has long championed Garfinkel's work as a pragmatic analysis of social cooperation, significantly influencing my own thinking on the subject. See McCarthy, "On the Pragmatics of Communicative Reason," in David Couzens Hoy and Thomas McCarthy, *Critical Theory* (Cambridge, Mass.: Blackwell, 1994).

36. Werner Güth, Rolf Schmittberger, and Bernd Schwarze, "An Experimental Analysis of Ultimatum Bargaining," *Journal of Economic Behavior and Organization* 3 (1982): 367–388. Richard Thaler, "The Ultimatum Game," *Journal of Economic Perspectives* 2.4 (1988): 195–206. Colin Camerer and Richard Thaler, "Ultimatums, Dictators, and Manners," *Journal of Economic Perspectives* 9.2 (1995): 209–219.

37. There are interesting gender differences in the results of the ultimatum game. Men attract higher offers as player 2 than women do. Reciprocally, players of both sexes demand higher offers when they know that player 1 is a woman. Sara Solnick, "Gender Differences in the Ultimatum Game," *Economic Inquiry* 39.2 (2001): 189–200.

38. E. Allan Lind and Tom Tyler, *The Social Psychology of Procedural Justice* (New York: Plenum Press, 1988). Tom Tyler, *Why People Obey the Law* (New Haven: Yale University Press, 1990). Tom Tyler and Steven Blader, *Cooperation in Groups: Procedural Justice, Social Identity, and Behavioral Engagement* (Philadelphia: Taylor and Francis, 2000).

39. Garfinkel, *Studies in Ethnomethodology*, chap. 2.

## Chapter Eight

1. Jean-Jacques Rousseau, *On the Social Contract* (1762), in *Basic Political Writings*, trans. Donald Cress (Indianapolis: Hackett, 1987), bk. 2, chap. 11, p. 170.

2. Henry Ireton in the Putney Debates. A. S. P. Woodhouse, ed. *Puritanism and Liberty* (Rutland, Vt.: Charles Tuttle, 1992), 53–55.

3. Immanuel Kant, *The Metaphysics of Morals*, trans. Mary Gregor (New York: Cambridge University Press, 1996 [1797]), AA 6:313–315; G. W. F. Hegel, *Elements of the Philosophy of Right*, trans. H. B. Nisbet (New York: Cambridge University Press, 1991 [1821]), secs. 300–314; John Stuart Mill, *Thoughts on Parliamentary Reform* (1859), in *Collected Works*, vol. 19 (Toronto: University of Toronto Press, 1977); and "Considerations on Representative Government" (1861), in *On Liberty and Other Essays* (New York: Oxford University Press, 1998), especially chap. 4.

4. Emile Durkheim, *The Division of Labor in Society*, trans. W. D. Hall (New York: Free Press, 1984 [1893]).

5. National Assembly of France, Declaration of the Rights of Man and of the Citizen (1789), trans. Thomas Paine, appendix to Thomas Paine, *Rights of Man* (Indianapolis: Hackett, 1992).

6. Jeremy Bentham, "Anarchical Fallacies" (1796), in *The Works of Jeremy Bentham*, vol. 2, ed. John Bowring (New York: Russell and Russell, 1962), 507.

7. T. H. Marshall, "Citizenship and Social Class," in *Sociology at the Crossroads* (London: Heinemann, 1963); Jürgen Habermas, *Between Facts and Norms: Contributions to a Discourse Theory of Law and Democracy* (Cambridge, Mass.: MIT Press, 1996), chap 3.

8. Habermas, *Between Facts and Norms*, chap 3.

9. Ibid., 110. Cf. Martin Luther King, Jr., "An unjust law is a code inflicted upon a minority which that minority had no part in enacting or creating because they did not have the unhampered right to vote." *Letter from Birmingham City Jail* (Philadelphia: American Friends Service Committee, 1963), 7.

10. Robert Alexy, *A Theory of Legal Argumentation* (Oxford: Oxford University Press, 1989), 192–195.

11. Kurt Vonnegut, Jr., "Harrison Bergeron," in *Welcome to the Monkey House* (New York: Delacorte Press, 1968).

12. Sidney Verba, Kay Schlozman, and Henry Brady, *Voice and Equality: Civic Voluntarism in American Politics* (Cambridge, Mass.: Harvard University Press, 1995), esp. table 12.5, p. 352. Also see section 6.3 of the present volume.

13. Verba et al., *Voice and Equality*, figure 7.7, p. 207.

14. Frances Fox Piven and Richard Cloward, *Regulating the Poor: The Functions of Public Welfare* (New York: Vintage, 1971), 45–119.

15. Walter Korpi, *The Democratic Class Struggle* (London: Routledge and Kegan Paul, 1983); Gøsta Esping-Andersen, *Politics against Markets: The Social-Democratic Road to Power* (Princeton: Princeton University Press, 1985).

16. Bismarck's political patronage state of the 1880s and Richard J. Daley's of the 1970s are two notable exceptions.

17. I take these observations to be contiguous with Frank Michelman's procedural concerns in "Law's Republic," *Yale Law Journal* 97.8 (1988): 1493–1537; "How Can the People Ever Make the Laws? A Critique of Deliberative Democracy," in *Deliberative Democracy: Essays on Reason and Politics*, ed. James Bohman and William Rehg (Cambridge, Mass.: MIT Press, 1997); and "Constitutional Authorship," in *Constitutionalism: Philosophical Foundations*, ed. Larry Alexander (New York: Cambridge University Press, 1998).

18. Verba et al., *Voice and Equality*, 208–209.

19. Ibid., 391–398, 411.

20. Jennifer Hochschild, *What's Fair? American Beliefs about Distributive Justice* (Cambridge, Mass.: Harvard University Press, 1981).

21. Martin Gilens, *Why Americans Hate Welfare: Race, Media, and the Politics of Antipoverty Policy* (Chicago: University of Chicago Press, 1999).

22. Verba et al., *Voice and Equality*, 189–191.

23. Ibid., 319.

24. Ibid., chap. 11.

25. Public Law 104–193, title I, section 402(a)(1)(B)(iii).

26. Public Law 104–193, title I, section 408(a)(7).

27. Public Law 104–193, title I, section 408(a)(2).

28. Public Law 104–193, title I, section 408(a)(1).

29. Denise Polit et al., *Is Work Enough? The Experiences of Current and Former Welfare Mothers Who Work* (New York: Manpower Demonstration Research Corporation, 2001).

30. Verba et al., *Voice and Equality*, chap. 11.

31. Ibid., 360–364.

32. Public Law 104–193, title I, section 407(d).

33. Public Law 104–193, title I, section 408(b)

34. Public Law 104–193, title I, section 408(b)(2)(A)(iii).

35. Groups rather than individuals. See Kevin Olson, "Distributive Justice and the Politics of Difference," *Critical Horizons* 2.1 (2001): 25–29; also the present volume, section 3.4.

36. Public Law 104–193, title I, section 401(b).

37. Public Law 104–193, title I, section 403.

38. Lawrence Mead, ed., *The New Paternalism: Supervisory Approaches to Poverty* (Washington, D.C.: Brookings Institution, 1997); and *Beyond Entitlement: The Social Obligations of Citizenship* (New York: Free Press, 1986).

39. See esp. Mead, *Beyond Entitlement*, 243. Cf. Hochschild, *What's Fair?* 252–254, 279.

40. See section 7.2.

41. Kant, *Metaphysics of Morals*, AA 6.211–214; Jon Elster, *Ulysses and the Sirens: Studies in Rationality and Irrationality* (New York: Cambridge University Press, 1984).

42. By analogy with Paul Samuelson's elegant work on consumer preference. Paul Samuelson, *Foundations of Economic Analysis* (Cambridge, Mass.: Harvard University Press, 1947).

43. See, for instance, Gilens, *Why Americans Hate Welfare,* 171–173, 192–195.

# Bibliography

"An Act for Erecting of Hospitals or Abiding and Working Houses for the Poor." 39 and 40 Elizabeth I, c. 5. 1598.

"An Act for the Punishment of Rogues, Vagabonds, and Sturdy Beggars." 39 and 40 Elizabeth I, c. 4. 1598.

"An Act for the Punishment of Vagabonds, and for Relief of the Poor and Impotent." 14 Elizabeth I, c. 5. 1572.

"An Act for the Relief of the Poor." 5 Elizabeth I, c. 3. 1563.

"An Act for the Relief of the Poor." 39 and 40 Elizabeth I, c. 3. 1598.

"An Act for the Relief of the Poor." 43 and 44 Elizabeth I, c. 2. 1601.

"An Act for the Setting of the Poor on Work, and for the Avoiding of Idleness." 18 Elizabeth I, c. 3. 1576.

Alexy, Robert. *A Theory of Legal Argumentation.* Oxford: Oxford University Press, 1989.

———. "Basic Rights and Democracy in Jürgen Habermas's Procedural Paradigm of the Law." *Ratio Juris* 7.2 (1994): 227–238.

"Americans with Disabilities Act." Public Law 101–336. 1990.

Anderson, Joel. "A Social Conception of Autonomy: Volitional Identity, Strong Evaluation, and Intersubjective Accountability." Doctoral dissertation, Northwestern University, 1996.

Aristotle. *On Interpretation.* In *The Basic Works of Aristotle.* Ed. Richard McKeon. Trans. E. M. Edghill. New York: Random House, 1941.

Baldwin, Peter. *Politics of Social Solidarity: Class Bases of the European Welfare State, 1875–1975.* New York: Cambridge University Press, 1990.

Barry, Brian. *Theories of Justice.* Berkeley: University of California Press, 1989.

Baude, Annika. "Public Policy and Changing Family Patterns in Sweden: 1930–1977." In *Sex Roles and Social Policy*. Ed. Jean Lipman-Blumen and Jessie Bernard. Newbury Park, Calif.: Sage, 1979.

Baynes, Kenneth. "Rational Reconstruction and Social Criticism: Habermas's Model of Interpretive Social Science." In *Hermeneutics and Critical Theory in Ethics and Politics*. Ed. Michael Kelly. Cambridge, Mass.: MIT Press, 1990.

Benhabib, Seyla. *The Claims of Culture: Equality and Diversity in the Global Era*. Princeton: Princeton University Press, 2002.

Bentham, Jeremy. "Anarchical Fallacies" (1796). In *The Works of Jeremy Bentham*. Vol. 2. Ed. John Bowring. New York: Russell and Russell, 1962.

———. "Pauper Management Improved" (c. 1797). In *The Works of Jeremy Bentham*. Vol. 8. Ed. John Bowring. New York: Russell and Russell, 1962.

Bergman, Helena, and Barbara Hobson. "Compulsory Fatherhood: The Coding of Fatherhood in the Swedish Welfare State." In *Making Men into Fathers: Men, Masculinities, and the Social Politics of Fatherhood*. Ed. Barbara Hobson. New York: Cambridge University Press, 2002.

Bergqvist, Christina. "Childcare and Parental Leave Models." In *Equal Democracies? Gender and Politics in the Nordic Countries*. Ed. Christina Bergqvist et al. Oslo: Scandinavian University Press, 1999.

———, Jaana Kuusipalo, and Audur Styrkarsdóttir. "The Debate on Childcare Policies." In *Equal Democracies? Gender and Politics in the Nordic Countries*. Ed. Christina Bergqvist et al. Oslo: Scandinavian University Press, 1999.

Beveridge, William. *Social Insurance and Allied Services*. London: Her Majesty's Stationery Office, 1942.

Björnberg, Ulla. "Equity and Backlash: Family, Gender, and Social Policy in Sweden." In *Organizational Change and Gender Equity*. Ed. Linda Haas, Philip Hwang, and Graeme Russell. Thousand Oaks, Calif.: Sage Publications, 2000.

Blackstone, William. *Commentaries on the Laws of England* (1765–1769). Chicago: University of Chicago Press, 1979.

Bohman, James. "Complexity, Pluralism, and the Constitutional State: On Habermas's *Faktizität und Geltung*." *Law and Society Review* 28.4 (1994): 897–930.

———. *Public Deliberation: Pluralism, Complexity, and Democracy*. Cambridge, Mass.: MIT Press, 1996.

———. "Deliberative Democracy and Effective Social Freedom: Capabilities, Resources, and Opportunities." In *Deliberative Democracy: Essays on Reason and Politics*. Ed. James Bohman and William Rehg. Cambridge, Mass.: MIT Press, 1997.

Bourdieu, Pierre. *Distinction: A Social Critique of the Judgement of Taste*. Trans. Richard Nice. Cambridge, Mass.: Harvard University Press, 1984.

Briggs, Asa. "The Welfare State in Historical Perspective." *Archives Européennes de Sociologie* 2 (1961): 221–258.

Brush, Lisa D. *Gender and Governance*. Walnut Creek, Calif.: Altamira Press, 2003.

Bibliography

Butler, Judith. *Gender Trouble: Feminism and the Subversion of Identity.* New York: Routledge, 1990.

———. "Merely Cultural." *Social Text* 15.3–4 (1997): 265–277.

Camerer, Colin, and Richard Thaler. "Ultimatums, Dictators and Manners." *Journal of Economic Perspectives* 9.2 (1995): 209–219.

Checkland, Sidney, and Olive Checkland, eds. *The Poor Law Report of 1834* (1834). New York: Penguin, 1974.

Chisholm, Roderick. "What Is a Transcendental Argument?" *Neue Hefte für Philosophie* 14 (1978): 19–22.

Cohen, G. A. "The Labor Theory of Value and the Concept of Exploitation." *Philosophy and Public Affairs* 8 (1979): 338–360.

———. "The Structure of Proletarian Unfreedom." In *Analytical Marxism.* Ed. John Roemer. Cambridge: Cambridge University Press, 1986.

Constant, Benjamin. "The Liberty of the Ancients Compared with That of the Moderns" (1819). In *Political Writings.* New York: Cambridge University Press, 1988.

Cruikshank, Barbara. *The Will to Empower: Democratic Citizens and Other Subjects.* Ithaca, N.Y.: Cornell University Press, 1999.

Dahl, Robert. *Democracy and Its Critics.* New Haven: Yale University Press, 1989.

Dean, Mitchell. *The Constitution of Poverty: Toward a Genealogy of Liberal Governance.* New York: Routledge, 1991.

Durkheim, Emile. *The Division of Labor in Society* (1893). Trans. W. D. Hall. New York: The Free Press, 1984.

Dworkin, Ronald. *Taking Rights Seriously.* Cambridge, Mass.: Harvard University Press, 1977.

———. "What Is Equality? Part 4: Political Equality." *University of San Francisco Law Review* 22 (1987): 1–30.

Elman, R. Amy. *Sexual Subordination and State Intervention: Comparing Sweden and the United States.* Oxford: Berghahn Books, 1996.

———. "Unprotected by the Swedish Welfare State Revisited: Assessing a Decade of Reforms for Battered Women." *Women's Studies International Forum* 24.1 (2001): 39–52.

Elman, R. Amy, and Maud Eduards. "Unprotected by the Swedish Welfare State: A Survey of Battered Women and the Assistance They Received." *Women's Studies International Forum* 14.5 (1991): 413–421.

Elster, Jon. *Ulysses and the Sirens: Studies in Rationality and Irrationality.* New York: Cambridge University Press, 1984.

———. *Making Sense of Marx.* New York: Cambridge University Press, 1985.

Engels, Friedrich. *Origins of the Family, Private Property, and the State.* New York: Penguin, 1985.

Esping-Andersen, Gøsta. *Politics Against Markets: The Social-Democratic Road to Power.* Princeton: Princeton University Press, 1985.

―――. *The Three Worlds of Welfare Capitalism.* Princeton: Princeton University Press, 1990.

―――. *Social Foundations of Postindustrial Economies.* New York: Oxford University Press, 1999.

Foucault, Michel. *Discipline and Punish: The Birth of the Prison.* New York: Vintage Books, 1979.

Frankenberg, Günter. "Why Care?—The Trouble with Social Rights." *Cardozo Law Review* 17 (1996): 1365–1390.

Fraser, Nancy. "Rethinking the Public Sphere: A Contribution to the Critique of Actually Existing Democracy." In *Habermas and the Public Sphere.* Ed. Craig Calhoun. Cambridge, Mass.: MIT Press, 1992.

―――. "After the Family Wage: A Post-Industrial Thought Experiment." In *Justice Interruptus: Critical Reflections on the "Postsocialist" Condition.* New York: Routledge, 1997.

―――. "From Redistribution to Recognition? Dilemmas of Justice in a 'Post-Socialist' Age." In *Justice Interruptus: Critical Reflections on the "Postsocialist" Condition.* New York: Routledge, 1997.

―――. "Social Justice in the Age of Identity Politics: Redistribution, Recognition, and Participation." In *The Tanner Lectures on Human Values.* Ed. Grethe Peterson. Salt Lake City: University of Utah Press, 1998.

―――. "Rethinking Recognition." *New Left Review* 3, 2nd ser. (2000): 107–120.

―――. "Recognition without Ethics?" *Theory, Culture and Society* 18.2–3 (2001): 21–42.

―――. *Adding Insult to Injury: Social Justice and the Politics of Recognition.* Ed. Kevin Olson. London: Verso, forthcoming.

Garfinkel, Harold. *Studies in Ethnomethodology.* Englewood Cliffs, N.J.: Prentice-Hall, 1967.

Gilens, Martin. *Why Americans Hate Welfare: Race, Media, and the Politics of Antipoverty Policy.* Chicago: University of Chicago Press, 1999.

Glendon, Mary Ann. *Rights Talk: The Impoverishment of Political Discourse.* Glencoe, Ill: Free Press, 1991.

Goodin, Robert. *Protecting the Vulnerable: A Reanalysis of Our Social Responsibilities.* Chicago: University of Chicago Press, 1985.

―――. *Reasons for Welfare: The Political Theory of the Welfare State.* Princeton: Princeton University Press, 1988.

―――. "Social Welfare as a Collective Social Responsibility." In Robert Goodin and David Schmidtz, *Social Welfare and Individual Responsibility.* New York: Cambridge University Press, 1998.

*Griswold v. Connecticut.* 381 U.S. 479 (1965).

Güth, Werner, Rolf Schmittberger, and Bernd Schwarze. "An Experimental Analysis of Ultimatum Bargaining." *Journal of Economic Behavior and Organization* 3 (1982): 367–388.

Haas, Linda. *Equal Parenthood and Social Policy: A Study of Parental Leave in Sweden.* Albany, N.Y.: SUNY Press, 1992.

Haas, Linda, and Philip Hwang. "Company Culture and Men's Usage of Family Leave Benefits in Sweden." *Family Relations* 44 (1995): 28–36.

———. "Programs and Policies Promoting Women's Economic Equality and Men's Sharing of Child Care in Sweden." In *Organizational Change and Gender Equity.* Ed. Linda Haas, Philip Hwang, and Graeme Russell. Thousand Oaks, Calif.: Sage Publications, 2000.

Habermas, Jürgen. "What Is Universal Pragmatics?" Trans. Thomas McCarthy. *Communication and the Evolution of Society.* Boston: Beacon Press, 1979.

———. *The Theory of Communicative Action.* Vol. 1. Trans. Thomas McCarthy. Boston: Beacon Press, 1984.

———. *The Theory of Communicative Action.* Vol. 2. Trans. Thomas McCarthy. Boston: Beacon Press, 1987.

———. *Moral Consciousness and Communicative Action.* Cambridge, Mass.: MIT Press, 1990.

———. "Philosophy as Stand-In and Interpreter." In *Moral Consciousness and Communicative Action.* Cambridge, Mass.: MIT Press, 1990.

———. "Reconstruction and Interpretation in the Social Sciences." In *Moral Consciousness and Communicative Action.* Cambridge, Mass.: MIT Press, 1990.

———. "On the Pragmatic, the Ethical, and the Moral Employments of Practical Reason." In *Justification and Application: Remarks on Discourse Ethics.* Trans. Ciaran Cronin. Cambridge, Mass.: MIT Press, 1993.

———. "Struggles for Recognition in Constitutional States." *European Journal of Philosophy* 1.2 (1993): 128–155.

———. *Between Facts and Norms: Contributions to a Discourse Theory of Law and Democracy.* Trans. William Rehg. Cambridge, Mass.: MIT Press, 1996.

———. "Reply to Symposium Participants." *Cardozo Law Review* 17 (1996): 1477–1557.

———. *Inclusion of the Other.* Trans. Ciaran Cronin and Pablo De Greiff. Cambridge, Mass.: MIT Press, 1998.

———. "Constitutional Democracy: A Paradoxical Union of Contradictory Principles?" *Political Theory* 29.6 (2001): 766–781.

———. "On Law and Disagreement: Some Comments on 'Interpretive Pluralism.'" *Ratio Juris* 16 (2003): 187–194.

Hardin, Russell. *One for All: The Logic of Group Conflict.* Princeton: Princeton University Press, 1995.

Heath, Joseph. *Communicative Action and Rational Choice*. Cambridge, Mass.: MIT Press, 2001.

Hegel, G. W. F. *Elements of the Philosophy of Right* (1821). Trans. H. B. Nisbet. New York: Cambridge University Press, 1991.

Hernes, Helga Maria. *Welfare State and Woman Power: Essays in State Feminism*. Oslo: Universitetsforlaget, 1987.

Hirdman, Yvonne. "The Gender System." In *Moving On: New Perspectives on the Women's Movement*. Ed. Tayo Andreasen, et al. Aarhus: Aarhus University Press, 1991.

———. "Women—From Possibility to Problem? Gender Conflict in the Welfare State—The Swedish Model." Working paper, National Institute for Working Life, Stockholm, Sweden, 1994.

———. "State Policy and Gender Contracts: The Swedish Experience." In *Women, Work, and the Family in Europe*. Ed. Eileen Drew, Ruth Emerek, and Evelyn Mahon. New York: Routledge, 1998.

Hirschman, Albert. *Exit, Voice, and Loyalty*. Cambridge, Mass.: Harvard University Press, 1970.

Hobson, Barbara. "No Exit, No Voice: Women's Economic Dependency and the Welfare State." *Acta Sociologica* 33.3 (1990): 235–250.

Hochschild, Arlie. *The Second Shift: Working Parents and the Revolution at Home*. New York: Viking, 1989.

Hochschild, Jennifer. *What's Fair? American Beliefs about Distributive Justice*. Cambridge, Mass.: Harvard University Press, 1981.

Honneth, Axel. *The Struggle for Recognition: The Moral Grammar of Social Conflicts*. Trans. Joel Anderson. Cambridge, Mass.: MIT Press, 1995.

Horne, Christine. "Sociological Perspectives on the Emergence of Social Norms." In *Social Norms*. Ed. Michael Hechter and Karl-Dieter Opp. New York: Russell Sage Foundation, 2001.

Jenson, Jane. "Who Cares? Gender and Welfare Regimes." *Social Politics* 4.2 (1997): 182–187.

Kant, Immanuel. *Critique of Pure Reason* (1781/1787). Trans. Norman Kemp Smith. New York: St. Martin's Press, 1965.

———. *The Metaphysics of Morals* (1797). Trans. Mary Gregor. New York: Cambridge University Press, 1996.

King, Martin Luther, Jr. *Letter from Birmingham City Jail*. Philadelphia: American Friends Service Committee, 1963.

Knight, Jack, and James Johnson. "What Sort of Equality Does Deliberative Democracy Require?" In *Deliberative Democracy: Essays on Reason and Politics*. Ed. James Bohman and William Rehg. Cambridge, Mass.: MIT Press, 1997.

Korpi, Walter. *The Democratic Class Struggle*. London: Routledge and Kegan Paul, 1983.

———. "Faces of Inequality: Gender, Class, and Patterns of Inequalities in Different Types of Welfare States." *Social Politics* 7 (2000): 127–191.

Kugelberg, Clarissa. "Swedish Parents at a Multinational Conglomerate." In *Organizational Change and Gender Equity*. Ed. Linda Haas, Philip Hwang, and Graeme Russell. Thousand Oaks, Calif.: Sage Publications, 2000.

Larner, Wendy. "Post-Welfare State Governance: Towards a Code of Social and Family Responsibility." *Social Politics* 7 (2000): 244–265.

Leo XIII. "Rerum Novarum" (1891). In *The Papal Encyclicals*. Vol. 2. Ed. Claudia Carlen. Ann Arbor: Pierian Press, 1990.

Lewis, Jane. "Gender and Welfare Regimes: Further Thoughts." *Social Politics* 4.2 (1997): 160–177.

Lind, E. Allan, and Tom Tyler. *The Social Psychology of Procedural Justice*. New York: Plenum Press, 1988.

Lister, Ruth. "'She Has Other Duties'—Women, Citizenship and Social Security." In *Social Security and Social Change: New Challenges to the Beveridge Model*. Ed. Sally Baldwin and Jane Falkingham. New York: Harvester Wheatsheaf, 1994.

Locke, John. "An Essay on the Poor Law" (1697). In *Political Essays*. Ed. Mark Goldie. New York: Cambridge University Press, 1997.

Macpherson, C. B. *The Political Theory of Possessive Individualism*. New York: Oxford University Press, 1962.

———. *The Life and Times of Liberal Democracy*. New York: Oxford University Press, 1977.

Manin, Bernard. "On Legitimacy and Deliberation." *Political Theory* 15.3 (1987): 338–368.

Marris, Peter, and Martin Rein. *Dilemmas of Social Reform: Poverty and Community Action in the United States*. 2nd ed. Chicago: University of Chicago Press, 1982.

Marshall, T. H. "Citizenship and Social Class." In *Sociology at the Crossroads*. London: Heinemann, 1963.

Marx, Karl. "On the Jewish Question" (1843). In *Karl Marx: Selected Writings*. Ed. David McLellan. New York: Oxford University Press, 1977.

McCarthy, Thomas. *The Critical Theory of Jürgen Habermas*. Cambridge, Mass.: MIT Press, 1978.

———. "On the Pragmatics of Communicative Reason." In David Couzens Hoy and Thomas McCarthy, *Critical Theory*. Cambridge, Mass.: Blackwell, 1994.

———. "Legitimacy and Diversity: Dialectical Reflections on Analytical Distinctions." *Cardozo Law Review* 17 (1996): 1083–1125.

Mead, Lawrence. *Beyond Entitlement: The Social Obligations of Citizenship*. New York: Free Press, 1986.

———, ed. *The New Paternalism: Supervisory Approaches to Poverty*. Washington, D.C.: Brookings Institution, 1997.

Michelman, Frank. "Welfare Rights in a Constitutional Democracy." *Washington University Law Quarterly* 1979.3 (1979): 659–693.

# Bibliography

———. "Possession vs. Distribution in the Constitutional Idea of Property." *Iowa Law Review* 72 (1987): 1319–1350.

———. "Law's Republic." *Yale Law Journal* 97.8 (1988): 1493–1537.

———. "How Can the People Ever Make the Laws? A Critique of Deliberative Democracy." In *Deliberative Democracy: Essays on Reason and Politics*. Ed. James Bohman and William Rehg. Cambridge, Mass.: MIT Press, 1997.

———. "Constitutional Authorship." In *Constitutionalism: Philosophical Foundations*. Ed. Larry Alexander. New York: Cambridge University Press, 1998.

———. "Morality, Identity and 'Constitutional Patriotism.'" *Ratio Juris* 14.3 (2001): 253–271.

Mill, John Stuart. *On Liberty* (1859). Ed. Stefan Collini. New York: Cambridge University Press, 1989.

———. *Thoughts on Parliamentary Reform* (1859). In *Collected Works*. Vol. 19. Toronto: University of Toronto Press, 1977.

———. "Considerations on Representative Government" (1861). In *On Liberty and Other Essays*. New York: Oxford University Press, 1998.

Mink, Gwendolyn. *Welfare's End*. Ithaca, N.Y.: Cornell University Press, 1998.

Moynihan, Daniel Patrick. *Maximum Feasible Misunderstanding: Community Action in the War on Poverty*. New York: Free Press, 1969.

National Assembly of France. Declaration of the Rights of Man and of the Citizen (1789). Trans. Thomas Paine. Appendix to Thomas Paine, *Rights of Man*. Indianapolis: Hackett, 1992.

O'Connor, Julia. "Gender, Class, and Citizenship in the Comparative Analysis of Welfare State Regimes: Theoretical and Methodological Issues." *British Journal of Sociology* 44.3 (1993): 501–518.

O'Connor, Julia, Ann Shola Orloff, and Sheila Shaver. *States, Markets, Families: Gender, Liberalism, and Social Policy in Australia, Canada, Great Britain, and the United States*. New York: Cambridge University Press, 1999.

Olson, Kevin. "Distributive Justice and the Politics of Difference." *Critical Horizons* 2.1 (2001): 5–32.

———. "Participatory Parity and Democratic Justice." In Nancy Fraser, *Adding Insult to Injury: Social Justice and the Politics of Recognition*. Ed. Kevin Olson. London: Verso, forthcoming.

Orloff, Ann Shola. "Gender and the Social Rights of Citizenship: The Comparative Analysis of Gender Relations and Welfare States." *American Sociological Review* 58 (1993): 303–328.

Paine, Thomas. *Rights of Man* (1791). Indianapolis: Hackett, 1992.

Pateman, Carole. *Participation and Democratic Theory*. New York: Cambridge University Press, 1970.

———. *The Sexual Contract*. Stanford, Calif.: Stanford University Press, 1988.

"Personal Responsibility and Work Opportunity Reconciliation Act." Public Law 104–193. 1996.

Phillips, Anne. *The Politics of Presence: The Political Representation of Gender, Ethnicity, and Race*. New York: Oxford University Press, 1995.

Pius XI. "Quadragesimo Anno." In *The Papal Encyclicals* (1931). Vol. 3. Ed. Claudia Carlen. Ann Arbor: Pierian Press, 1990.

Piven, Frances Fox, and Richard Cloward. *Regulating the Poor: The Functions of Public Welfare*. New York: Vintage, 1971.

Polit, Denise, Rebecca Widom, Kathryn Edin, Stan Bowie, Andrew London, Ellen Scott, and Abel Valenzuela. *Is Work Enough? The Experiences of Current and Former Welfare Mothers Who Work*. New York: Manpower Demonstration Research Corporation, 2001.

Power, Michael. "Habermas and the Counterfactual Imagination." *Cardozo Law Review* 17 (1996): 1005–1025.

Putnam, Robert. *Bowling Alone: The Collapse and Revival of American Community*. New York: Simon and Schuster, 2000.

Rawls, John. "Kantian Constructivism in Moral Theory." *Journal of Philosophy* 77 (1980): 515–572.

———. "Themes in Kant's Moral Philosophy." In *Kant's Transcendental Deductions*. Ed. Eckart Förster. Stanford: Stanford University Press, 1989.

———. *Political Liberalism*. New York: Columbia University Press, 1993.

———. *A Theory of Justice*. Rev. ed. Cambridge, Mass.: Harvard University Press, 1999.

Roemer, John. *A General Theory of Exploitation and Class*. Cambridge, Mass.: Harvard University Press, 1982.

———. "New Directions in the Marxian Theory of Exploitation and Class." In *Analytical Marxism*. Ed. John Roemer. New York: Cambridge University Press, 1986.

———. *Free to Lose*. Cambridge, Mass.: Harvard University Press, 1988.

———. *Egalitarian Perspectives: Essays in Philosophical Economics*. Cambridge: Cambridge University Press, 1994.

Rose, Nikolas. *Powers of Freedom: Reframing Political Thought*. New York: Cambridge University Press, 1999.

Rousseau, Jean-Jacques. *On the Social Contract* (1762). In *Basic Political Writings*. Trans. Donald Cress. Indianapolis: Hackett, 1987.

Sains, Ariane. "Charting the Papa Index." *Europe* (2001): 44.

Sainsbury, Diane. *Gender, Equality, and Welfare States*. New York: Cambridge University Press, 1996.

Samuelson, Paul. *Foundations of Economic Analysis*. Cambridge Mass.: Harvard University Press, 1947.

Sandqvist, Karin. "Swedish Family Policy and the Attempt to Change Paternal Roles." In *Reassessing Fatherhood*. Ed. Charlie Lewis and Margaret O'Brien. Newbury Park, Calif.: Sage Publications, 1987.

Sen, Amartya. "Equality of What?" In *The Tanner Lectures on Human Values*. Vol. 1. Ed. Sterling McMurrin. Salt Lake City: University of Utah Press, 1980.

————. *Commodities and Capabilities*. Amsterdam: North-Holland, 1985.

————. "Well-Being, Agency, and Freedom: The Dewey Lectures 1984." *Journal of Philosophy* 82.4 (1985): 169–221.

————. *Inequality Reexamined*. Cambridge, Mass.: Harvard University Press, 1992.

————. "Capability and Well-Being." In *The Quality of Life*. Ed. Martha Nussbaum and Amartya Sen. New York: Oxford University Press, 1993.

Solinger, Rickie. *Beggars and Choosers: How the Politics of Choice Shapes Adoption, Abortion, and Welfare in the United States*. New York: Hill and Wang, 2001.

Solnick, Sara. "Gender Differences in the Ultimatum Game." *Economic Inquiry* 39.2 (2001): 189–200.

Steedman, Ian, ed. *The Value Controversy*. London: Verso, 1981.

Taylor, Charles. *Multiculturalism: Examining the Politics of Recognition*. Ed. Amy Gutmann. Princeton: Princeton University Press, 1994.

Taylor-Gooby, Peter. *Social Change, Social Welfare and Social Science*. New York: Harvester Wheatsheaf, 1991.

Thaler, Richard. "The Ultimatum Game." *Journal of Economic Perspectives* 2.4 (1988): 195–206.

Thomas, Marlo. *Free to Be. . . You and Me*. Ed. Carole Hart. New York: McGraw-Hill, 1974.

Titmuss, Richard. *Social Policy*. London: Allen and Unwin, 1974.

Tocqueville, Alexis de. *Democracy in America*. Trans. Harvey Mansfield and Delba Winthrop. Chicago: University of Chicago Press, 2000.

Tyler, Tom. *Why People Obey the Law*. New Haven: Yale University Press, 1990.

Tyler, Tom, and Steven Blader. *Cooperation in Groups: Procedural Justice, Social Identity, and Behavioral Engagement*. Philadelphia: Taylor and Francis, 2000.

Verba, Sidney, Kay Schlozman, and Henry Brady. *Voice and Equality: Civic Voluntarism in American Politics*. Cambridge, Mass.: Harvard University Press, 1995.

Vonnegut, Kurt, Jr. "Harrison Bergeron." In *Welcome to the Monkey House*. New York: Delacorte Press, 1968.

Wallulis, Jerald. *The New Insecurity: The End of the Standard Job and Family*. Albany, N.Y.: SUNY Press, 1998.

# Bibliography

Webb, Sidney, and Beatrice Webb. *English Poor Law History*. 3 vols. Hamden, Conn.: Archon Books, 1963.

Weber, Max. *Economy and Society*. 2 vols. Berkeley: University of California Press, 1978.

Weldon, S. Laurel. *Protest, Policy, and the Problem of Violence against Women: A Cross-National Comparison*. Pittsburgh: University of Pittsburgh Press, 2002.

Wittgenstein, Ludwig. *Philosophical Investigations* (1953). Trans. G. E. M. Anscombe. Oxford: Blackwell, 1997.

Woodhouse, A. S. P., ed. *Puritanism and Liberty*. Rutland, Vt.: Charles Tuttle, 1992.

Young, Iris Marion. *Justice and the Politics of Difference*. Princeton: Princeton University Press, 1990.

# Index